# Gender and Stratification

# Gender and Stratification

*Edited by*
Rosemary Crompton and Michael Mann

Polity Press

© Polity Press, 1986.
© Chapter 2, David Lockwood, 1986. © Chapter 12, Leonore Davidoff, 1986.

First published 1986 by Polity Press, Cambridge, in association with Basil Blackwell, Oxford.

Editorial Office: Polity Press, Dales Brewery, Gwydir Street, Cambridge CB1 2LJ, UK.

Basil Blackwell Ltd, 108 Cowley Road, Oxford OX4 1JF, UK.

Basil Blackwell Inc., 432 Park Avenue South, Suite 1503, New York, NY 10016, USA.

British Library Cataloguing in Publication Data

Gender and stratification.
1. Sex role
I. Crompton, Rosemary          II. Mann, Michael, *1942—*
305.3          BF692.2

ISBN 0-7456-0167-7
ISBN 0-7456-0168-5 Pbk


Library of Congress Cataloging in Publication Data

Gender and stratification.

Bibliography: p.
Includes index.
1. Sex role—Addresses, essays, lectures.
2. Social status—Addresses, essays, lectures.
3. Social classes—Addresses, essays, lectures.
I. Crompton, Rosemary.     II. Mann, Michael, 1942—
HQ1075.G46   1986          305.3          85—28342
ISBN 0-7456-0167-7
ISBN 0-7456-0168-5 (pbk.)


Typeset by Pioneer, Perthshire
Printed in Great Britain by
TJ Press Padstow

# Contents

# List of Contributors

Frank Bechhofer is Director of the Research Centre for the Social Sciences at the University of Edinburgh, author (with others) of *The Affluent Worker* and editor (with B. Elliott) of *The Petite Bourgeoisie*.

Rosemary Crompton is a Senior Lecturer in the School of Economic and Social Studies at the University of East Anglia. She is author (with Gareth Jones) of *White-Collar Proletariat: Deskilling and Gender in Clerical Work*.

Cynthia Cockburn is a Research Fellow at The City University and author of *Brothers: Male Dominance and Technological Change*.

Leonore Davidoff is a Lecturer at the University of Essex and author (with C. Hall) of *Family Fortunes: Men and Women of the English Middle Class, 1780–1850*.

Christine Delphy is Chargé de Recherches at CNRS in Paris and author of *Close to Home*.

Christopher Harris is Professor of Sociology at University College of Swansea, the University of Wales. He is author of *The Family in Industrial Society*.

Diana Leonard is a Lecturer at the University of London Institute of Education and author of *Sex and Generation*.

David Lockwood is Professor of Sociology at the University of Essex and author of such classic studies as *The Black-coated Worker* and (with others) *The Affluent Worker*.

Michael Mann is Reader in Sociology at the London School of Economics and author (with R. M. Blackburn) of *The Working Class in the Labour Market* and *The Sources of Social Power*.

Lydia Morris is a Lecturer at the University of Durham and author of 'Renegotiation of the domestic division of labour' in *New Approaches to Economic Life* edited by B. Roberts et al.

Ken Prandy is Senior Research Officer at the Department of Applied Economics, Cambridge and co-author of DAE studies including *White Collar Unionism.*

Alison Scott is a Lecturer at the University of Essex and author of 'Economic development and Urban Women's Work: the case of Lima, Peru' in Richard Anker and Catherine Heins's *Sex Inequalities in Urban Employment in the Third World.*

Janet Siltanen is a Lecturer at the University of Edinburgh and author (with Michelle Stanworth) of *Women in the Public Sphere.*

Margaret Stacey is Professor of Sociology at the University of Warwick and author (with M. Price) of *Women, Power and Politics.*

Sylvia Walby is a Lecturer at the University of Lancaster and author of *Patriarchy at Work.*

# 1

## Introduction

### Rosemary Crompton and Michael Mann

The documentation, interpretation and explanation of structured social inequality has always been a central focus of the sociological enterprise and, indeed, of the social sciences generally. British sociology is no exception, as evidenced by eighteenth- and nineteenth-century political economy and surveys of social conditions by such as Eden, Booth and Rowntree, Glass's work on social mobility and Marshall's on social citizenship after the Second World War, Townsend's research on poverty and Goldthorpe and Lockwood's theoretical and empirical work from the 1960s to the present.[1] However, like sociology everywhere (although there have always been honourable exceptions) the topic of gender has been relatively neglected in 'main-stream' stratification research and theory. Indeed, although the Social Stratification Research Seminar which intiated this volume met throughout the seventies, it was not until 1984 that the question of gender was addressed directly as the topic of a single meeting.

The explanation of this delay is, we think, of more than just passing historical interest. Although intellectual sexism no doubt plays a part in any explanation — an important point to which we will return — the situation is more complex in its totality. In addition, its investigation supplies a useful background against which to set the papers in this volume.

Sociology in Britain has developed in relation to the traditions of both European and American social thought and social research. However, it is probably true to say that stratification *theory* in Britain since the Second World War has taken its major inspiration from Europe. Two of the most influential books of the late fifties and early sixties — Lockwood's *The Blackcoated Worker: A Study in Class Consciousness* (1958) and Dahrendorf's *Class and Class Conflict in an Industrial Society* (1959), drew upon the European traditions of class analysis as represented by Marx and Weber. These approaches sought to distinguish themselves from both the theory and practice of stratification sociology in the United States. American sociology was identified with a 'consensus model' of contemporary society; that is, as over-emphasizing the extent to which advanced industrial societies were held together by common values — for example, the Parsonian 'social system', and the functional theory of stratification of Davis and Moore (1945), etc. In contrast, sociologists such as Bottomore (1961) and Rex (1961), as well as Lockwood and Dahrendorf, stressed the extent to which conflict persisted, even in societies basking in (temporary) post-war affluence. Secondly, and within the same general approach, these theorists, in contrast to class analysts such as Centers and Warner in the United States, drew a sharp distinction between the concepts of 'class' and 'status'.[2] Social class, it was argued, could not be measured in the same way as status or 'prestige'; rather it represented, and was necessarily a structure of, social *relationships* which were not simply embodied in individual or family characteristics. Such measurements produced statistical *categories*, but could not identify social collectivities or *class*.

This stress on relationships, rather than individual attributes, can be argued to reflect a 'Marxist' strand of the attempted synthesis of Marx and Weber which, in various combinations, represented the 'main-stream' stratification theory of this period. In this perspective on class relationships therefore, the structures of capital and labour, power and the market, have occupied a central place. *Class* relationships have been distinguished sharply from the documentation of social inequality *per se*. One consequence of this broad theoretical approach however, has been a tendency to 'depersonalize' the agent who, in consequence, also appears to be non-gendered. This outcome might seem paradoxical given that much stratification sociology throughout the sixties was neo-Weberian and committed, to various degrees, to an 'action' approach. The major empirical research of this period — the 'affluent worker' volumes of Goldthorpe, Lockwood, Bechhofer and Platt (1969) — gave the 'normative' aspect of class equal emphasis with the 'economic' and the 'relational'. The legacy of Weber can also be detected in an emphasis on the individual actor. Thus for many stratification theorists, an important question was — and is — whether the life-chances of the individual were (are) crucially affected by the kinds of structures identified at the beginning of this paragraph.

It is not the case, therefore, that gender has been simply omitted from stratification analysis by default. Parkin is worth quoting at some length on this topic, his clear expression of the orthodoxy being repeated by both Goldthorpe (1983) and Lockwood in chapter 2 in this volume.

> Female status certainly carries many disadvantages compared with that of males in various areas of social life including employment opportunities, property ownership, income, and so on. However, these inequalities associated

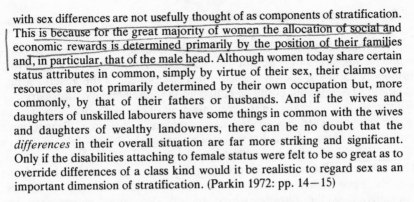

with sex differences are not usefully thought of as components of stratification. This is because for the great majority of women the allocation of social and economic rewards is determined primarily by the position of their families and, in particular, that of the male head. Although women today share certain status attributes in common, simply by virtue of their sex, their claims over resources are not primarily determined by their own occupation but, more commonly, by that of their fathers or husbands. And if the wives and daughters of unskilled labourers have some things in common with the wives and daughters of wealthy landowners, there can be no doubt that the *differences* in their overall situation are far more striking and significant. Only if the disabilities attaching to female status were felt to be so great as to override differences of a class kind would it be realistic to regard sex as an important dimension of stratification. (Parkin 1972: pp. 14—15)

Similarly, Goldthorpe's defence of the 'conventional view' is presented as stemming from 'a clear recognition of major sexual inequalities, especially in regard to opportunities for labour market participation, and of the consequent relationship of dependence that generally prevails between married women and their husbands' (Goldthorpe 1983: pp. 469—70). As female life-chances are not market-determined, women cannot be said to constitute a 'class', but the status differences between women, *as women*, are too considerable for them to be considered a meaningful status group.

If 'depersonalization' can be detected as a tendency in the approaches to class and stratification we have discussed so far, it emerged as a central tenet of another major European contribution which was influenced strongly by British and American sociology throughout the seventies, i.e. structural Marxism as represented by the work of Althusser, Poulantzas and their followers. This approach was dissociated, quite explicitly, from the 'idealism' of the Weberian tradition. 'Classes' were conceived as essentially *positions* in the social organization of production rather than collections of actual individuals. The 'structure' was of 'empty places', and moreover, the characteristics of the individuals who 'filled the slots' were relatively unimportant (Wright and Perrone 1977). These characteristics included both gender and race. The stress on *production* — which has been much criticized — characteristic of European structural Marxism, was also paralleled from the mid-seventies onwards by a resurgence of academic interest in the labour process, originating in the United States with the publication of Braverman's *Labor and Monopoly Capital: The Degradation of Work in the Twentieth Century* (1974). In this work, as Braverman makes clear, 'No attempt will be made to deal with the modern working class on the level of its consciousness, organization, or activities. This is a book about the working class as a class *in itself*, not as a class *for itself*' (p. 26—7). The debate on the labour process which has followed Braverman's work has tended to focus primarily on the structuring of places in the capitalist labour process, rather than on the individuals who fill them. The topic of gender as such, as in structural Marxist approaches, is again obscured, at least in part.

Braverman, however, did not ignore the question of women's employment. He suggested that, within a broadly Marxist framework, women in a monopoly capitalist society are a central component of the 'reserve army' of labour. Their labour could be called upon to facilitate expansionary 'de-skilling' — as, classically, in the routinization of clerical work — as well as in periods of acute labour shortage such as in wartime. Braverman's analysis therefore, although explicitly an account of class 'places' rather than of individuals, *did* suggest that some of these places might be gendered. This solution, however, raises problems for any argument which seeks to identify 'class position' with position in the social division of labour. Logically, it is the *position* which should 'determine' rather than the characteristics of the individual who fills it. However, if positions are in fact 'gendered' — in the sense of being either 'male' or 'female' occupations — then gender 'overdetermines' position — do 'reserve armies' have a 'class position' of their own? In the nineteenth century, Marx and Engels had argued that the material basis of women's subordination would be overcome as women were integrated increasingly into social, as opposed to domestic, production. In this model, the liberation of women is seen as part and parcel of the liberation of the 'working class' in general. A similar assumption — that the oppression experienced by women is symptomatic of the broader oppressions of capitalist society — underlies the 'domestic labour' perspective which developed parallel to Marxist theory throughout the seventies. It has been argued (Dalla Costa, Himmelweit, Zaretsky) that, even though production has been shifted from the home to the 'public' sphere, women's labour in the home, (although not offered on the market) makes an indirect contribution to the extraction of surplus value from the working class as a whole. That is, by caring for and reproducing the labour force both on a day to day basis and over the generations, women's work reduces the overall cost of labour to capital.

We have not been able, in this short introduction, to give more than the briefest of sketches of class and stratification theory. It is possible to suggest, however, that the subject of women within class and stratification theory has perhaps not been ignored deliberately. With massive over-simplification, it may be noted that as far as Weberian or neo-Weberian approaches are concerned, if female 'life-chances' are *not* largely market-determined, then it is logical (albeit limiting) to regard such individuals as 'beyond' the boundaries of class theory. Similarly, within Marxist approaches, the class situation of women is not *inherently* problematic — women are members of a class if they occupy the relevant position within the social organization of production; and more generally, the particular form of the oppression (or otherwise) of women is seen, to various degrees, as a reflection of the prevailing economic mode and its associated patterns of exploitation.

This view of the 'woman problem' as essentially an artefact of the prevailing system of economic exploitation has been resisted strenuously by many feminists. They have argued that the oppression of women is not to be viewed as 'secondary' to — and therefore, by implication, less important than — class oppression as a whole. Women, they argue, are oppressed as a class by *men*, and patriarchal structures are geographically and historically almost universal, predating capitalism and persisting in the so-called 'socialist' societies. In short, the major axis of differentiation in contemporary society is not class as such, but gender and it is women who face the 'longest revolution'.

Many feminists however, appear reluctant to abandon class theory in its entirety, and this is particularly the case as far as some aspects of the Marxist approach are concerned. In recent years, there has emerged an increasing emphasis on what has come to be called 'dual-systems' theory, exemplified in the work of Heidi Hartmann (see chapters 6 and 9 in this volume). Hartmann agrees with the feminist critique that Marxist theory is inadequate to deal with the 'woman question' and argues that the way ahead is to treat capitalist and patriarchal structures as two separate, if interrelated, systems: 'Capitalist development creates the places for a hierarchy of workers, but traditional Marxist categories cannot tell us who will fill which places. Gender and racial hierarchies determine who fills the empty places' (Hartmann 1976: p. 18). In this 'dual-systems' approach, we have an interesting echo of the 'multidimensional' approach to social stratification, where gender, age, race, etc. are seen as independent dimensions which cross-cut each other, giving rise to a complex structure of inequality (Lenski 1966). The problem with such approaches is that societies are not built up of independent 'dimensions' or 'levels'. 'Capitalism', 'gender', 'race', are not homogeneous totalities interacting externally with one another. Hartmann is wrong to see capitalism as producing the places; gender and race the persons. The character and speed of the development of capitalism and its 'places' was itself influenced by 'gender' and race-associated processes such as inheritance systems and the availability of colonial plantation labour. It was also affected internally by other social structures such as the state, war, religion and urban/rural struggles. In turn, capitalist processes affected their 'internal' developments. Thus dual-systems theorists, while criticizing rightly the limitations of previous stratification orthodoxies, have not taken their criticisms far enough.

Thus far, our remarks have been concerned mainly with the attention, or lack of it, given to gender in class stratification *theories* — that is, attempts to uncover the *sources* of structured inequality and social change. However, within the large canvas which is stratification sociology, the documentation of inequalities is also an integral part. Both Marxists and Weberians have engaged in empirical research which both documents *and* attempts to explain structures of inequality.[3] In contemporary capitalist societies, the occupational structure is used widely as an approximate index of class membership. There are many problems associated with its use — most notably that it provides us with no reliable guide to the distribution and power of capital — but as it is one of the few national measures available to stratification sociologists, it is unlikely to fall into disuse. Research by industrial sociologists and others has provided a body of evidence which enables occupations to be classified according to the characteristic 'life-chances' they afford, and/or position in the social organization of production. The systematic consideration of gender however, raises serious problems for occupational classifications, whether neo-Marxist or neo-Weberian.

Two particular problems may be identified:

(a) Should the individual or the household properly be the 'unit' of stratification analysis? (This is most problematic for neo-Marxists).
(b) The 'life-chances' associated with the same occupation may be very different depending upon whether it is carried out by a man or a woman. (This raises more problems for neo-Weberian approaches).

As we have seen, it has been assumed widely by sociologists of various 'theoretical' persuasions that the family is the basic unit of stratification analysis. On this reading, the class situation of family members — including women — is 'derived' from that of the main breadwinner who is usually a man. This assumption has been criticized widely. Empirically, the proportion of households without a male 'head' — and thus a class 'identifier' — is increasing. Additionally, since the sixties, women have participated increasingly in the labour force as employees in their own right (Martin and Roberts 1984).

Should these women in formal employment therefore be 'declassed'? Critics of the orthodox view of the 'male breadwinner' have advocated two rather different solutions, although both would include giving a 'class situation' to women who work. One solution would reject the household as the unit of class analysis as Garnsey has observed: 'In a system of individual wage labour, families are not engaged as units in the occupational division of labour' (Garnsey 1978: p. 429). Thus Stanworth (1984), in her critique of Goldthorpe, argues that women in employment are not 'declassed' by marriage and should be considered as having a 'directly determined' class position. The other solution would retain the household as a unit of measurement, but include, where the woman is in formal employment, her 'class situation' as contributing to that of the household overall — thus we have the increasing phenomenon of 'cross-class' families (Britten and

Heath 1983).[4] Recognizing the contribution which the wife's employment might make to the family unit as a whole however, still side-steps an important question — is it valid to assume that members of a family share an identical 'class situation'? As Leonard and Delphy remind us in chapter 5, this is certainly not the case as far as the distribution of property is concerned.

The second major problem associated with measurement and classification that we have identified stems from the fact that, as we have noted already, men and women in the same occupations may in practice have very different 'life-chances'; that it is the gender of the occupant, rather than the occupation itself, which determines the outcome.[5] If this phenomenon is widespread, then it will obviously have serious consequences for any class analysis which 'begins with a structure of positions, associated with a specific historical form of the social division of labour' (Goldthorpe 1983). The most frequently cited empirical example is clerical work. Men who begin their working lives as clerks, it is argued, will almost certainly be promoted to managerial positions, whereas women — the majority of the clerical labour force — will not (Stewart, Prandy and Blackburn 1980). That the same occupation may have a different status and/or different life-chance outcomes, depending on the gender of the occupant, is obviously a serious threat to the entire strategy of using occupational classifications in empirical work on social stratification. Overcoming the practical problems raised is likely to be a massive task — one which calls for a completely revised occupational scheme, parallel classification for 'male' jobs and 'female' jobs or just piecemeal modifications? (see, for example, Martin and Roberts 1984: p. 21).[6]

We can see therefore, that the question of gender raises serious problems for both theoretical and empirical work in social stratification. The pressure to confront these issues has been increasing since the sixties, with the growth of the number of households without an official male 'breadwinner', the increasing participation of women in employment and in the passing of legislation which has, to a considerable extent, removed formal barriers to the participation of women in almost all areas of social life. However, (and paradoxically), perhaps the sheer magnitude of the difficulties raised by gender, and which we have tried to indicate in our discussion so far, has served to inhibit the debate (Allen 1983).

There is another explanation, however, of the neglect of gender by the stratification 'mainstream' which requires systematic attention. As Newby has noted 'The issue of gender inequality was not, primarily, one which arose from debates within stratification research but one which arose external to it, via the women's movement' (1982). It is noteworthy that, with very few exceptions, the most prominent figures in stratification research and theory in Britain and elsewhere are, and always have been, male. Is the neglect of gender by stratification theorists therefore a

reflection of the conscious or unconscious action (or inaction) of
'malestream' sociology?

One of our contributors has already developed this argument and she
develops it further in chapter 13. Stacey distinguishes between the 'public'
and the 'private' domains of contemporary society: the 'public' domain
including the world of waged work, industry and production for the
market; of politics, warfare, etc.; and the 'private' domain including the
domestic world of the family, of production for use rather than production
for exchange, and of course, of the reproduction of human beings
themselves.[7] She argues:

> Our present problem . . . stems from the early male domination of sociological
> theory which led to exclusive attention being paid to the public domain, to
> affairs of state and the market place which in the mid-nineteenth century
> were not affairs with which women were allowed to be concerned. (Stacey
> 1981: p. 173)

The concepts developed which purported to analyse 'society' (and this
would include class and stratification concepts) were therefore, and are in
reality, only partial as they do not examine 'society' as a *whole*, but only the
'public' sphere. Indeed, they are not only partial but positively misleading.
In particular, the division of labour has been examined almost entirely
using 'public' domain concepts of production and the market which are
inappropriate both for work carried out in the private domain and 'private'
domain work in the 'public' sphere, i.e. the 'people work' of caring and
nurturing: nursing, teaching, etc. Stacey argues, therefore, that sociology
(and this would include stratification sociology) must develop new theories
and concepts 'which can articulate the private and public domains and
address those activities which straddle both domains' (1981: p. 182).

This, then, was the background to the Symposium on Gender and
Stratification which met at the University of East Anglia in the summer of
1984. The papers presented there, and which form the chapters in this
volume, touched upon all aspects of the debate.[8] Davidoff, in her historical
analysis (chapter 12), provides empirical evidence as to how the agricultural
and industrial revolution in England separated the 'public' from the 'private'
sphere and domesticated and feminized the wives and daughters of capitalist
farmers. Scott (chapter 11) provides a broad comparative perspective on
the gender division of labour in Britain, Egypt, Ghana and Peru. Leonard
and Delphy (chapter 5) emphasize the role of the family and especially the
hereditary transmission of property, in class formation.

Others focus more closely on contemporary society. Prandy (chapter 10)
addresses himself to the 'measurement problem'. He illustrates the
difficulties presented by the non-comparability of men's and women's
occupations and suggests that a more coherent theory can be provided by
moving outside of the economic to the 'social' sphere, and especially to

patterns of intermarriage. Although not addressing the problem directly, and arriving at rather different solutions, two further chapters also attempt to move away from orthodox occupational categories. Harris and Morris (chapter 7) argue, on the basis of a study of redundant South Wales steelworkers and their families, that the neglect of gender in stratification theory is a consequence of concentrating on 'occupation' rather than power in the labour-market. Siltanen's study (chapter 8) shows how domestic responsibilities, rather than gender *per se*, affects location in the occupational structure of the Post Office — an argument which might also be taken to suggest that rewards are not strictly 'market-determined'. Crompton (chapter 9) raises the question of the possible consequences for 'service class' formation and development if the current trend of increasing vocational qualifications for women in Britain is maintained, and Cockburn (chapter 6) explores the relevance of physical skills and of the culture and power that surround them, for theories of patriarchy.

Three other chapters address themselves more explicitly to the theoretical problems for stratification theory and practice raised by the systematic consideration of gender. Lockwood (chapter 2) provides a robust defence of the stratification orthodoxy, arguing that while gender (and its attendant concepts such as patriarchy) may provide interesting problems for analysis, it has little direct relevance to either social class or status which remain the core of stratification theory. In contrast, Walby (chapter 3) argues for a radical theoretical revision, taking class and status into the household and arguing that housewives and husbands *are* classes. Mann (chapter 4) provides a historical perspective on the restructuring of theory, tracing the historical interrelations of various stratification 'nuclei': 'persons'; household/families/lineages; genders; classes and nations. He argues that whereas patriarchy has become *less* important as an organizing principle, stratification itself has become 'gendered'.

Finally, Stacey (chapter 13) and Bechhofer (chapter 14) record their reflections and conclusions on the main body of the text. In addition to their original contributions to the topic of gender and stratification, both chapters provide useful summaries of the Symposium itself.

This book does not simply reproduce 'feminist' and 'main-stream' stances on the gender and stratification debate although neither does it present a 'consensus' view. In chapter 13, Stacey distinguishes various positions which have emerged in the discussion so far: firstly, a division between those concerned mainly with how and why class is measured; and secondly, the 'structuralists', described as having a more 'theoretical' focus on uncovering the 'crucial characteristics of the social order' and thus the sources of structured inequality and social change. (As we have suggested, too rigid a distinction cannot be maintained between these enterprises in practice, because clearly, *what* is measured will reflect the measurer's underlying assumptions as to which characteristics are crucial.) The debates amongst the 'structuralists' tended to crystallize into two groups holding different opinions: those for whom the relations of class and the market are ultimately of most significance; and those who would emphasize the predominance of patriarchal structures. The former stance corresponds to the stratification main-stream (broadly conceived to include the range of Marxist and Weberian theories), the latter to the feminist. Finally, Stacey identifies a third category — the revisionists — also discussed by Walby (chapter 3) as the 'new feminist stratification'.

As Stacey identifies us as 'revisionists', perhaps we should be cautious of abusing our editorial discretion. Nevertheless, we would suggest that the revisionist strategy may well prove to be the most useful way forward in the present context, even though it may not, ultimately, provide a final set of answers. The explicit recognition of the fact — common to all the 'revisionists' — that the subject-matter of social stratification theory and research includes the private sphere of the household as well as the public world of employment and the market, is, we would suggest, highly significant. The theoretical explanation of relationships within what has been described variously as the 'domestic economy', 'the family', the 'private sphere' (and which should have been central even to traditional stratification debates) has been marginalized sociologically. However, 'the family' is no longer viewed uncritically as a 'natural' phenomenon by most sociologists; in particular, it may be a site of conflict and exploitation by men of women. The process of 'simply adding on' questions raised by gender to the existing concern of stratification theory may therefore, finally transform the theory itself. As we have suggested, one reason for the previous neglect of gender may have been the fact that a direct confrontation of the problems raised threatens some of the most cherished assumptions of the stratification orthodoxy.

The lesson of the Symposium therefore, was to continue to work on a range of issues relating to conceptualization, measurement and empirical research in both the domestic and public spheres. As far as stratification theory is concerned, these chapters demonstrate, at the very least, that 'gender matters' (although Lockwood may have reservations!). If in this respect only, we hope that stratification research will never be the same again.

# 2

## Class, Status and Gender

### David Lockwood

Since the study of social stratification deservedly occupies the central place in macrosociology, it is perhaps not surprising that its explanatory purpose should have become the target of feminist critiques which concur in the view that traditional approaches to social stratification have been misconceived because they have failed to take into account the fact that the structure of social inequality has at least as much to do with gender, as with class or status, relationships. It is with the validity of this thesis, and its implications, that the present chapter is exclusively concerned.[1] But before attending to it directly, it is necessary to distinguish three separate kinds of enquiry that are generally subsumed under the heading of social stratification analysis. Only then will it be possible to identify the precise respects in which a recognition of the significance of gender relations and sexual inequality calls for changes in accepted modes of thinking about the subject.

#### THE AIMS OF STRATIFICATION ANALYSIS

Weber's observation (1968) that societies can be distinguished according to their degree of class or status formation provides the most convenient summary of the range of facts that social stratification theory is called upon to explain.[2] A vast amount of historical and comparative evidence supports the conclusion that 'communal' and 'corporate' social interactions of a class or status kind constitute more or less systematic properties of total societies. For example, the fact that the Ruhr insurrection of 1920 approximated a situation of class war is as indisputable as the fact that the caste system in Tanjore in 1962 still represented a highly developed form of status-group consolidation (Eliasberg 1974; Beteille 1965). The first form of enquiry, then, concerns the extent to which class or status systems are the predominant modes of social action at the societal level.[3] This is why the study of social stratification is of such pre-eminent importance in sociology. Since class and status formation are modes of social interaction which are not only empirically identifiable as variable configurations of total societies, but analytically distinguishable from the 'economy' and the 'polity', it is understandable why, within the division of labour of the social sciences (including Marxist theory), 'social stratification' should have come to be regarded as the distinctive subject-matter of macrosociology. Furthermore, since status-group consolidation and class polarization can be taken as limiting cases of social order and conflict, it is once again not hard to understand why the study of social stratification should be regarded as the specific sociological contribution to the analysis of social (as opposed to system) integration.

Theories of social stratification, then, presuppose as their explanatory object the inter- and intra-societal variability of class and status formation. From this viewpoint, the most important question regarding claims about the significance of sexual inequality is whether societies can be differentiated according to the predominance of systems of gender relations, that is, structures of social action comparable to those within the range of class polarization and status-group consolidation. If they cannot, the thesis that the aims of 'sex-blind' stratification theory are misconceived because they neglect gender relationships must be rejected. In that case also, the further question arises of exactly what kinds of social interactions a gender-informed study of social stratification does in fact seek to explain.

A closely-related kind of enquiry subsumed under the study of social stratification attempts to generalize about the determinants of class and status formation.[4] This is often referred to as the analysis of class (though seldom, status) 'structure' or 'structuration'. Weber's judgement — that economic and technological change favours class stratification and pushes status stratification into the background — is prototypical of this endeavour, which has by now become highly complicated in terms of the independent variables under consideration (consider explanations of why there is no socialism in the United States? as an hors d'oeuvre and with why has the Western working class not been revolutionary? as the entrée). But since the extent of class and status formation is one major measure of social integration, it should come as no surprise that explanations of its variability encompass the widest set of factors. At the structural level, these are what are conventionally (and even in some 'advanced' formulations) thought of as the economic, political and ideological. At the situational level, they refer to the basic elements of the schema of social action: the determinants of actors' ends, their choice of means and their conditions of action, which naturally include the unintended consequences of their interactions. Additionally, and not least, there are factors having to do with a society's history or what is now sometimes called the 'social formation'. To seek to add to this embarrassment of riches the factor of gender is something that could hardly be objected to. But that would mean no more than claiming that class and status formation is significantly affected by the variability of the structure of gender relations. It would not mean that the latter is a 'stratification' phenomenon in its own right: that is, a structure of social relations quite distinct from class and status interactions. The acceptance of this limitation would seem to be implicit in much of the feminist critique of conventional stratification analysis. But it would not be accepted by those who adhere to the idea of patriarchy. For them, gender relations are not part of the explanation of something else; they are the thing that deserves and requires explanation.

Since the determination and explanation of the variability of class and status formation have been the central concerns of the study of social stratification, the documentation of the inequality of opportunities and outcomes — according to socially (though not necessarily sociologically) relevant categories — has occupied a subordinate place. This relegation is justifiable on several grounds. First, because the interest in the distribution of unequal rewards, life-chances, or whatever, is primarily one of social policy, of how different social arrangements could procure 'better' outcomes and opportunities. This is clearly revealed by the 'theoretical' object of such investigations, namely, a set of outcomes that is intelligible only in the statistical sense that it conforms to, or deviates from, some 'ideal', random, or category-neutral, distribution. *Inter alia*, gender-based inequalities will naturally be such an object of interest and are well attested to (see for example Reid and Wormald 1982). What is called the 'sexual division of labour' is one facet of this. But the second reason why this sort of empirical regularity is peripheral to the study of social stratification proper is that the outcomes in question are explicable only in terms of the same factors that can also account for the extent of class or status formation: explaining 'outcomes' is, so to speak, a by-product of stratification analysis. Thirdly, and most importantly, in themselves such 'outcomes' are not necessarily immediately relevant to the explanation of class or status formation. For example, there is now a great mass of evidence that refutes the obstinate idea (never entertained by a De Tocqueville or a Trotsky) that economic deprivation is a necessary or even a sufficient condition of radical, if not revolutionary, class action. Moreover, many of the outcomes that fascinate sociologists are not outcomes whose effects are so immediately tangible to the individuals concerned. For example, it is doubtful that publicizing the precisely documented fact that relative mobility opportunities are highly unequal would arouse a deep and widespread sense of social grievance (see Goldthorpe *et al.* 1980: p. 266). Although such knowledge is an indispensable indication of the persistence and location of status-group stratification, it throws no light on the social actions by which these boundaries are maintained. Matters are not dissimilar when, for example, it comes to interpreting the meaning of conventional measures of working-class radicalism (a good example of how such misinterpretation can arise is provided by Geary 1981). It is then no more than sociological common sense to assert that, whether outcomes are taken either as conditions or as manifestations of class or status-group formation, their significance inheres entirely in the ways in which they are understood and evaluated by those who, through their actions, maintain or change these forms of social relationships.

From these considerations it follows that arguments indicting conventional stratification analysis on the ground that sexual inequalities of opportunity or outcome have escaped its attention are of small weight. The fact that something should be of concern to the Equal Opportunities Commission does not thereby guarantee its sociological relevance.

### HAS STRATIFICATION ANALYSIS NEGLECTED GENDER?

Having outlined the three fairly distinct kinds of enquiry subsumed under the heading of stratification analysis, it is now possible to define more precisely the nature of the objection that this field of study is deficient because it has ignored the importance of gender relations. The least significant possible thesis is that the statistical study of the distribution of opportunities or outcomes has been insufficiently concerned with documenting gender (as opposed to a whole range of other) inequalities. Ignoring the questions of how far this is the case, and whether this sort of study fulfils mainly a social-policy or political function, it is fairly clear that the mere accumulation of such data is of sociological relevance only to the extent that it provides certain (though not the most interesting) 'raw materials' which can presumably be explained by theories of the structural determinants of class and status formation. It is not, therefore, the kind of study that deserves extended comment here; but it does lead on to another possible line of criticism, which is that stratification theorists have paid far too little attention to the importance of gender relations as determinants of class and status formation. This is a much more serious, and probably the most crucial objection; also, one that is, *prima facie* least disputable.[5]

But it is distinct from the last, and much more ambitious, possible claim that, as structures of social interaction, gender relations are somehow comparable to the kinds of societal configurations that have been thought of traditionally as lying between the limits of class polarization and status-group consolidation. It is of course necessary to be cautious in formulating the problem in this way because, for any particular society at any given time, it may be difficult to establish the exact extent to which it is, in Weber's terms, 'class' or 'status' formed, that is, by reference to the predominant modes of social interaction. Nevertheless, since it has not been found useful to conceptualize the possible range of social formation in other than these broad terms, it seems appropriate to begin by asking whether, judged by the forms of their communal and corporate interactions, men and women constitute anything analogous to 'classes' and 'status groups'.

The objection to even beginning to pursue such thoughts are commonplace. Outside of the pages of *Lysistrata*, the war between the sexes does not eventuate in society-wide 'class struggle'; and even in those instances where there is some slight approximation to such a conflict, the basis of it has been far from enduring or systematic.[6] Again, the cases in which men and women can be said to make up anything approaching identifiable status groups, whose boundaries are maintained by conventional, legal or religious sanctions, are far too exceptional to require a revision of the traditional approach to this subject.[7] Both of these objections rest on the simple fact that gender relations are usually heterosexual (though often homosociable) and are therefore cross-cut by class and status relations.[8] This prevents men and women having economic interests that could lead them to organize collectively against each other in any 'class' action. Furthermore, since some degree of endogamy and commensality is what marks one status group from another, any comparable form of gender interaction is also ruled out. Taken together, these are powerful objections to the claim that gender relations are macrosocial phenomena of the same order as classes and status groups. It is, of course, always possible to argue that gender relationships partake of some kind of ubiquitous, class- or status-oriented interaction at the situational, as opposed to the societal, level: so that they are, so to speak, of only 'subterranean' importance. But a retreat to this position would be identical in its implications to that apparently accepted by those Marxist theoreticians who, faced with the fact that the Western working class has failed to be revolutionary, have sought to redefine 'class struggle' in order to encompass almost all forms of everyday social conflict.[9] In both cases, the price to be paid is much the same: the dissolution of any distinction between gender or class action and social action *per se*.

These considerations also have a bearing on the view that gender relations are somehow similar to ethnic relations.[10] This affinity is no doubt discoverable in the visibility of both types of actors and the saliency of ascriptive properties in governing their relationships with others. But beyond this surface resemblance, the argument does not have much force, particularly as it refers to questions of group formation. Ethnic divisions, far more frequently than those of class, do provide the basis of acute communal conflicts, especially when ethnicity is associated with 'differential incorporation' (Kuper and Smith 1971), or the unequal distribution of citizenship rights. Such conflicts are naturally even more intense when the political domination of one ethnic group by another is accompanied by its economic exploitation and public derogation. Ethnic discrimination and the communal strife to which it often gives rise are therefore best understood as forms of status- rather than class-based stratification and antagonism. This conclusion is supported by the fact that the lack of coincidence of ethnic and class boundaries does not prevent the eruption of communal conflicts which are class-indiscriminate in their scope (Kuper 1974: ch. 7, 8). In general, the consciousness of ethnic belonging is far more widespread, continuous and intense than class-consciousness. And in these respects it is certainly similar to gender consciousness. But for reasons already adduced, gender differences (unless they are also associated with highly visible forms of differential incorporation) are unlikely to eventuate in anything at all comparable to ethnic solidarity and conflict. In this century, the struggle for the enfranchisement of women has provided the only significant example of mass mobilization of this kind, and once that single status interest was achieved the movement collapsed.[11]

## MARXIST CLASS THEORY, PATRIARCHY AND GENDER

The foregoing observations may now be tested by examining the only two major lines of thought that might possibly lead to different conclusions. One is the attempt to accommodate gender relations to Marxist class theory. The other is the idea that gender relations constitute a distinct form of stratification, namely patriarchy.

Since the most recent phase of feminism originated in left-wing movements in the United States (and was motivated partly by the sexism and relative status deprivation that women experienced at that level of the 'class struggle') it is not accidental that attempts to formulate the place of women in the class structure should have become a major concern of Marxist theoreticians. It is also natural that the present orientation of this school of thought should have led to the conceptualization of sexual divisions in terms that have less to do with actual social relationships, or patterns of social interaction, than with the determination of the 'place' of female labour within the class structure and of its 'functions for capital'. The 'woman question' in Marxism then, is partly just another aspect of the 'boundary debate', i.e., the analysis of 'objective' class positions and class interests, which it is assumed provides a correct understanding of the potentialities of class action. A major question from this perspective is whether or not female domestic labour is part of the working class or proletariat, and, less orthodoxly, whether it is in some sense a class which is exploited domestically, rather than capitalistically. But the 'woman question' (unlike some other issues arising from the 'boundary' debate) is also closely related to the Marxist economic theory of system contradiction via such questions as whether or not domestic labour is a source of surplus value, and whether or not women constitute a 'reserve army of labour'.

To a large extent then, discussion of women's place(s) in the class structure has been dominated by conceptual debates whose energy derives more from their political significance for the protagonists than from the explanatory power of the vying arguments. Certainly the sociological value of such work has yet to be shown. Mere observers of these debates are unlikely to be excited by such belated recent discoveries, as that the whole domestic labour debate throws no light on the fact that it is usually women who do housework, or that the 'reserve army of labour' thesis appears to be vitiated by the fact of sexually-segregated job markets. Nor will they be impressed with the explanatory power of a theory whose main counter-factual appears to be that the withdrawal of women from housework would mean the collapse of capitalism. And if internal critics can level powerful charges of 'functionalism' and 'reductionism' against the basic terms of the debate, it is still not clear what in the way of a more discriminating and positive analysis these condign criticisms lead to.[12]

The domestic labour debate has shown signs of diminishing returns for some time. But from the beginning, it represented a conceptual investment whose profitability was highly questionable, simply because of the 'essentialist' activity in which it engaged and which focused on such questions as what sort of labour *is* domestic labour? Is it really labour that contributes to surplus value? Are women domestic workers really exploited by capital or by their husbands? And so on. In this respect it shares the same features as the 'boundary debate' and the debate on productive and unproductive labour. Marxism has always had difficulties in formulating a stable and coherent theory of action which could relate the analysis of objective class position and of system contradictions to class formation. This is another reason for scepticism about the explanatory power of the theories that are likely to issue from the current domestic labour debate. It is not clear what this debate seeks to explain, although, like all Marxist theory, it is ultimately oriented to an understanding of the development of the class struggle. Nevertheless, its starting point (and perhaps its finishing point) is the analysis of class 'structure' or 'structuration'; it is not concerned primarily with explaining forms of class action or class conflict (except in the sense, already noted above, in which Marxism now views these as endemic in class relations, whether at the economic, political or ideological level).

In this respect, it differs fundamentally from the kind of analysis that has accreted around the concept of 'patriarchy', which, despite the 'essentialist' tendency it shares with Marxist debates, does refer to patterns of behaviour

*David Lockwood*

or forms of social interaction, that is, gender relations. The two approaches also differ in that whereas the orthodox Marxist position holds that women do not constitute a class,[13] while patriarchy is seen as a structure of social relations in which men are privileged systematically and women dis-privileged in such a variety of social contexts that it makes sense to think of gender relations as a form of 'stratification', and hence one may suppose of 'gender situations', 'gender interests' and 'gender conflicts'.

The arguments against current uses of the concept of patriarchy have been well rehearsed (see especially Elshtein 1981: pp. 204—28; Beechey 1979). One important objection is that, since patriarchy refers to a quite specific historical form of household relationship and societal ideology, its application to modern societies is quite misleading, and results in the concept losing any possible explanatory value and acquiring instead a merely liturgical character. While matters of terminology are never crucial, it is plain that the highly generalized meaning that patriarchy has acquired tends to preclude serious historical and comparative study of 'gender stratification'. This is partly because all concepts of invariant societal properties tend to regress towards forms of explanation that derive from some kind of 'positivistic' or 'idealistic' action schema.

This is certainly evident in discussions of patriarchy. Those who regard the ubiquity of this phenomenon as more impressive than its historical and social variability have sought to account for its pervasiveness by a whole range of reductionist, extra-sociological explanations, be they biological, cultural, or psychoanalytical, or simply in terms of men's (presumably innate) drive to dominate women. Whatever in other respects might be seen to be the merits of these various theories and their respective redemptory promises, it is clear that they afford no basis for a systematic, comparative, study of gender relations and inequalities. And yet, even among those who eschew the search for origins and who are more interested in bringing women back into the detailed study of societies past and present, it is still commonly assumed that the oppression of women by men is a global feature of social life manifesting itself in every institutional sphere, and therefore in need only of particularization.[14] Thereby, the historical and sociological objective is once again misconceived. It is by now well recognized that if patriarchy is to be a useful concept it must take account of the variability in gender relations. But this discovery of sociological essentials merely echoes what, for example, Mills (1963: p. 344) argued for thirty years ago: 'some sort of classification of women according to their condition'. This hardly exists, and the documentation of 'instances' of patriarchal domination, however detailed this may be, is no substitute for the prior work of decomposing the idea of patriarchal domination itself. For, *contra* Mills, what is needed is not an empirical classification of types of women (such as that provided, for example, by Parsons' categories of 'wife', 'mother', 'good companion', 'career' woman and 'glamour' girl) but rather an analytical differentiation of gender relations; and, naturally, hypotheses about the determinants of the variability of these components.[15] No amount of illustration of the institutionally imbricated nature of patriarchal domination will guarantee this result.

Moreover, it is doubtful that further conceptual and empirical investigation of the structure of gender relations would lead to the conclusion that patriarchy constitutes a type of social formation that has been improperly ignored by conventional stratification analysis. Certain theories in which men and women, or husbands and housewives, appear as the subjects of a new ground of the class war, are highly factitious. Nevertheless, despite the more extravagant claims of some of its adherents, the idea of patriarchy does represent a challenge to accepted notions of status stratification and indeed poses a rather interesting problem. This is that, although the status situations of men and women differ in certain significant respects, and fairly systematically so in a variety of institutional contexts, it is at the same time true that men and women are not, in any meaningful sense of the term, status groups. Why this should be the case merits further discussion.

## STATUS GROUPS AND GENDER

It is convenient to begin with Weber, who defines status situation first negatively as that of 'men whose fate is not determined by the chance of using goods or services for themselves on the market', and then positively, so as to include 'every typical component of the life situation of men that is determined by a specific social estimation of honour' (1968). While the life-chances of populations of modern Western societies are status-determined — in the strict sense of the term — mainly by the institutional complex of citizenship, it may be thought that, in so far as opportunities to acquire, dispose of, and benefit from, marketable skills are limited by estimations of social worth then this liability is far more evident in the 'fate' of women than in that of men. Weber's second criterion is that status stratification goes hand in hand with the 'monopolization of ideal goods and opportunities' and that 'material monopolies provide the most effective motives for the exclusiveness of a status group.' Among the latter, the most relevant in the present context is the right to pursue certain types of occupations. Thirdly, such monopolization is guaranteed by conventional, or legal, or religious, sanctions.[16] By these criteria also it can be argued that women occupy a fairly distinctive status situation because their life-chances, including their chances of entering employment, and specific kinds of employment, are determined substantially by customary and ideological (if not juridical) constraints; and, furthermore, because these outcomes may be interpreted in significant measure as the result of men's deliberate attempts to monopolize positions of occupational authority and to secure domestic benefits.[17] On these grounds then, it is reasonable to think of the sexual divisions of labour and of other aspects of sexual inequality as being status-determined, that is, as outcomes of the differentiation of status situations specific to men and women. Yet at the same time, it is fairly clear that in itself, sex or gender is a relatively insignificant basis of status-group formation. As Shils (1967) puts it, 'the deference accorded to a woman or to women as a category or to a man or to men as a category is at the margin of macrosocial deference.'

Part of the explanation of this is to be found in the fact that the status a woman inherits or acquires from particular men (or that which she achieves on her own account), is, or appears to be, far more significant than the status she shares with women in general *vis-à-vis* men in general. But there is another, no less important, reason why men and women do not form separate status groups, and this has to do with the fact (so much emphasized by proponents of the idea of patriarchy) that the subjection of women to men tends to occur in every institutional context.

Simply because the relations between the sexes have no specific institutional expression outside of the nuclear family, they are at once the locus of an ever-present potential for discrimination and an unstable basis of status-group formation. For all practical purposes, sexual identity is as unmistakable as the gender connotations attaching to it are unavoidable. Only a few other properties of persons, such as skin colour and age, are of equally direct and pervasive social significance. Many ethnic identifying marks, such as apparel and hair-style are optional, and some ethnic groups are not outwardly distinct at all. But the sheer visibility of maleness and femaleness means that the relations between the sexes are charged with (among other sentiments) moral expectations that derive from estimations of the relative social worth of men and women in general. Naturally, the extent to which such predispositions are expressed in acts of deference and derogation will vary, according to the formality or informality of the relationship, on its degree of anonymity and so on. But the second, elementary point in need of emphasis is that the relationships in which women customarily defer to men and men derogate women are predominantly dyadic. These relationships may be private, personal or domestic; they may be public, anonymous and ephemeral; or they may be interspersed among bureaucratically organized activities. But in all instances, they are most commonly status interactions involving a particular man and a particular woman, and not groups of men and women. It is precisely the highly particularized and limited scope of such relations that has called forth the feminist slogan 'the personal is political.' At the same time the latter recognizes, at least tacitly, that the structure of macrosocial deference has very little to do with the relations between the sexes.

In contemporary Western societies, whose stratification systems are based on class relations and the relations of a common legal status of citizenship, the status hierarchy is, by any historical comparison, relatively unpronounced, its boundaries identifiable principally through patterns of social inclusion and exclusion, of intermarriage and informal association. While for some purposes it is convenient to assume that non-legal status is a function of position in the occupational hierarchy, this formulation is elliptical in that it fails to reveal that the status order is a system of social action. Shils (1982), who has been foremost in giving due recognition to this fact, has also shown that status is determined fundamentally by proximity to the creative and charismatic 'centre' of society, so that the positions and activities that have highest status are those that are imbued with the greatest 'authority' (in the original sense of that word). Now as always, position in the hierarchy of authority of corporate groups, whether these be armies, churches, parties, business enterprises, or whatever, is what is decisive for status ranking (and for that matter, other rewards as well, including income to a large extent). Status-defining ceremonies and rituals, as well as the interest in publicly recognized status as an end in itself, become more noticeable at the higher reaches of corporate groups; and the equivalence of these variously based high statuses is established by meticulously graded, national honours. All this is more or less well understood, recognized or acquiesced in by those who inhabit the middle and even the lower reaches of the status order, and whose own modes of status-group demarcation are modelled on those of their respective, immediate superiors from whom they seek recognition. Indeed, the stability of the status system as a whole depends on the existence of intersecting status groups throughout its various levels; this is the social mechanism by which conceptions of authority and creativity are transmitted from the centre to the periphery.

Such considerations might appear far removed from a question such as whether conventional stratification analysis has erred in assuming that the social status of women is determined by the occupational position of their fathers and husbands. But this is not so. A recent and keen debate on whether the occupations of women should be taken into account in defining the status of family units has focused on the extent and significance of 'cross-class' marriages (see Goldthorpe 1983; and replies by Britten and Heath 1983; Erikson 1984; Goldthorpe 1984; Heath and Britten 1984; Stanworth 1984). But these matters serve simply to bring into prominence the fact that it is the position of an occupation within some hierarchy of authority that is decisive for its status and not the sex of the person who happens to be in it. This does not mean that the sex (or any other ascriptive property) of the incumbents of these positions has no status implications whatsoever, but merely that these effects are marginal in the sense that they do not disturb the familiar rank order of broad occupational strata.[18] At any rate, there is no evidence to suggest, and no reason to believe, that a 'sex-neutral' distribution of persons among occupations would fundamentally alter their relative social standing.[19] In societies where kinship relations are no longer a principal mode of social organization and a major type of corporate group, sexual differentiation lacks a status-conferring institutional basis. This is a basic reason why men and women do not, and cannot, form status groups; and there is no ground for believing that this would not still hold even if heterosexual, monogamous marriage were not the norm.

In the end therefore, the idea of patriarchy serves to draw attention to some of the ways in which the sexual division of labour is reproduced by what has been called the 'subterranean' status relations between men and women. This is an important subject, a part of the study of the distribution of social inequalities. At the same time, patriarchy has not proved to be a concept that entails any radical revision of conventional stratification theory, whose purpose is to explain variations in the degree of class and status formation. It is possible that gender relations may prove to be a more important part of such explanations than has been recognized hitherto. But this again does not mean that the purpose of stratification theory has been misconceived.

# 3

## Gender, Class and Stratification
### Towards a New Approach

### Sylvia Walby

#### INTRODUCTION

It has become almost a truism that main-stream stratification studies deal
inadequately with gender inequality (Acker 1973; 1980; Allen 1982; Delphy
1981; Garnsey 1978; Murgatroyd 1982a; 1982b; Newby 1982; West 1978).
In response to these critiques there have been attempts to revise the
conceptual and empirical tools used in stratification studies (e.g. Britten
and Heath 1983; Murgatroyd 1982a), and at defending the old position
(Goldthorpe 1983). I am going to argue that those criticisms did not go far
enough, that their weaknesses left the way open for revisions which failed
to tackle the most important problems concerning gender and stratification.[1]
I shall then suggest a revised framework which would permit a more
adequate theorization of gender inequality and suggest some of the new
questions this raises for stratification theory.

The early criticisms (with few exceptions) were too cautious, criticizing
stratification studies only on their own terms, rather than challenging their
narrow problematic. The questions asked by stratification theory were
accepted as defining the parameters of the terrain; only the neglect of the
impact of women on those issues was questioned. The critics challenged
the use of the household as the unit of stratification primarily on the
grounds that it dealt inadequately with those people who did not live in the
conventional 'male breadwinner, dependent housewife and children' groups,
such as households without an adult male, or where the adult male earned
either less than his wife or did not work at all. These critics argued that
women's paid work was important too, and increasingly so and could be
ignored only at the cost of gross inaccuracy in the class map of capitalist
societies. They argued against the neglect of gender inequality within the

household and emphasized the problems of taking the class of the man to indicate the position of that unit. Overall, they stressed the importance of taking adequate account of women's participation in class relations and not deriving these from that of their husband or father.

These critics laid the ground for a flowering of work which tried to elucidate the position of women in a class society and their impact on it. This work has taken two main directions: first, a close examination of women's paid work, and attempts to produce a classification of women's occupations which takes better account of the divisions between them (Arber, Dale and Gilbert 1984; Murgatroyd 1982a); and secondly, an exploration of the implications of taking women's paid work into account in determining the class position and work strategy of the household (Britten and Heath 1983; Pahl and Wallace 1983). These and many other pieces of work have reached a high level of technical sophistication in working out the issues generated by the critique of the old approach.

These critiques have recently, at long last, provoked a defence of the conventional view, in which the traditional position has received a sustained explicit justification (Goldthorpe 1983). In view of the importance of this intervention, it is appropriate to consider Goldthorpe's article in some depth. This will be followed by a discussion of the initial response to it drawn from the new feminist critique (Stanworth 1984).

## THE 'CONVENTIONAL' VIEW AND ITS CRITIQUE

Goldthorpe's (1983) article is a strong attempt to justify the conventional position by arguing that women's paid work is of such limited significance that the class position of married women is determined by that of their husbands. Goldthorpe criticizes two 'groups' of critics: those who attack the use of the household as the unit of stratification, and those who, while retaining this as the unit, try to include women's activities as one of the determinants of the position of the household. He suggests that the derivation of a woman's class position from that of her husband is not a sign of sexism, but claims that it is in recognition of sexual inequality that stratification theory derives a woman's class position from that of her husband.

Goldthorpe argues that sexual inequality means that wives are dependent upon their husbands for the determination of their life-chances and that the paid employment of wives has little impact on their situation. He suggests that gender inequality means that a wife's participation in paid employment is so limited that this employment is an inappropriate basis for a woman's class identification.

Goldthorpe attempts an empirical substantiation of these claims using data collected in the Oxford Mobility Survey. He examines the paid work histories of women for support for his suggestion that women's labour-force participation is 'intermittent' and 'limited' and 'conditioned': 'The labour market participation of married women is typically of an intermittent and limited kind, and is moreover conditioned by the class context in which it occurs' (p. 472). Goldthorpe uses this data to try to show that a wife's paid employment is so insignificant in the determination of her own life-chances that it can properly be ignored. In a later article Goldthorpe (1984) tries to suggest that his point is conceptual rather than merely factual but this makes little difference to the main thrust of his argument.

Goldthorpe (1983) suggests that wives' participation in the labour market is intermittent and limited on the basis of data which shows that the majority of wives are not in continuous employment and that 'a sizeable proportion will withdraw from participation . . . on more than one occasion' (p. 473–4). Further, he supports his argument that this employment, such as it is, is conditioned by their husband's class position, by analysing the variations in the timing of this employment in relation to the husband's class. He examines the number of years which elapse between marriage, the first withdrawal from the labour-market of the wives, the birth of the first child, and the first re-entry into the labour-market after the birth, and argues that, since these timings are to some extent correlated with husband's class, women's employment can be said to be conditioned by the husband's class.

Goldthorpe's defence of the conventional view of women and class analysis is flawed for two reasons. First, his empirical evidence is insufficient to support his contention that women's paid work is so 'intermittent, limited and conditional' that it should not be taken into account in examining the position of the family as a whole. Secondly, and more importantly, I would argue that his theoretical arguments for his narrow focus and restrictive definitions of class are not justified. This is because definition of the issues under dispute is drawn from a framework which, as I shall show later, excludes from theoretical view issues which are central to the changing social division of labour and social stratification.

The first problem with Goldthorpe's work is that he stretches his evidence too far; it does not sufficiently support his claim that women's paid work is insignificant for the woman's life-chances and the position of the household. While Goldthorpe claims that married women's paid employment is intermittent and limited, his evidence shows that only a minority of married women will take more than one break from paid employment; that is, the majority pattern is merely for one break for child-care. I would argue that this shows a large commitment to paid work, and it is not appropriate to describe this participation as intermittent since this word suggests repeated moves in and out of the labour-market. Further, while Goldthorpe emphasizes the greater employment discontinuity of longer-married women as supporting evidence, this pattern is, on the contrary, evidence that the

newer pattern for married women is one of greater continuity in paid
employment (cf. Elias and Main 1982).

Goldthorpe's contention that the participation of married women in the
labour force is heavily conditioned by the class of their husbands, receives
but little support from the very slight correlation in his small sample
between the times of first birth and the woman's withdrawal from the
labour force, and the husband's class. This support is particularly fragile
since Goldthorpe does not make the obvious comparison with the impact
of the woman's own occupation on the timing of such withdrawals (Elias
and Main 1982; Mincer 1962).

Stanworth (1984) writing in the new critical tradition, subjects
Goldthorpe's (1983) defence of the conventional view of women and class
analysis to careful scrutiny. It is typical of such critical work in that it
combines technical excellence with a rather limited view of the questions
to be asked. Stanworth picks up on the details of Goldthorpe's account of
the significance of married women's paid employment. She is able to
demonstrate quite convincingly that, on his own terms, Goldthorpe
underestimates the importance of this employment for class analysis. She
shows that Goldthorpe fails to consider the impact of the extra income of
the wife on matters which affect the behaviour of the male, including for
instance house purchase, and suggests that it is necessary to ask what
impact this has on the men's acceptance of existing social relations.
Further, she suggests that the conditioning of a spouse's employment
pattern is a two-way affair, and that the wife conditions the husband's
employment as well as vice versa (Stanworth 1984: p. 163).

Stanworth's most telling point is her refutation of Goldthorpe's attempt
to deny the existence of cross-class families. Stanworth accepts Goldthorpe's
claim that women in routine non-manual jobs (largely clerical workers)
should be classified as working-class, but goes on to show that this
recategorization of these workers as working-class merely changes *which*
families are cross-class families, rather than demonstrating that there are
no such entities. She suggests that after this reclassification, cross-class
families are not those in which routine non-manual women workers are
married to male manual workers, but rather those in which working-class
women (including routine non-manual workers) are married to service-
class or intermediate-class men.

However, a major problem in Stanworth's article is that she does not
consider the class position of full-time housewives. Certainly the implicit
assumption is that they are theoretically insignificant, almost as if they did
not exist. For instance, in her reworking of Goldthorpe's data on cross-class
families, Stanworth omits women who never had paid work from
categorization as participating in either homogamous or cross-class
marriages, while categorizing other women by their longest period of paid
employment, whether or not they were currently full-time housewives. So,

*[handwritten: only w/ respect to class]*

while Goldthorpe treats all married women as full-time housewives and considers their paid work to be insignificant, Stanworth treats all women as paid workers and considers full-time housewives to be insignificant. In arguing against Goldthorpe's suggestion that women's paid work is irrelevant in the determination of married women's class position, Stanworth goes to the opposite extreme and regards this work as the sole determinant of married women's class position. This must be considered as a serious problem in Stanworth's analysis.

In failing to address the issue of the theorization of housewives, she fails to comment upon the inadequacies of Goldthorpe's own position on this. I shall now look at some of these problems.

In his article Goldthorpe has largely ignored the issue of gender inequality by linking class relations with a structure of positions associated with a *social* division of labour which excludes the *sexual* division of labour within the household (1983: p. 467). Goldthorpe's notion of the social division of labour is restricted to that between and among employees, employers and self-employed within the money sector of the economy. It incorrectly omits the (unpaid) division of labour performed within the home. I would argue that it is the lack of incorporation into class analysis of the structured positions associated with this domestic division of labour that is the major flaw of the conventional approach. Yet Goldthorpe does not address this issue seriously. While he notes the sexual inequality in the family, and indeed patriarchal institutions more generally (p. 486 n.13), he does not address the question of its theorization because he has defined it as an issue outside the ambit of class analysis. So, while refusing rightly to subsume sexual inequality to a narrowly outlined class inequality, Goldthorpe rejects the utility of the concept of class to conceptualize the relations between husbands and wives. Yet Goldthorpe makes no argument for the restriction of class analysis to such a narrowly defined social division of labour: it is merely an unquestioned assumption.

While Stanworth argues for a 'radical reworking of the categories of class analysis' (1984: p. 165) this reworking is not radical enough. Stanworth sees women's subordination as primarily the outcome of capitalist class processes. I think these are very limited aims for class analysis. They constitute only a very small widening of the questions and issues which constitute class analysis. They do not address adequately the full range of gender inequality and its significance for stratification theory as a whole.

I shall now go on to look at other examples of this new critical feminist school of which Stanworth is an example.

*Sylvia Walby*

## THE NEW FEMINIST STRATIFICATION THEORY

### *Occupational Classification*

At present the measurement of social class is based on men's occupations. A major concern of the new feminist critique has been to consider what modification of class boundaries would be necessary if women in paid work were to be considered as well (Arber, Dale and Gilbert 1984; Dale, Gilbert and Arber 1984; Murgatroyd 1982a; 1982b; 1984a; Stanworth 1984; West 1978). Issues involved in this debate include whether the class position of particular job-slots is affected by the gender of the occupant of that slot, and whether the existing distinctions between occupations are both fine enough and appropriate for discriminating between women workers.

Many of these discussions focus on the class location of clerical workers, or 'routine non-manual workers'. These writings draw upon an existing debate in the literature on the class location of such workers of both sexes, who have been classified by the Registrar-General and some social theorists as middle-class, while others have argued that they are more properly categorized as working-class because the work is de-skilled, routinized and involves little authority (see Abercrombie and Urry 1983; Braverman 1974; Carchedi 1977; Crompton and Jones 1982; Giddens 1973; Lockwood 1958; Poulantzas 1975; Stewart, Prandy and Blackburn 1980). Recently some attention has been paid to the fact that many of these clerical workers are women, and debates have begun as to whether this is significant for their class location (Crompton and Jones 1984; West 1978; Murgatroyd 1982a).

Further, it has been suggested that the category of clerical worker is differentiated insufficiently, and that this disguises important differences between women workers (Arber, Dale and Gilbert 1984; Murgatroyd 1982a). Workers with such significantly differing amounts of autonomy and authority as a typist in a pool and a managing director's secretary need to be distinguished. A further suggestion is that shop assistants are incorrectly classified by the Registrar-General as non-manual rather than manual workers, thus placing them inappropriately in the middle class rather than the working class.

### *Women's Contribution to the Family*

The second major attempt to revise stratification theory on the basis of the arguments of the feminist critique is based on a re-evaluation of the contribution of women's work to the family (eg. Britten and Heath 1983;

Pahl 1980; Pahl and Wallace 1983). These writers retain the household as the unit of stratification, but argue that its position is not determined solely by that of the adult male, but rather by the resources of both husband and wife.

Britten and Heath (1983) argue that such an analysis shows the frequency and importance of the cross-class family in which a woman with a routine non-manual job is married to a man with a manual job. They suggest that this should be a category in its own right and that such households should not simply be considered working-class.

Pahl and Wallace have emphasized the work strategies of households (Pahl 1980; Pahl and Wallace 1983). They have taken seriously the feminist argument that work is done within households and attempt to reconceptualize the division of labour to include this. The distinctions made here provide tools which have some powerful uses. Gershuny (1983) has drawn attention to the movement of tasks between the market and household economies and the importance of this for changes in the overall pattern of the division of labour. The redefinition of the social division of labour to include household work as well as paid work is a vital part of the reconstruction of social analysis in order to take account of gender divisions. The movement of work between the market and household economies is a highly significant part of the changes in the division of labour and its implications for social stratification are immense.

However, while these developments provide an advance over those writings which simply ignored women's situations they are flawed by inadequate attention paid to gender inequality. By still treating the family as the unit, the inequality between men and women within the family is hidden conceptually. The exploration of this inequality is hindered rather than helped by a theoretical framework which does not provide central conceptual space for this unequal relationship. Within these analyses such inequality remains on the level of an incidental quantitative empirical finding, rather than a theoretically central phenomenon. This leads the questions being asked by researchers operating within this framework away from what I would argue are central issues in the understanding of gender inequality. The focus on the household as the unit draws attention away from the theoretical links between different aspects of women's oppression. We need to place analyses of the household division of labour and work strategy within a theoretical framework adequate to understanding gender inequality. Existing stratification theory does not provide that.

## The Limits to the New Feminist Stratification

I have argued, therefore, that recent attempts to revise stratification theory do not go far enough. They are limited by their failure to re-examine the questions which lie at the heart of the conventional stratification theory. These are derived from a male-centred problematic which has no space for a proper consideration of issues pertaining to gender inequality. Existing work has attempted to demonstrate its validity in relation to these old questions rather than rethinking the central questions of stratification theory. This is a result of trying to demonstrate immediate relevance at the expense of carrying out a thorough critique.

Much British stratification theory has been concerned with the debate between the different approaches derived from Marx and Weber over the nature of the working class as a political actor in contemporary capitalist society. The issue has traditionally taken the form of asking why the working class is not revolutionary, and indeed why it often does not even support the party that claims to represent its class interests. The debate over embourgeoisement, for instance, was a classic example of this form of debate. These questions have little if any direct relevance to an understanding of gender relations. Rather than reviewing the relevance of this question for feminists the new revisionists have merely asked what impact women have on it. The questions at the centre of conventional stratification theory have not been criticized and replaced; rather women have simply been added on to existing concerns. Gender inequality is not examined *in its own right* in these analyses, despite claims that women are being put back in. While these critiques are necessary revisions, they are not sufficient. Any adequate attempt at a theory of stratification must also attempt to explain gender inequality and changes in its form and degree. Stratification theory should be seeking to specify and explain the changing nature of relations and inequality between men and women as well as that between conventionally defined classes.

One strength of British stratification studies which I do not wish to reject is its concern with the relationship between material position and political action. The debates as to what constitutes class position have usually been informed by the question of explaining class action, and not merely class categorization. I believe the same concern should inform stratification theory when its attention is turned to gender relations. That is, we should be asking: what is the relationship between the material position of each gender and their political actions on gender issues? So far, attempts to develop typologies of women's class position, although technically excellent, have not been informed by this question. (e.g. Arber, Dale and Gilbert 1984; Dale, Gilbert and Arber 1984).

GENDER, CLASS AND POLITICS

*A Critique*

An analysis of gender and class demands that the concept of class that is
utilized be examined and defined carefully. Part of the existing controversy
stems from different usages by the protagonists in the debate. One definition
is that of a collectivity of individuals who share a similar set of life-chances
on items of a material kind (e.g. Arber, Dale and Gilbert 1984; Dale,
Gilbert and Arber 1984; Murgatroyd 1982a; 1982b). This draws on a
tradition, more common in America than Britain, of studying social
stratification by ranking individuals on a scale. This tradition is quite
different from the more European tradition of defining classes in relation
to each other, as one group of people who benefit at the expense of others.
Embedded also in this latter problematic is a research agenda which
demands an analysis of the relation between class position and political
action. Despite the fact that much of the British stratification theory has
drawn on the European tradition in its analyses of men and class, many
British writers on women and class have tended to draw on the ranking
tradition. Their emphasis is on an accurate clustering of women into
categories which can be ranked according to life-chances of a certain
standard of living or economic position, rather than the more interesting
question of the relationship between work and market situation and political
action. This concept of class involved in 'ranking' is not 'wrong', rather it
has very specific uses, but these uses are limited, and they do not facilitate
an analysis in the European tradition.

The attempt to derive a woman's class position from that of her husband
assumes a notion of class in which the standard of living is the determining
factor. That is, it assumes work or market situations to be the determinant
of an individual's class location. The idea of derived class is incompatible
with any analysis in which class location is determined by the *individual's*
market or work position. Thus, the conventional approach to women's
class position belongs to the ranking tradition, rather than to the European
tradition. However, even within this approach, the issue of whether a
woman takes the same position in the ranking order as her husband should
remain an empirical question rather than one determined a priori. Since a
wife may not have the same level of consumption as her husband the
assumption that a woman should take the rank of her husband must be in
doubt. Proponents of the 'conventional view', however, who purport to
follow the European tradition can only argue for a 'derived class' for
women at the expense of both theoretical inconsistency and empirical
error.

## 32                     Sylvia Walby

So, while there have been attempts to develop typologies of women's occupations these have not been related to political action on gender issues. This raises the question of what the relevant issues of gender politics are. It is here that existing feminist critiques and revisions of stratification theory are weakest. Almost all the writers either ignore the issue (e.g. Murgatroyd 1982a; Arber, Dale, Gilbert 1984), or they operate with very conventional notions of class politics, such as voting behaviour (Britten and Heath 1983).

Despite many attempts to rethink the conceptualization and theorization of the political as it affects gender relations (see for example Allen 1974; Feminist Anthology Collective 1982; Koedt et al. 1973; Millet 1977; Redstockings 1975), there has been no integration of this work with that of stratification studies. Indeed, some recent writers on women and politics stick to a narrow and conventional view of gender politics and do not even integrate the new feminist issues into their work, retaining the old concentration on parliamentary party politics and those of the workplace (e.g. Currell 1974; Siltanen and Stanworth 1984).

### Redefining the Political Issues

Yet the classic arenas of class politics, the workplace and the state, have different relations to gender politics than they do to conventional class politics. Parliamentary parties represent different class interests to a much greater extent than they represent different gender interests. It is clear that a vote for Labour is not a vote for feminism and that the three major parties in Britain at least do not have policies which differ on gender issues as much as they do on conventional class issues.

Thus analyses such as those of whether the cross-class family is more or less likely to vote Labour miss the most important point. They ask questions which are too narrow and are drawn from an overall framework which has not been rethought enough to include gender issues properly.

The most appropriate starting point in defining the relevant issues in gender politics is that of the seven demands of the contemporary British Women's Liberation movement. These are: equality in employment and education; child-care facilities; control over fertility through contraception and abortion; legal and financial independence; and an end to sexual oppression and male violence.[2] This list was developed at annual national conferences over a period of years and represents the nearest thing there is to a consensus among British feminists as to the relevant issues in gender politics. While feminists may disagree on the relative importance of the demands I think this list would be agreed by most and is the best agenda available.

So my question has become: what is the relationship, if any, between economic position and participation in collective action around the issues of equality in employment and education; child-care facilities; the provision of contraception and abortion; women's financial and legal independence; sexual oppression and male violence against women?

I would emphasize, as a point of logic, that it is not sufficient to consider only women in this context, since men may be active politically (although usually on the other side), in these political issues (Friedman and Sarah 1982). Gender politics is not an issue fought by women against some non-gendered subject. Further, it is not to be expected that all women would simply support all feminist demands and all men oppose them. The question is rather, under what circumstances do which groups of men or women support or oppose particular actions on these political issues? To what extent does their position in the patriarchal and capitalist class systems determine their involvement in these politics? What effect do we expect contemporary changes in patriarchal and capitalist relations to have on gender politics?

I am not arguing that the questions raised by the new feminist critique are irrelevant or unimportant. They are necessary for an adequate analysis within the conventional framework of the relation between classes within capitalist relations. Rather, this set of questions is only part of stratification studies. Gender inequality needs more direct attention *in its own right*, not just in respect of how it affects conventional class relations. However, since my space is limited I shall confine my attention to issues of gender relations and gender politics.

## AN ALTERNATIVE APPROACH

### *Housewives, Husbands and Class*

I seek to explain the patterns of gender inequality and changes in these patterns. Can the theoretical tools and methods developed within conventional stratification theory be mined usefully for this project? Are any of the various concepts of class and status adequate to the task of theorizing gender relations?

I am going to argue that housewives and husbands can be conceptualized as classes, when class is defined in terms of a distinctive work and market position, but that gender should not be reduced to class. That is, while husbands and housewives are classes, women and men are not. The distinctive material position of housewives is the major determinant of gender relations, but not the only one, and the extent of this determination should be considered an empirical question in need of exploration. Other relevant sets of patriarchal relations include those at the workplace, in the state, in sexuality and in male violence.

I do wish to argue that the sexual division of labour is crucial to patterns of gender relations, but not that the two can be simply equated.

I shall, in the ensuing discussion of housewives and husbands as classes, utilize a definition of class as a set of positions with a common work and market situation. This is because I wish to operate with a conceptual distinction between material position and consciousness and action, so as to facilitate asking the question of the relationship (if any) between the two. Hence I would reject, for my project, the concept of class which embodies notions of consciousness and action around a common set of interests, on the grounds that it is heuristically confusing.

The starting point for my approach is a recognition that housework is a distinctive form of work. It is hard work and the fact that it does not receive a wage should not be held to disqualify it from the status of work (Gershuny 1983; Gilman 1966; Oakley 1974; Schreiner 1911; Seccombe 1974). The domestic labour of the housewife comprises the production of the labour power of the husband, herself and children and other dependents (if any). However, I would argue that it is a mistake to identify the distinctiveness of domestic labour in the nature of the tasks (for instance O'Brien 1981); rather this should be seen to reside in the distinctive nature of the relations of production under which the housewife labours (Delphy 1977). The content of housework changes over time and varies according to the income and wealth of the household, yet the essential nature of the relations of production hold constant despite this. For example, two centuries ago a housewife in Britain would include many of the stages of the making of clothing among her tasks while today this is unusual (Schreiner 1911; Pinchbeck 1981); but changes in the content of the tasks have little effect on the underlying relations of production. These movements of tasks from the household economy to the market economy (and sometimes back again) are common (Gershuny 1983; Schreiner 1911). Yet whatever the precise nature of her tasks the housewife is involved in an unequal exchange relationship in which she receives maintenance for her labour — which is most unlike exchange relationships under capitalist relations of production.

The typical married woman in the UK in 1974—5 performed more work (paid plus unpaid) than her husband, although there are some categories of couples in which the husband does more work (Gershuny 1983: p. 155). However, unlike Gershuny, I would argue that it is not just the quantity of work which is important here. More significant is the distinctive social relations under which the work is performed by the woman. It is neither exchanged in a calculated bargain for a wage which varies in proportion to the effort expended, nor with an employer who may be changed easily; rather the exchange is indirect, although nonetheless present (since a wife who refused to perform domestic services of various sorts is liable to be divorced), and changing the employer (the husband) is much more difficult than for a wage labourer. The social relations which induce a wife to part with her labour for less return than her husband are again distinctive to the patriarchal household. The circumstances in which the labour contract under marriage and under waged labour are made and broken, and the implications of this for the nature of the labour contract itself, serve to differentiate significantly the social relations of production under which these forms of labour are performed.

It is sometimes argued that the differences between housewives are too great for them to be included in the same class (e.g. Molyneux 1979). However, this is merely a quantitative difference in the standard of living and does not affect the position of housewives in the relations of production in which they are engaged. The housewife married to a middle-class man is still engaging in the same relations of production as that married to a working-class one; each exchanges her labour with him indirectly for her maintenance. Even a woman with servants is still working under patriarchal relations of production, since she is still dependent upon her husband for maintenance in return for her efforts at household management. This is not to deny that there is reason to distinguish between housewives according to the class position of their husbands, merely that it is not sufficient to deny their common subordination to patriarchal relations of production in the household.

The position of the husband should be taken into account when issues such as the standards of living, access to resources and sources of political influence are considered, but this is not the same as suggesting that married women should take the same class position as their husbands.

Thus I would argue that housewives (both full-time and part-time) are a class exploited by their husbands who also constitute a class. This is not, however, a sufficient characterization of the class position of women. I do not believe that it is appropriate to designate all women as a class. Not all women are housewives, and thus not all women have a class position in the patriarchal mode of production. This applies only to those women who perform unpaid domestic labour for a husband (or father)[3] in a household and not all women are in this position. It is not appropriate to accord to all women a common class-position on the basis that most women will expect, at some point in their lives, to be housewives (as does Delphy 1977). I have argued earlier for the position that class location is dependent solely upon an individual's direct work and market situation.

However, while all women do not constitute a class, they do nevertheless have some features of their social situation which are common to all women. Women share a large variety of economic and non-economic circumstances. For instance, sexual choices are affected crucially by gender divisions; gender is the first characteristic to be taken into account in the process of selecting a sexual partner. Further, significant forms of violence and harrassment are organized socially by gender in that all women are vulnerable to male attack in the form of rape and other forms of sexual molestation in ways which affect the conduct of women significantly. Again, forms of discrimination in the workplace affect all women, regardless of their actual marital status. Still further, access to rights of citizenship such as suffrage and some legal rights, have often, historically, been withheld from all women on the basis of their sex alone. Thus there are many illustrations of the ways in which gender is a significant organizing principle in society.

Nevertheless, I would argue that it is not consistent with the principles of class analysis to suggest that women rather than housewives form a class since these common statuses do not follow directly from a shared economic position. Rather they have a certain degree of autonomy from the economic. I would suggest that in Weberian terminology this would mean that while housewives and husbands are classes, women and men are status groups.

A further important issue in the class location of women is that many women also have a class position deriving from their participation in waged labour. Thus many women have a dual class position. Many women are engaged in two distinct sets of relations of production, and to try to conflate these or ignore one of them by emphasizing the primacy of the other (cf. Goldthorpe 1983; Stanworth 1984) is, in my opinion, a serious mistake for social theory. Sometimes this dual class location will be contradictory, sometimes in harmony: there are no a priori conclusions to be drawn here.

Having argued that housewives and husbands are two classes in a patriarchal system, it is now necessary to make some suggestions as to their relationship to political action. Stratification studies which investigate the links between economic position and political action might then consider the following issues. Are women without husbands likely to be more radical in gender politics than those with husbands? Indications of the composition of the contemporary women's movement — that it contains a high proportion of women without husbands (single, separated and divorced) — would lend support to this suggestion.[4] Why should marriage make a woman more conservative on the issue of gender politics? Why does not the more direct experience of the particularly virulent form of patriarchal oppression that women suffer in marriage make these women more discontented, in a manner parallel to the way that male manual workers have been more radical in conventional class politics than male non-manual workers? Is the answer to be found in the forms of control exercised over women in marriage, or is it due to a woman's assessment of the dependence of her life-chances upon a husband? Does the need to sustain the existing marriage lead to a greater likelihood of opposition to policies and practices surrounding issues such as divorce, non-marital sexuality and fertility control which might make it easier for her husband to become involved with another woman? This is merely informed speculation (cf. Dworkin 1983; Finch 1984), but suggests some pertinent questions as to women's participation in certain sorts of gender politics.

What impact does the increase in the number of single-parent families have on gender politics? What difference does it make to a man's gender politics whether he is married or not? How do contemporary changes in the age of marriage, rate of divorce, rate of remarriage and increase in cohabitation affect women's and men's consciousness and action concerning gender politics?

To what extent was the expansion of the higher education open to women significant for the development of feminist politics because it provided a rare opportunity for women to live independently from men, as neither daughters nor wives? A further question is that of the impact of the husband's class position on his wife's gender politics. Under what circumstances does having a rich husband lead to an easing of the woman's position and make her contented, and under what circumstances does such a situation free her from time-consuming labour so that she may take on a leading political role? These are all important questions about the relationship between contemporary changes in social structure and politics which have received little attention, partly because of the overwhelming dominance of conventional views of class analysis and the failure of the critiques to push the criticism far enough.

## Women in Capitalist Class Relations

The second possible determinant of women's class position was that of her waged labour, if any. We need to ask questions as to what impact various levels of participation in paid work have on women's political consciousness and action. We need to know what difference it makes to women's political attitudes and, more importantly, actions, whether they are full-time housewives, engage in full-time or part-time paid work in addition to being housewives, or are not housewives at all. Existing literature is inadequate on this issue, but there are some suggestions that paid work is important in the political mobilization of women around their own demands (Liddington and Norris 1978; Mark-Lawson, Savage and Warde 1984), although this is by no means a necessary condition (cf. many leading suffragettes). Is there a significant difference between women in full-time and part-time paid work? (cf. Martin and Roberts 1984).

It is necessary to return to the question of the classification of women's and men's waged labour. I have suggested earlier that the distinctions being made by the new feminist school, while possessing relevance for class relations within the capitalist system of social relations, did not have such relevance for relations within the patriarchal system. Women and men face two major systems of social inequality within paid work, and classifications of their work needs to be able to make discriminations relevant to both. Some work has been done in trying to produce discriminations which are relevant to women's place in the class relations in the capitalist system (Arber, Dale, Gilbert 1984; Murgatroyd 1982a; 1982b; 1984b) but very little on women's and men's places in a wider system of patriarchal relations. What are the issues that I think need to be integrated into the classification and analysis? How are these to be determined? I will suggest two examples and then make suggestions for how further items might be identified.

The first item that needs identification in these classifications is the relationship between men and women in the workplace. What is the nature of the sex-ordered hierarchy in the workplace? Are there both men and women, or is the workplace confined to one sex? If workers of both sexes are present do they work side by side, or are they segregated? Martin and Roberts (1984) have shown that this makes some difference to attitudes to the gender division of labour. What is the sex of the supervisors?

There are indications that participation in waged labour contributes to women's activism on their own behalf, especially when large groups of women work together (cf. Liddington and Norris 1978). However, this is by no means a sufficient condition, since not all groups of women in paid work have organized in this way. Mark-Lawson, Savage and Warde (1984) and Mark-Lawson (1984) have argued that it is not merely the existence of waged labour for women which facilitated their organization around political issues of concern to women such as child and maternal welfare, but also that the extent and success of this organization varied according to whether the women worked alone or alongside men. Savage (1984) has argued further for the significance of the forms of control at work, especially the relationship between a female workforce and its supervisors, in determining the kinds and success of political action around their interests. These studies indicate that the relations between men and women within the workplace have important effects upon women's organization around their own interests. These issues would not be captured by the distinction made in conventional discriminations between women workers. They need to be.

A further issue is that of men, paid work and gender politics. Usually the role of men in gender politics is ignored completely as if they had nothing to do with it. Yet this is clearly not the case: men have organized actively around gender issues, usually, though not always, to the detriment of women. What are the workplace circumstances which are likely to produce patriarchal organization among men? I would suggest that a workplace in which men and women do not work together, i.e. either a highly segregated workplace with men in the dominant position, or consisting of men only, is more likely to produce this than workplaces where men and women work side by side (Walby 1983b; 1985).

CONCLUSION

In this chapter I have argued that while the conventional position on women and class is hopelessly flawed, that of the new feminist critique does not go far enough. I have argued that these critics have tried to add women into a framework, the questions of which are only relevant for analysis of the system of class relations under capitalism. While the critiques have shown that the conventional view is flawed in its own terms, they have balked at challenging the questions of that old problematic. Stratification theory, in order to be truly about stratification rather than limited forms of inequality between white men, needs to reassess the question of what 'including gender' would properly mean. I have suggested that it entails taking inequality between men and women as a key feature of contemporary society and which is in need of explanation, along with the forms of political resistance to, and support of, this patriarchal domination. The new feminist stratification theory should retain the traditional interest of British stratification theory in the relationship between material position and political action, between social structure and social change, and not confine itself to merely elaborating more accurate rankings of life-style and prestige, which include women as well as men.

With these notions in mind I have tried to elaborate a more adequate account of gender and stratification, arguing that while single women in waged labour should take their class positions from their own occupation, married women have a dual class-position in possessing both a class position derived from their paid work and a class location as housewives in relation to their husbands. Married men likewise have a dual class-position: one from their waged labour and one from their position as husbands in relation to their wives. Drawing on a reconstructed notion of gender-based politics and some existing literature on gender-political activity I have suggested some questions concerning the relation between women and men's class position and political action on gender issues.

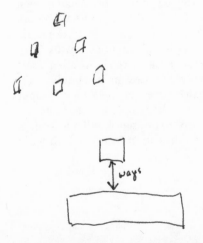

# 4

## A Crisis in Stratification Theory?
### Persons, Households/Families/Lineages, Genders, Classes and Nations

### Michael Mann

Society would be captured perfectly by sociological theory if it consisted merely of atomic particles clustering around the nuclei provided by our theoretical concepts. We know social reality is not so neat, but at some point we must act as if it were. After we elaborate our central theoretical concepts, we must assume that other social influences are randomly, contingently related to them. Social stratification, with its strong theoretical traditions, has done this fairly explicitly. Its two main orthodoxies, Marxian and Weberian, define three nuclei: social class, social status/ideology and political power. Though aware of the complexities of social life, theorists treat other aspects of stratification as ultimately contingent and non-structural. They may admit that gender relations are 'neglected', interesting and important. But gender relations are not part of the core of stratification (such is Lockwood's argument in chapter 2.) Beneath classes, status and political power lie actors who, in the last resort, resemble atomic particles.

Certain aspects of stratification have never fitted easily into this model — for example, ethnic and religious struggles have not usually been reducible to class and status as (respectively) the Marxian and Weberian traditions assert. My own unease has stemmed principally from nations and nation-states, which are not reducible to political phenomena (as both orthodoxies have it). Gender relations present a third area in which a set of properties intersects with the orthodox categories in a peculiar yet structured way. In this case, the orthodoxies have spawned what Popper would call an *ad hoc* auxiliary hypothesis, changing the basic atomic particles of the theory from individual persons to households. Thus women are said to obtain their position in social stratification from the dominant

male of their household. Making that assumption we can proceed with the
traditional model, as it is asserted, for example by Goldthorpe (1983).

I believe that all three areas present fundamental difficulties for current
stratification theory. I do not provide an alternative general theory here. I
attempt a more limited, descriptive and historical task. I identify and trace
the interrelations of five principal stratification nuclei — five collective
actors who have impacted on gender/stratification relations over the recent
history of the West. They are: the atomized 'person' (not strictly a collective
actor, but nonetheless a social identity conferred by the core structures of
liberal society); the connected networks of household/family/lineage;
genders (the male and female sexes given social power-significance); social
classes (viewed broadly in a Marxian perspective and so comprising
principally capitalist and working classes and their fractions in modern
Western society); and nations and nation-states. To adopt such a
'multidimensional building-block' approach to stratification theory reveals
that I believe the theoretical crisis to be serious. It is more serious than
Cockburn indicates in chapter 6 for example. It is not just a question of
finding a theory to relate the two theoretical nuclei she suggests —
capitalism and patriarchy. Capitalism is too limited a concept to deal with
the totality of non-gendered stratification relations in modern society.
And, as I will indicate in this chapter, patriarchy no longer exists, even if a
different form of gender domination does.

Obviously in one short chapter I have not the space either to define
carefully all my nuclei or to document fully all my assertions regarding
their interrelations. Much of the supporting material for my concepts and
generalizations can be found in the first two volumes of my book, *The
Sources of Social Power* (1986, forthcoming). I start with the origins of
modern gender relations.

## PATRIARCHY IN AGRARIAN SOCIETIES

A patriarchal society is one in which power is held by male heads of
households. There is also clear separation between the 'public' and the
'private' spheres of life. In the 'private' sphere of the household, the
patriarch enjoys arbitrary power over all junior males, all females and all
children. In the 'public' sphere, power is shared between male patriarchs
according to whatever other principles of stratification operate. No female
holds any formal public position of economic, ideological, military or
political power. Indeed, females are not allowed into this 'public' realm of
power. Whereas many, perhaps most, men expect to be patriarchs at some
point in their life cycles, no women hold formal power. Within the
household they may influence their male patriarch informally, but this is
their only access to power. Contained within patriarchy are two

fundamental nuclei of stratification: the household/family/lineage and the dominance of the male gender. These coexist in any real society with social classes and other stratification groupings.

This is an ideal-type. Yet it has not been so far from historical reality, from the first written records emerging from Mesopotamia around 2,500 BC, to western Europe up to the eighteenth century AD. These historic societies have distinguished the public from the private; in the public sphere power relations have been overwhelmingly between male household-heads (patriarchs); and the private sphere has usually been ruled formally by a patriarch. Families/households were the primary social units. Their relations with their own broader lineage and with other lineages constituted most of the formal structure of social stratification. That is why the label 'patriarchy', though much disputed nowadays (for a review, see Beechey 1979), seems apposite to most of our history.

This must be qualified in three ways. First, in almost all societies custom and law generally protected women from their patriarchs at some basic level — and the woman's own lineage could uphold her rights against an unjust husband (see below). Secondly, less was in the public sphere in the past than now, except amongst the highest social class. The 'private' family was the main unit of economic production and of socialization, and for almost the whole lifetime: there were few households of single, childless, 'post-child', or retired persons. Far more was unpenetrated by public power. Thus there was greater scope for private, informal power according to personal influence and force of character. Modern studies of comparable private activities (sexual relations, household budgeting etc.) show greater variations in power between men and women than do public power relations. This would matter more in historic societies because more was private.

Thirdly, and most significantly, women (and men) belonged (and still do) to more than one household/family in their lifetimes. Power is transmitted hereditarily through intercourse between a man and a woman drawn from separate households, usually from separate lineages. So power must make a journey, potentially fraught with difficulty, between two families of origin and one family of procreation. Most historic societies, precisely because family and lineage are so crucial to their stratification, confer on the woman trusteeship over power resources transferred from her family of origin. In early modern Europe spinsters and widows could formally control most of the resources they inherited; and married women could retain some control of land (but not of moveable chattels) they brought into the marriage. In the upper classes women could be legal agents, manage estates, defend castles and succeed to thrones; lesser, equivalent rights existed among merchants, guilds and propertied peasants. Such women were not exercising power as 'persons' or even just as members of classes, but as trustees for their previous lineages. They were 'honorary patriarchs'.

These are qualifications, not refutations, of patriarchy. Customary protection, informal powers and exploitable spaces between families provided no basis for collective action by women. If they sought to influence public power, they had to go through patriarchs. Gender, though fundamental to stratification, was asymmetric: men could act, women could not. Exceptions can be found — but how many sociological generalizations spread out over 4,000 years of global history can do even half as well?

Social stratification was thus two-dimensional. One dimension comprised the two nuclei of household/family/lineage and the dominance of the male gender. The second dimension comprised whatever combination of 'public' stratification nuclei (classes, military elites etc.) existed in a particular society. The latter dimension was connected to the former in that public power — groupings were predominantly aggregates of household/family/lineage heads. But apart from this, the two dimensions were segregated from each other. Thus, to analyse 'public' stratification in patriarchal society, we can largely ignore gender. We could write a history of power relations almost up to the eighteenth century and confine it to men, as long as we add the defensive proviso 'Oh, by the way, remember that this is a story of relations between male patriarchs. Underneath them all the time were women (and junior men, and children).' This can be validated with the aid of Acker's (1973) list of the assumptions made by orthodox stratification theory. She lists six.

1 The family is the unit of the stratification system.
2 The social position of the family is determined by the status of the male head of the household.
3 Females live in families.
4 Females' status is equivalent to that of their man.
5 Women determine their own social status only when not attached to men.
6 Women are unequal to men in various ways, and are evaluated differentially on the basis of sex, but this is irrelevant to the structure of stratification.

These assumptions would be broadly true of most historic societies (later I shall agree with Acker that they are not true of modern societies). My only quibble would concern what we were to label 'social stratification'. For there were two incommensurate structures of stratification linked through families/households/lineages: the 'orthodox' structures of (male)classes etc., and the relations between the two genders. But as almost the whole recorded history of society concerns the first, public realm, perhaps we should concede even this point. The internal structure of public stratification was not gendered.

So the more patriarchal the society, the better orthodox theory performs. If orthodox theory does worse in modern societies, then they must be less patriarchal. This is what I argue in the rest of the chapter: as the particularism of agrarian societies gave way before the universal, diffused stratification of modern society, stratification became gendered internally. It is outside of my scope here to weigh the many and varied causes of this transformation. It is sufficient to group them around three major power configurations of modern times — capitalism, liberal citizenship and the nation-state. I argue that these three configurations transformed gender/ stratification relations in successive historical phases of modern Western society, the first two then becoming institutionalized, the third remaining unfinished. Cumulatively they add up to a contemporary stratification structure which has moved beyond patriarchy and become gendered internally in both its economic and political aspects.

## THREE MODERN TRANSFORMATIONS OF GENDER AND STRATIFICATION

### I: The Capitalist Economy — Neo-patriarchy and Gendered Classes

The events described here are well documented in the literature. I draw particularly on Branca (1975); Casey (1976); Chodorow (1979); Degler (1980: pp. 362—435); Hartmann (1979); Matthaei (1982); and Tilly and Scott (1978).

From about the sixteenth to the nineteenth centuries in Western Europe, under the pressure of emerging capitalism, first in agriculture then in industry, more of economic life became a part of the public realm. Among the lower classes, the rise of wage labour and the loss of customary rights to land meant that the peasant family was no longer the main unit of production. People went out to work for others. The lineage weakened, the nuclear family grew stronger and became characterized by what Stone (1977) calls 'affective individualism' between husband and wife. As labour was becoming an abstract commodity, it was possible that men and women could become interchangeable as labourers, so ending gender particularism in the economy. But, as Hartmann (1979) argues, patriarchy was so well entrenched in European society that it withstood this capitalist pressure. Male workers and employers together contrived to create a labour-market in which priority was given to males. Patriarchy acquired a new colouration: almost all men worked in the public sphere, at least half the women looked after the private household. The remaining women did work in the public sphere. But their wages could barely support a household; their occupations could be regarded as extensions of their private domestic roles — preparing and serving food, fashioning textiles and clothes, and caring for the young, the elderly, the indigent and the infirm, in educational, health and charitable occupations; they would fit employment around their family life cycles; and even if they worked they also undertook most domestic labour. The simple divide between the public and the private gave way to a more subtle gender segregation, diffused right through the traditional barrier between public and private spheres. We might well term these employment arrangements 'neo-patriarchy'.

Among the capitalist class parallel transformations occurred from the end of the 18th century. As Davidoff shows in chapter 12, the business enterprise moved out of the household into the office, the exchange and the club. Women members of capitalist households lessened their active participation in the economy. They became domesticated. Because under law women could not retain control of moveable chattels they brought into marriage, they were also affected adversely by the change from land to capital. But this also meant that their own families of origin lost control over such capital. So a formidable lobby emerged to change matrimonial law to favour women. In Britain the Married Women's Property Act of 1870 was one of the first achievements of the feminist movement. Yet it was also assisted (and probably won decisively) by forces emanating from the heart of the old society. Lineage has remained fundamental to the inheritance of class position but, in this respect, classes reduced their patriarchal colouration.

By about 1850 in Britain the change in employment was virtually complete: more women in the public sphere, but under neo-patriarchal arrangements. These arrangements have subsequently become institutionalized. Looking back over employment trends (as Scott does in chapter 11), it is astonishing how little has changed over the last 135 years. Occupational segregation and the confinement of most women to those 'semi-domesticated' occupational areas just mentioned still persists. The most significant general change has probably been the post-1940 increase in married women working before and after their child-rearing phase. Most women now divide their lifetimes into private and part-public phases (I return to this later). Nor are women generally active users of capital. Their greater longevity, plus the Property Acts, ensure that they own more of capitalism than men do. Yet they tend to be passive rentiers, leaving managerial control of capital to publically employed men. If we followed Marxian orthodoxy, and reduced stratification relations to direct 'relations of production' and to 'the labour process', we would have to conclude that little has changed and that at least a 'neo-patriarchy' remains.

But the adjustment of patriarchy to capitalism involved other changes. The privacy of the household had diminished and in the public sphere the fourth of my nuclei — classes — became more significant collective actors. In place of 'classes' as aggregates of particularistic networks of lineages, in place of the asymmetry whereby only the ruling class was capable of extensive and political action, came universal symmetric classes. A

conscious, organized capitalist class was in place in Britain by about 1880, a
middle class slightly later, a working class by about 1914. Women, still
dependent on their patriarchs, became members of such classes. This
affected the character of nineteenth-century feminist movements (as we
will see), intensifying middle-class liberal feminism, dividing it somewhat
from a working-class socialist feminism around the beginning of this century.
But it affected women in employment especially. Women were generally
subordinate to men. But they also derived a class position from their
patriarch, and this might raise them above other men. In an agrarian
patriarchal society this had not mattered because men and women were
largely kept apart in their spheres. But employment is public and waged.
Wage hierarchies are institutionalized, and the large corporations and state
departments of the twentieth century are organized with charts showing
integrated hierarchies. Perhaps these would undermine the particularism
of patriarchy and generate a single hierarchy covering at least occupational
stratification and including both men and women?

Sociologists have long attempted to create a single hierarchical scale,
normally based on occupation, along which to distribute the entire
population. But they have had little success in combining men's and
women's occupations in a single scale. Traditional orthodoxy has been to
assign a woman's position in this hierarchy on the basis of the occupation
of her relevant patriarch (husband or father). A recent polemic has
illuminated the strengths and weaknesses of this approach. Goldthorpe
(1983; 1984) has shown that, *if* you wish to construct a single scale based on
occupation, the orthodox method is probably the best. Yet Britten and
Heath (1983) and Heath and Britten (1984) have also demonstrated that the
woman's own occupation 'makes a difference', improving the prediction of
voting behaviour, for example. Erikson's (1984) Swedish data also support
both arguments. But men's and women's occupations cannot be combined
meaningfully into a single scale. Few jobs are occupied interchangeably by
men and women and their career patterns differ. Their jobs are just
'different'. They also aggregate into different social groupings as
Murgatroyd (1984a) shows. She constructs indices of dissimilarity between
the jobs of husbands and wives (data from the 10 per cent sample of the
1971 England and Wales Census). Whereas the Registrar-General's 'social
classes' discriminate quite well between the men's occupations, they do not
among the women's. Murgatroyd constructs a rather different set of
'women's social groups' to provide the best solution to the results of her
multidimensional scaling. The orthodox scale does better where the
woman's occupation contributes fewer resources to the household. It will
do worse where the woman contributes as much as or more than the man.
But it may also perceive incorrectly the hierarchical position of a woman
who is effectively independent of patriarchs. How significant are these
problems? How many are the women involved? I delay my answers until

later because the questions introduce political as well as economic aspects of stratification.

But we should not become obsessed with constructing scales on which to distribute individuals. Stratification is more than the sum of individuals, or indeed of households. If our stratification theory sees its task only as assigning women as individuals to jobs or households, it will miss any collective impact women might have on stratification. And this has been considerable. There is a significant clustering of women's occupations. A kind of compromise between patriarchy and a more gendered stratification hierarchy has emerged. Women in the economy now form a number of quasi-class fractions. In each main case they occupy a 'buffer zone' between the men of their own class grouping and the men of the next class grouping down the hierarchy. At the bottom large numbers of women in part-time and unskilled manual employment are a buffer between the unemployed (who are mostly men, because many women are not registered as unemployed) and the 'skilled' manual workers above them (who are overwhelmingly male). The second largest female concentration is in clerical and sales work, inhabiting a buffer zone between manual and non-manual male workers. Third are the 'semi-professions', whose lower reaches are predominantly staffed by women with substantial educational qualifications in caring occupations. They form a buffer around an important educational divide within the middle class. Fourth — though this is a somewhat different distinction — are the passive rentier widows, spinsters and divorced women, and the 'sleeping-partner' wives and daughters, buffering capital from all labour. All told, this looks uncommonly like a systematic role for women in what many regard as the core of stratification — the economy and the occupational division of labour. Gender is no longer segregated from the rest of stratification: its segregating mechanisms have become a central mechanism of economic stratification.

Each one of these female buffer zones impacts upon social stratification in general and social class in particular. Here I have space to touch on only one zone, the second. One of the 'hardy perennials' of stratification theory has been whether lower white-collar work has been 'proletarianized' during the twentieth century. The research of the Cambridge Department of Applied Economics group enables us to see that this is a false issue. Lower white-collar work is undertaken by three segregated groups of people: women, young men and older men. The older men are former manual workers who have moved sideways in the employment hierarchy; the young men are careerists expecting promotion. The lifetime trajectories of both differ from that of the women, who typically interrupt their employment for *seven* years while they rear children and who cannot expect promotion. Moreover, women would not have 'noticed' deskilling of white-collar work during most of the twentieth century, since — unlike the men — they are largely new to this employment. Women, new to the

labour force, have predominantly staffed the expansion of lower white-
collar employment (Stewart, Prandy and Blackburn 1980). Gender has
prevented the proletarianization of white-collar workers, both by dividing
them from each other and by preventing deskilling having social significance
for them. This is a definitive answer to a central concern of stratification
theory, one that depends upon considering class stratification as being
gendered. Explanations of comparable scope would follow from analysing
the other gender buffers I identified. Economic stratification has become
gendered.

## II: Liberal Citizenship — Enter the Person and the Nation

In this section I discuss the rise of two more social nuclei, both more
universal than the household/gender particularism of patriarchy. Both
were conveyed primarily by Western liberalism and by the bourgeoisie. So
their universalism was in practice restrained by the compromises which
liberalism made with class and with particular national states.

The roots of individualism can be traced back to the early Christian
notion of universal individual salvation. Christ's message in and immediately
after his own time was broadly egalitarian, stressing that all were spiritually
equal before God, capable of communicating directly with Him without
going through the particularistic authority structures of Jewish or Roman
society. There is some evidence of an early Christian 'feminist' movement
(Pagels 1980; Mann 1986: ch. 10). However, this was soon suppressed, and
the famous doctrines of Saint Paul and of the pseudo-Pauline epistles took
over. Women were to obey their masters to achieve salvation. According
to Stone (1977: pp. 151−218) and Hamilton (1978: pp. 50−75),
Protestantism at first gave ideological reinforcement to the patriarchy of
the husband, while also increasing social respect for the status of the wife
in her private sphere. But extreme Protestantism could stir up feminism,
both in the Civil War period and at the end of the eighteenth century in the
Evangelical movement. By 1800 many upper- and middle-class women
were involved in moral-improvement projects among the masses. They
began to see the implications for themselves of their faith in universal
education. Evangelicals provided much of the leadership of the first feminist
movements in Britain and the United States (Banks 1981: pp. 13−27).
Grimes (1967) argues that a Puritan ethic of moral individualism lay behind
the women's suffrage movement in the western United States (where it was
most successful) right up until 1914.

But by this time Protestantism was not alone. Over several centuries
institutions of political power had been developing away from the
particularistic 'territorial federalism' characteristic of most agrarian
societies, towards the emergence of universal 'ruling-class/nations'. Estates-

General and Councils of the Realm gave way to enfranchised parliaments or massed courtiers; personal royal patronage gave way to the institutionalized sale of state offices; nobles, and sometimes merchants and yeomen, viewed themselves as a single 'nation' (even if still connected by lineage); monarchs ruled with the cooperation, and sometimes the formal consent, of this class/nation. Underlying much of the change was the growth of capitalism. The universal commodity form, the 'invisible hand' of the market, the 'free' wage labourer without particularistic ties to land or lord, the abstract rights of property — all encouraged the drift of Western culture toward 'individualism'.

This was reflected in political doctrine. Political rights and duties had hitherto been conceived predominantly in a particularistic way; obedience was due to a particular sovereign, ordained either by God or by original acclamation by the community and legitimized through dynastic succession. From him descended further networks of particularistic dynastic duties. But from about the time of Locke, there was greater interest in tracing political rights and duties to the qualities of abstract individuals. Free persons, not communities webbed together by custom, had entered into contracts to institute states. Sovereigns must uphold not custom, but the life, liberty and property of the individual, the abstract 'person'. And persons aggregated into a second novel nucleus, the nation. The nation became, not a community based on territory or blood, but a political community of free, participating citizens (Kohn 1967). Such theories were exemplified in the founding charters of the modern liberal era, those of the American and French Revolutions. Here we find declarations grounding all political rights in the sum of universal, abstract individuals — that is, in nations and persons.

It is true to say that most of the doctrines, when elaborated, made clear that the person and the nation were not universal: servants, almost always, and usually labourers and those without property, were not to be an active part of the political community. Thus liberalism was confined by class, just as was the parallel current of Evangelical Protestantism. Liberalism and moral improvement were opposed to the particularism of the old regime, called by them in Britain 'Old Corruption'. They sought a more universal basis for legal and political participation in the national state, but one confined by property. They wanted to enlighten and improve the morals of the lower classes, but through charity. Their legal and political universalism was the product of the emergence of a more extensive and universal bourgeoisie, but there, for the moment, it rested.

Women got similar treatment. Despite the rhetoric of liberalism women were not included in the nation. Was not the French founding charter entitled *Declaration of the Rights of Man and Citizen*? Nevertheless, from the 1680s to the 1980s the same liberal rhetoric has been used by radicals to achieve legal and political equality for all men and even for all women.

*Michael Mann*

Feminism, like socialism, built on top of the rhetoric. Each of the founding charters was rephrased in detail by leading feminists: for the text of Olympe de Gouge's 'Declaration of the rights of woman and citizen' see Riemer and Fout (1983: pp. 62—7); for the Seneca Falls Declaration (of Independence) see O'Neill (1969: pp. 108—10).

The main characteristic of the feminist movement in the late nineteenth and early twentieth centuries was its overlap with liberalism — added to at the end of this period by an overlap with socialism (for historical accounts, see Banks 1981; Degler 1980; Dubois 1978; Flexner 1974; Grimes 1967; Morgan 1972; 1975; O'Neill 1969; Rover 1967). Thus it was assisted by radical-liberal surges (e.g. the Progressives' surge in the western United States before 1914), but hindered by liberal defeats (e.g. the defeat of 'Reconstruction radicalism' in the United States in the 1870s). In Britain the switch from Asquith to Lloyd George as Liberal Party Leader was a considerable boost to the women's suffrage movement. Social democracy also shared social policies with the feminists (especially over education and recognition of workers' rights). So in the countries dominated by liberalism and contending with emerging socialism, feminists converted a considerable number of men who already had legal and political rights, especially the intellectuals. Liberalism was essentially universal within the bounds of the nation-state, and it could erect no powerful ideological defences against enfranchising either subordinate classes of women.

This was not sufficient, of course. To achieve suffrage, a widening of educational opportunities and legal equality, a large and troublesome women's movement was also required. This happened in two principal phases. From about 1870 the few feminist agitators acquired substantial numbers of middle-class followers, drawn principally from the expanding female occupations of teaching and social work (more of this later). Then, from around 1910, we can talk of the emergence of 'mass' movements, as socialists and trades unions began to stir up women workers more generally, and as women's penetration of education and clerical work widened. By 1915 membership of the principal suffrage organization in the United States was two million. Though British numbers were smaller, the militancy of the suffragettes became far greater.

So by about 1912 legal and political citizenship for all men and women was only a matter of time. Liberalism and socialism had no good reasons for resisting feminist pressure, once this was brought to bear. The Great War probably sealed it, for women now contributed greatly to the national effort. The vital British Suffrage Acts came in 1918 and 1928; the United States Constitution was captured in 1919—20. Most accounts of the suffrage movement stress its slowness. But, considering that the vote had to be achieved from all-male legislatures and that the feminist movement could never wield anything like the mass numbers and violence of the male suffrage movements, this surely amounts to comparatively rapid and steady progress.

Full legal and political citizenship in the nation-state were achieved and then maintained comparatively easily by women. They have not been 'virtually represented' (in the words of the eighteenth-century conservative doctrine) for over 50 years in most of the West. Women have entered as 'individual citizens' into the legal and political institutions of social stratification. The Marxian tradition of analysis has played down the achievement of 'bourgeois democracy'. Feminists have generally followed this line when viewing modern gender relations, partly because of the fact that, having achieved the vote, the feminist movement seemed largely to disappear until the 1960s. However, as Banks (1981: pp. 153—79) points out, the most active remaining feminists in Britain transferred their energies into the politics of welfare. This is the clue which moves us to the third phase of the story. National citizenship has indeed made a considerable impact on gender and by that route political stratification now also became gendered. As women were now a part of the state, and as the role of the state was enlarging enormously, gender became politicized, again subverting traditional patriarchy. Such is the argument of the next section.

### III: The Nation-State — Gender Politicized

In 1880 state expenditures in the United Kingdom represented well under 10 per cent of GNP; by 1980 it was well over 40 per cent. Such a phenomenal rise, typical of advanced capitalist countries, indicates a sea-change in the life of the state, from a small specialized agency making laws and engaging in foreign wars, to a massive redistributor of the resources of (national) society. The state now co-ordinates most social activities, provides their infrastructures and redistributes between economic sectors, geographical areas, age- and life cycle groups and social classes. The state became a nation-state, not merely in the liberal sense of political participation, but as the main collective nucleus of everyday life-experience. Gender was not an active agent in this transformation, but it could not help but be affected, and then react back upon the state. Gender became politicized.

The first main expansions, in the second half of the nineteenth century, were of transport and communications infrastructures, which did not particularly impact on gender, and of symbolic infrastructures (i.e. education) and care/control of the poor, which did. Both reduced the privacy of the household, removing some of its socialization functions, controlling the family life of the poor and expanding the occupations of teaching and social work. These immediately provided most of the activists of the first substantial feminist movements. Education and social welfare have continued as state growth-areas through the twentieth century.

First, education has expanded enormously, to consume around 10—15 per cent of state budgets through the twentieth century and to play a substantial role in allocating persons to class positions. The history of what Parkin (1979: pp. 54—60) has termed 'credentialism' has been uneven. The effects of its most recent spurt, the expansion of higher education in the 1950s and 1960s, are still working their way through social stratification. Meritocratic ideology claims that educational credentials are available to all talented persons. Of course, we know that class origins limit meritocracy quite substantially. But it has given a distinctive route up the stratification hierarchy to the *middle* class — distinct from the hereditary transmission of 'upper-class' capital. Though there is also gender discrimination, middle-class women have benefitted from their traditional role as socializers within the family and from liberal ideology (which always saw literacy as necessary to citizen participation). Thus women have penetrated education as teachers and pupils more successfully than they have most other 'public' areas of society. Thus, where credentialism is strongest — in the professions and, especially, in education itself — women have become relatively well qualified (as Rosemary Crompton shows in chapter 9), they have come closest to achieving equal pay and equal jobs and they continue to predominate amongst feminist activists. Segregation is not ended, equality not achieved, even here. But the growth of education has provided women with one of their furthest points of entry into the public sphere and into economic stratification.

Secondly, social welfare expanded as social democracy replaced liberalism, and as Poor Law became Welfare State. Social services, excluding education, consumed about 20 per cent of the state budget in 1920. Today it consumes over 40 per cent. What Marshall (1950) termed 'social citizenship' now covers all women as well as men. It is still expressed in liberal terms — the rights of all persons in the nation to adequate subsistence. But persons also still live in households/families (though less in lineages). So the Welfare State has blown right through the private walls of the household. We subsist in the modern nation-state only by allowing state scrutiny of our income and wealth through taxation and by demonstrating our need and 'worth' for welfare. This is quite unlike the relationship between state and person-household in historic societies: states could not penetrate the locality or the household to know the incomes of their inhabitants, let alone tax them (except crudely) or provide generally for their welfare. But now my income and wealth, the value of my fixed property and moveables, the number and circumstances of other household members, my familial and/or sexual relations with them, and the sincerity of our attempts to find employment are all scrutinized by the nation-state.

State scrutiny implies that all these circumstances have become politicized. General rules are laid down by parliament concerning our welfare rights and duties, including familial and marital roles. These straddle a contradiction between the values of patriarchy and of citizenship. The result is again a sort of compromise between patriarchy and a more gendered stratification, in this case gendered political stratification. The state recognizes that a man should normally head the household, earn a family wage, be the public person. This is the neo-patriarchal aspect of the state, bringing notions of domesticity and femininity into politics. But the state also ensures that the woman-citizen can subsist, even if this contradicts the power of the patriarch. The state's dilemmas have been increased by the decline in infant mortality and birthrates, and the rise in divorce and remarriage. The duties of men to their ex-wives and absent children; the plight of single-parent families; who is to count as a 'dependent'? — these complex and contentious issues are now politicized, to generate perennial legislation. Sometimes the legislation protects women from men; sometimes it reproduces conditions of patriarchy. But it always generalizes and politicizes gender relations. Much legislation also recognizes *in extremis* the autonomy of women from any particular patriarch. Daughters have quite similar rights as sons in relation to their fathers; women who separate or divorce have a financial claim on their former joint household extending to their ex-spouse's present income; and single parents receive a state subsistence income. Subsistence is often meagre and embodies subtle discriminatory provisions against women, but most women derive some, and some derive most, of their subsistence from state welfare or legislative protection, rather than from a patriarch.

We can now put together economic and political transformations, to see the force of Acker's 'head-counting' criticism of the distributional scales of orthodox theory. Most of its six assumptions no longer apply to many women. For example, she says, 40 per cent of households in the 1960 United States Census did not have a male head in the conventional sense — being female, or female-headed or husband-wife families in which the husband is retired, unemployed or working only part time. This proportion had become even higher by the time of the 1980 United States Census. In such a context categorizing distributional scales by the occupations of male head will leave a lot out.

But the household types that do not fit into orthodox theory are extremely varied. Women who are relatively autonomous from, or equal to, their men might be thought unlikely to form a single collective actor. They are divided by class and by whether their situation results from employment or state dependence. Around 7 per cent of women in the UK earn more than their husbands, many doing well out of credentialism. About 10—15 per cent of employed women live alone or with someone not related to them. Their earnings (at least in the United States, with better census data in this respect) are not far short of the national average (and they are higher if we

divide total household earnings by number of persons in the household), so
they are comfortably off. About one in eight families with dependent
children — the expected ideal-typical site of patriarchy — are headed by a
single parent, of whom nine-tenths are women. Most are relatively poor, 40
per cent being below the current official poverty level (both here and in the
United States).

Nevertheless, there are two common threads, one in employment, one
outside of it, which together explain most of the economic circumstances
of women. The first is that women receive less for their work than men in
similar jobs. This is so transparent to all, so contradictory to liberal and
social democratic notions of equality of all persons, and so economically
disastrous to many autonomous women, that a new feminist politics of
equal employment has arisen. This has a dual core of professional and
trade-union women. The second is that women do the domestic work,
especially child-rearing. Yet this worsens a woman's job prospects in
virtually every occupational category and makes her either more dependent
on her husband or drastically reduces her standard of living. Child-rearing
now seems to lessen women's earnings more than direct gender
discrimination does, at least in United States Census figures. In 1980 the
average household income in the United States was $24,656; that of
households without children headed by a woman was $18,528 (and by a
man $23,473); while that of households with children headed by a woman
was only $11,639 — despite the fact that over half these women were
working (Hacker 1983: table 2). The number of childless women has
declined greatly since the beginning of the century. Child-rearing unites
almost all women, for many of the variations between households, noted
above, turn out to be between different phases of the life cycle. During the
child-rearing phase the rational economic strategy would seem clear: stick
close to your patriarch, or face poverty. This strategy would place women
within the protective cover of their husband's social class (and validate
orthodox theory), But woman does not apparently live by bread alone.
Divorce rates among couples with dependent children, and illegitimacy
rates where the woman keeps her child, both continue to rise. But if
women do want more bread, there is an alternative political strategy:
include child-rearing in social citizenship and reward it. This broad strategy
also appeals to those whose success in employment is threatened by the
child-rearing phase.

This commonality of experience and political strategy among autonomous
and/or state-dependent women, is increasingly generating distinctive
pressure-group politics. A 'social feminism' couples the old liberal 'person',
claiming equality in education and employment, to state recognition of
child-rearing, centring on the provision of day-care facilities. These politics
are discussed by Sylvia Walby in chapter 3. In this country these pressure-
group politics achieved an obvious impact on the manifestos of both major

parties in the 1983 general election, especially on the Labour Party's. How effective are these new politics remains to be seen. But unless the variety of macrostructural trends, to which I have referred, are put into reverse, such pressures are likely to increase in stridency and mobilizing powers. Political stratification has become more gendered and this seems likely to continue. Though class of father and husband, and a woman's own occupational attainment, continue to divide women, the intersection of employment and Welfare State also provide gender solidarity. Gender is classed: but so too is economic and political stratification gendered.


CONCLUSION:

### Beyond Patriarchy and Neo-patriarchy, to Gendered Stratification

Do we still have patriarchy? No, because the particularistic distinction between the public and the private sphere has been eroded, first by employment trends and the emergence of more universal classes, secondly by universal citizenship by all persons in the nation, and thirdly by the nation-state's welfare interventions in the 'private' household/family.

Do we still have what I defined as 'neo-patriarchy'? Yes, to some extent, particularly in the extension of notions of 'domesticity' and 'femininity' into the public realms of employment and the Welfare State. Thus patriarchal values and practices still permeate many aspects of the culture of contemporary nation-states.

But we have also gone beyond even neo-patriarchy into two distinct and even opposite forms of gendered stratification. First, men and women have become in certain ways abstract, interchangeable 'persons' with equivalent rights as legal and political citizens, limited of course by the other stratification nuclei around which they might cluster — in this chapter, class and nation, but also (in some contexts not discussed here) ethnicity and religious affiliation. Persons have equality before the law and freedom of choice as individuals in few historic societies have done. One right that has expanded particularly for women is the right to choose a marriage partner, to terminate that marriage freely in divorce and to hold on to a portion of its material resources thereafter. These derivatives of liberalism, reinforced by social democracy and by feminist movements, represent fundamental changes in gender relations — whether or not feminists regard them as significant when compared to the transformations they would ideally like to see.

If this were the sole change, the other modern nuclei would be strengthened. Classes and nations would be homogenized and fortified by the collective experience and action of men and women together. Indeed, this has happened in certain respects, as, for example, in the gradual convergence of their rates of trade-union membership and their voting patterns (see various essays in Siltanen and Stanworth 1984).

But such trends are contradicted by a second type of gendered stratification. Even where men and women are not interchangeable, the pattern of their segregation and inequality has become integral to the structure of 'public' stratification. In patriarchal society the dimension of gender stratification was largely segregated from the dimension of 'public' stratification (classes etc.). This still persists but has diminished greatly. The participation of women in the public realm, particularly in employment and through the Welfare State, now affects the core stratification relations in our society. I gave examples of groups of women 'buffering' and 'fractionalizing' economic and political stratification both in employment and out of it. Some sociologists who minimize the impact of gender on stratification point to the relative absence of cllective action by all women, when compared to the frequency of action by collectivities like classes (as Lockwood does in chapter 2). I have argued against this with respect to political stratification, where the politics of employment and child-rearing unite a broader range of women. But to stress only this would be to miss the converse point: that the differential impact of gender in modern employment relations may reduce the impact of traditional (predominantly male) collectivities like class. Gender may cut across class; or gender and class may each fractionalize the impact of the other. As both trends are occurring simultaneously, a more complex form of stratification is now emerging.

To end thus is to end inconclusively, but it is also to report accurately on contemporary stratification. Patriarchy, even neo-patriarchy, was a relatively simple stratification structure. But modern capitalist nation-states present a more complex, uneven and probably unfinished array of stratification nuclei. Persons, families/households/lineages, genders, classes and nations (and others) all exist and interact. None can be assigned primacy, each has relevance for, and influences the shape of, the others and the whole. Two points are quite clear, however: stratification is now gendered and gender is stratified. We can no longer keep them in separate sociological compartments.

# 5

## Class Analysis, Gender Analysis and the Family

### Christine Delphy and Diana Leonard

Many authors in recent years have pointed out, with varying degrees of ire, that sociology has largely ignored women. We want in this chapter, however, to use the insight of Nicole-Clause Mathieu (1977), that the one place where this has *not* been true is the sociology of the family. She suggests that this is because this has been an area which sociology, like the rest of society, regards as largely natural. We want to develop this idea and to argue, first, that sociological accounts when they do touch on gender still base many 'social' explanations on 'natural' foundations; secondly, that as a result sociology supports the view that the world consists wholly or sufficiently of men and that women are 'extras', the detached reproductive organs of men or a marginal, lumpen group; and thirdly, that this has had serious consequences for sociological analyses of society. Given the focus of this book, we shall concentrate here on how this has happened in work on social stratification, though obviously the problem is not limited to this area alone.

Few sociologists would disagree with the general contention that the term class (or socio-economic category) is used in two senses: a narrow usage, applying to the collectivity of individuals who hold positions which define the class; and a broader usage, applying to a whole social milieu, around and including (*and required by*) the individuals who hold the positions. Thus, for example, 'the peasant class' can refer to the assembly of positions of small farmers, and the 'working class' to the assembly of positions of individual workers, *or* to whole populations, social strata, many of whose members are not heads of farms or actual wage-workers.

However, while sociologists may accept this as a statement, they virtually never put it in quite this way. This means that they don't recognize that using the same term to designate two distinct social groups, one of which is perhaps two or three times larger than the other, confuses the two. It also hides the fact that individuals who are 'in' a class but who do not occupy the positions which define the class, find themselves in a very different situation from those who do. The problem of 'non-holders' of positions — who they are and what their status is within the class — thus remains largely unbroached and unvoiced in sociology. We have a situation where the majority of the population are the concern of a few specialists — feminists, those concerned with the old or young or unemployed — but ignored by 'the mainstream'.

The majority of social scientists, whose chief focus is class divisions or stratification, have gone about things subtly, not bringing 'the problem of non-holders' to light, or, if challenged, arguing 'expedience', and relying on a shared set of presumptions (only certain men *really* matter) to shield them. But even those who *have* turned their attention directly to 'the woman question' or 'women and class' have asserted, Marxist and non-Marxist alike, that we must examine principally: 'the . . . link between women's oppression and the system of exploitation of our society' (Broyelle 1979); or 'the link between the forms of oppression of women and the organisation of production in the society' (Beechey and Allen 1982); and that analysis must 'begin with a structure of positions, associated with a specific historical form of the division of labour' (Goldthorpe 1983: p. 467). They agree that 'lines of class division and conflict run between but not through families' and that 'the position of the family as a whole within the system of stratification . . . derives from that of the family "head" . . . the separation of sex roles within the family . . . being itself the expression of a major form of inequality existing between the sexes' (1983: pp. 468, 469).

Authors thus assert that the oppression of women is not an integral part of '*the* system/organization of exploitation/production' of our society (which for them is the exploitation of the proletariat/the capitalist labour process), but is rather separate and linked; or that sex roles are not part of '*the* division of labour' or '*the* system of stratification', nor are they forms of 'class division and conflict', though they are connected thereto.

These statements all rest upon the presumption that capitalism, and the occupational structures it generates are *the* source of *systematic* inequalities (exploitations, stratification) in our society. If taxed with this, authors will agree that there *are* other inequalities; but the way they frame the problematic means that one set of inequalities is seen as primary, and, whatever the other inequalities, the explanation will always be under tension to revert back to a particular viewpoint and particular concerns. Other inequalities, when recognized, are always going to be secondary and derived, to be understood by their relationship to class inequalities, and explicitly less systematic or not systematic at all. Although some studies have been published which actually try to demonstrate the primacy of class division empirically (e.g. Westergaard and Resler 1975), class is more generally simply asserted to be self-evidently predominant over gender.

We believe that the reasoning underlying such approaches is in fact the opposite of what is presented generally, and indeed that it is an instance of patriarchal thinking. The primacy of the exploitation of the proletariat by the capitalist labour process, the primacy of the market in economic affairs, the primacy of employment relationships and functions and conditions of employment, apparently 'explain' why class inequalities should be the inequalities to which others are to be related. But it is rather sociologists' concern with the processes of interaction and antagonism between *men* which explains their focus upon certain inequalities.[1] The 'conclusion' is in fact the premiss underlying the reasoning, which in any event is circular, as figure 5.1 demonstrates.

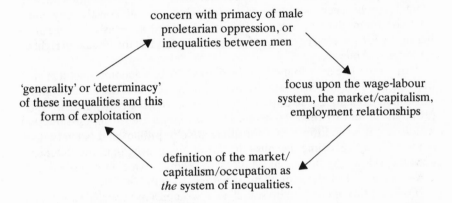

concern with primacy of male
proletarian oppression, or
inequalities between men

'generality' or 'determinacy'
of these inequalities and this
form of exploitation

focus upon the wage-labour
system, the market/capitalism,
employment relationships

definition of the market/
capitalism/occupation as
*the* system of inequalities.

*Figure 5.1   Patriarchal Chain of Reasoning in Mainstream Sociology*

Since women were marginal to the starting premisses, they stay marginal. For a long time they were pushed out of sight altogether in studies of the labour-market and only men were considered in class analyses. Any oppression women suffered which was non-capitalist (i.e. in non-market and domestic areas) was either neglected totally or decreed to be non-economic or secondary. Nowadays the predominance of the male sector is still set out in such a way as to legitimize a focus upon the protagonists (or rather on the 'main' protagonists) in *this* system. We are obviously not arguing that it is not an important system, but we are taking issue with why it is the only system, in theory and in practice, and with *how it is conceptualized.*

We are suggesting that 'class', in its narrow usage, is not the general system of inequalities in a statistical sense, since it concerns a minority of the population; nor is it necessarily general in a determining sense, since its relationship to very many types of inequality has yet to be shown (as opposed to asserted). We are suggesting rather that it is general in the sense of following the usual cultural representation of gender diversities in our society, where one gender is both the part and the whole and the other is the minority, the specific. It has been pointed out (de Beauvoir 1949; Spender 1980), that our everyday language reveals this clearly: 'man' and 'humanity' are synonymous. Women are never general, never universal, but always particular, always located in relation to men. We believe this applies also to much sociological language and conceptualization.

Class is seen as the primary social division in Western societies. It is also seen as systematic, as *the* system. And it is seen also as unquestionably social — indeed it has pre-empted the very term. We speak of 'social stratification' and 'social class'. This means that other inequalities have to struggle to be seen not only as systems but also as social: they must describe themselves as 'sex classes' or 'age-based systems'. One form of hierarchy is therefore not only the most studied, it has the linguistic right to be *the* social hierarchy.

This use of 'social' is found in a developed form in accounts, such as that of Engels (1884) and his many followers, which explain the subordination of women as being caused by their restriction to private life and domestic production; and by their exclusion from an arena and from a production which is called indifferently and alternatively 'public' and 'social'. This usage is very revealing because it shows so clearly that the scientific account follows the dominant ideology in seeing private/family life as less social, as more based on the facts of nature, than public life.

If we add this opposition of 'social' and 'women's oppression' to what we argued earlier, it appears that there is in sociology, as in our society generally, a belief that gender inequalities are not (fully) social, but are in some way and to some extent natural, whereas class oppression is entirely social and due to a system of exploitation. Furthermore it is held that in so far as gender inequalities *are* social, it is because they are linked to the oppression of the proletariat, to capitalism, to the mode or organization of production and to class.

This sort of thinking has led to a series of impasses in the study of gender and in the politics of the women's movement. It has led, for example, to a series of attempts to look at the oppression of women more or less exclusively in terms of its relationship/usefulness to capitalism; and to a sense of bewilderment as to what it is that radical feminists see as the reason for women's oppression. If it is not due/attached to class, they must be saying men are *naturally* oppressors.

These are obviously highly important debates for all those concerned with the analysis of gender in society and with attempts to change the position of women. This present collection requires, however, that whatever its shortcomings for the study of gender, we start within the 'class analysis' frame. We shall suggest, however, that there are *(at least)* two major patriarchal biases within the theoretical foundations of stratification theory; that both involve instances of naturalistic presuppositions — first that the family is a natural, affection-based, sharing, egalitarian unit; and secondly that inheritance naturally follows blood/genetic links — and that these biases have very serious consequences for the adequacy of stratification studies/class analyses in their own terms.

## THE FAMILY AS 'THE UNIT OF THE CLASS STRUCTURE'

Much important work has been done in the last ten years in developing theories of the labour-market which take account of *all* holders of class positions and not just the 'main' holders (adult, white males in full-time employment). Class analysis has been greatly enriched and improved thereby.

Unfortunately, the issue of what to do with non-holders, or how to see the relationship between households and class structures, has advanced little. There is a marked unwillingness to look at the internal structure of the family in mainstream sociology — as much as there is in real life to intervene in individual instances in 'a man's private life'. Although the women's movement has focused attention on wife abuse, sexual dual standards, the invisibility of housework and caring work and the experience of financial dependency, the stress even in recent sociology is still on the unit/the unity of the couple (cf. C. C. Harris 1983).

On the one hand there have been new analyses of the myriad ways in which '*the family* is functional' — now seen in terms of being 'functional for capitalism' rather than 'for society' (as in sociology in the United States in the 1950s and 1960s). We have discussed these analyses in an earlier paper (Delphy and Leonard 1982), arguing that they look fleetingly if at all at the structure of families and that they see divisions between the sexes as merely secondary effects of the oppression of the working class.

On the other hand there have been restatements of the 'conventional view', which in Goldthorpe's recent paper, for example, accepts that 'the separation of sex roles' within the family is 'an expression of a major form of inequality existing between the sexes', but which says this is offset by the 'large area of shared interest between husband and wife' (1983: p. 469).

Sociology is stymied because its practitioners cannot stop seeing heterosexual couples and their children as natural 'units'. Sociologists have still not recognized that 'the family' is a particular form of *social* relationship. It is not an organic whole: *it is a hierarchical system*. Marriage and parenthood and kinship are no more natural, no less social institutions than, say, parliament or factories, and women do housework and child care not because of natural abilities, or for love, or as a hobby, or from choice, but because this is how they earn their living and secure protection for themselves (from other men) and gain rights to have children (their major, if two-edged resource as society is currently constituted) in a particular form of society — Western, industrial, patriarchal.

If we were to use the same formal terms to analyse the family as have been developed for class analysis, namely, to see it as 'a structure of positions associated with a specific historical form of the social division of labour' (Goldthorpe 1983: p. 467), we think it would be recognized that the family is a social system in which subordinates work unpaid for a head (generally a husband/father) and are in return maintained by him (or provided with a contribution to their maintenance when they are in employment and earn some of their own keep). Dependants are also usually entitled to an inheritance on the death of their family head. The number and nature of family dependants is regulated by kinship and marriage (i.e. this is the idiom in which these work relationships are located). Dependants today are recruited mainly by marriage (they are mostly wives), the possibilities for family production having been much reduced. In the past, however — and still in certain sectors such as agriculture and shopkeeping — a range of kin worked in return for their keep, in particular children and unmarried siblings.

A whole variety of tasks are done by different members of different families.

1 These range from cleaning toilets to breadwinning; they carry different prestige and can be ranked roughly on a scale;
2 They are distributed among individuals according to the status of the individuals (i.e. according to their relationship to the head and their sex, age and marital status); and finally
3 The value given to a task depends on the status of the person who actually does it.

In general in the family (as in the labour-market) prestigious tasks are reserved for adult men, and conversely any task done by adult men is more prestigious than other tasks (or indeed than the same task) when done by women and children. It is often asserted, both by the actors and all too often by sociologists, that certain tasks are intrinsically of higher prestige (for example breadwinning) because they are functionally more important to the family; or that the division of labour is based on technical differences in capacities or abilities (for example physical strength or childbearing). We feel sure we do not need to rehearse the counter-arguments around the problems of functionalism and skill here (see Cockburn 1983a). These legitimize, but do not explain, family hierarchy.

The division of labour in our society is not, however, one of a rigid division of tasks; it is not a question of women cooking and cleaning and caring for children and men never doing these things. Such tasks are 'women's work', are not valued highly, and are often invisible; but men sometimes do them. Rather, domestic work is women's work in the sense that the status, the conditions of doing it, the relations of production of this work are now nearly specific to wives. What makes it wives' work is not the tasks or even the sum total of the tasks, but their particular organization. There is not a division of tasks, but a division of jobs, of labour — tasks *plus* their conditions of performance and remuneration and status.

The actual attribution of who does what within a family is regulated by tradition, by external circumstances (which include men's privileged position in the labour market and hence greater earning power) *and* by the head of the family. The head of the household is, as the title implies, the overall manager and decision-maker. He decides what needs doing and assigns labour to individuals — including sometimes delegating responsibility for particular areas to another member.

At times this is concealed because 'custom' seems to prescribe who does what (household members will come under sanction from kin and community if they break norms) and circumstances seem to constrain choices so the head has little leeway. But there is always room for some decision-making — even if it is simply a choice to continue as before or to refuse to take responsibility and to leave other family members to shift for themselves, or to delegate. And whatever the actual limits within which choice can be exercised, they lie in the hands of the head.

Such decisions involve both the distribution of work within the family *and* commercial choices; what to put on the market, where and to whom to sell it. This includes the sale of labour power — his own, that of his wife and children. If a father wants to he can let his son or daughter continue in education, or he can send him or her out to work at sixteen. Commercial decisions are usually much more extensive than is imagined. Within the constraints of local conditions and possibilities, the head determines the cash income of the household and what it is to be used for (in general if not in particular). For example he may or may not 'let his wife work', or he may, if he is relatively well off, prefer that she looks after dependants and produces at home rather than using nurseries or nurses, cleaning agencies, bakeries, frozen foods and take-aways, or servants (au pairs, domestic cleaners etc.). These decisions may be made in consultation with his wife — and she may even be able to persuade him to change his mind, but the mind to *be* changed is his.

If dependants have their own access to paid employment, or if they produce things within the home which they sell on a market, they have their own source of income. Their paid work will have to be undertaken in addition to their domestic responsibilities, however (or they have to pay for, and be responsible for, seeing that the latter are replaced). But the household head budgets for their income — which he can gauge in advance — and he stipulates what it is to be used for; for example commonly, the purchase of certain commodities, or so he can reduce the amount he pays for housekeeping, or to provide the dependant with some money 'of her own'. The dependant's income is seldom of the scale, nor is it as unequivocally the earner's to use as she pleases, as the head's is for him.

The labour extracted from the different categories of dependants, and the maintenance and transmission of property and status provided for them, is managed by the head — but obviously he doesn't have absolute control. As we have said, what can be expected and what must be given is governed by law and custom, and backed up with community control. Also, like all managers, the head must persuade his dependants to at least acquiesce and ideally to work with wholehearted enthusiasm. He must motivate them — which in the family, unlike the labour-market, characteristically involves manipulation of personal emotional attachment, ideologies of love, sexual attraction and self-sacrifice and, conversely, violence or its threat. The dependants in turn resist and/or try to manipulate their situation in various ways and with varying degrees of success.

Finally, it is worth commenting that, of course, as with any other enterprise, the head and his dependants do have interests in common which serve to minimize friction. Their joint project gives positive experiences; they are all generally better off (economically, socially, sexually) in a family than without one, in our culture; they can all work to enhance the family's position by contributions of various kinds, and all benefit thereby — albeit not equally or identically. Many husbands are very benevolent despots: they may choose to forego many privileges — though they can have them again at any time.

Before leaving the division of labour in the family to look equally briefly at the benefits received by various family members, we need to stress that there isn't a gap between the two: there isn't on one side a division of labour with a series of tasks on a scale of prestige, and on the other differential consumption — because the division of labour carries its own rewards. It is a system of rewards in itself. Since some jobs in the family are deemed important and prestigious (e.g. breadwinning), doing them is a benefit; conversely doing 'simple', trivial, invisible, 'light' work — especially when such work is actually arduous and time-consuming — is a deprivation. In particular, being the head and having decision-making power and the right to manage, in itself constitutes a benefit, which can even be considered a form of differential consumption (consumption of prestige — symbolic reward).

This then is linked to another system of rewards, the consumption system proper, where again the head of the family is in control of what comes into, or is produced within, the family and how it is distributed. He gets the dominant share again here — this being 'justified' by his decision-making power and his performing the important task of breadwinning and managing — and again he consumes the prestige and the intrinsic rewards attached to the wielding of power.

Because the family has been taken to be 'the major unit of reward and class fate' by sociologists and 'of consumption' by economists, very few people have bothered to look at distribution *within* it. They have assumed, against all the evidence of their own lives, that there is a simple per capita division of money, goods and services. But there are also moralistic influences at play. On one hand, although secondary poverty has long been recognized, it has been forgotten as constantly because people do not want to think about the possibility of there not being equality of misery (natural socialism?) among the poor: that when there is not even enough food to go round, some still take the lion's share. On the other hand, people cannot be bothered if the wives of middle-class men consume less than their husbands — they are 'spoilt bitches' anyway, who already get more than they deserve for their idle lives.

However, existing evidence suggests that there is a marked hierarchy of consumption within families:

1  different resources are available which carry different valuation;
2  these resources are distributed to individuals not according to criteria of need (e.g. the work people do or their appetites) but according to their familial status;
3  the value attached to a resource is dependent upon the status of the person who enjoys it. What adult men get carries prestige, and vice versa.

In poor families, even food and other essentials (medical care, leisure, pocket money) are distributed differentially. In richer families, new and increased areas of differential consumption open up (transport, especially cars; leisure activities; food and drink of high quality; etc.).

It should be noted also that consumption cannot be reduced to quantitative issues alone. Ways of consuming are as, if not more, important than quantities consumed. Up to now, however, the study of consumption has been preoccupied with volumes and varieties. The very existence of forms of consumption hasn't been broached. But driving one's own car is different from being driven; buying, cooking and clearing up after a meal means eating a very different meal from one served to you. Individuals can consume the same things (a car journey, a meal) in the same place at the same time without their consumption being identical. Thus at the same time as dependants consume less, they also consume a negative portion of choice, freedom and power over their own lives.

Because modes of consumption as such have not been studied and housework itself has been pretty well invisible (a condition of its being done efficiently is that it is not seen to be done, cf. Davidoff 1976), the enormous extent of the *services* produced in the home has been ignored. Sociology has presented 'production' as what the family *used* to do in its glorious past — but now does no more. But families in fact produce a lot for their own consumption, and this production is an important part of the resources which determine the standard of living (and life-style) of all members and their prestige *vis à vis* other families in the local community. And the consumption by family members is intrinsically different precisely because one member does most of the servicing for the others (and is not serviced herself): the wife's consumption is necessarily different qualitatively from her husband's. Those who argue for the 'socializing' of domestic work as a way of overcoming the domestic oppression of women, forget that having things done for you individually, 'in the comfort of your own home', with full attention to personal tastes, is precisely one of the key features of domestic work (Glastonbury 1978).

Class analysis, when faced with the internal hierarchy of the family and the significance of its production for self-consumption, should no longer keep willing the problem to go away. How it responds depends on whether it wants to work with the narrow or the broad definition of class.

If class analysis were to be concerned strictly with class in the narrow sense, then it might not concern itself with the family, since its focus would be employment relationships and situations. It would recognize that some individuals in employment are less freely contracting agents than others (because of overriding prior familial commitments); but it would not try to push non-holders of positions, and families-as-units, into the procrustean bed of their head's position in the social division of labour. It would leave non-holders in limbo, as being outside its frame of reference.[2]

But, of course, most class analysis is *not* just about class in the narrow sense. It may be concerned *principally* with employment relationships and employment functions, but it is also concerned with 'the distinctiveness of members of identifiable classes in terms of their life-chances, their life-styles and patterns of association, and their socio-political orientations and modes of action'; and with 'establishing how far classes have formed as relatively stable collectivities through the continuity with which individuals and families have been associated with particular class positions over time' (Goldthorpe 1983: pp. 467, 483). This inevitably involves concern with class in the wide sense.

As far as concern with class stability and continuity over time is concerned, class analysis has wished its way out of various problems by following the naturalistic ideology of society itself: i.e. by not seeing family relationships, including inheritance, as social and hierarchical.

HEREDITARY TRANSMISSION AND THE CONSTITUTION OF CLASSES

Because of human mortality, the material world possessed by one generation must fall to the next in one way or another; and when individuals die, the positions they occupy within the structure of society must be filled by new people, recruited in some accepted fashion. But these ends can be achieved in various ways. In our culture, however, transmission of property, status, customs and habits, as much as of physical traits, is implicitly hereditary. It takes place, not between any two or more persons, but between relatives and more particularly between forebears and descendants. Unless the term 'transmission' is qualified, it connotes familial transfers.

Other methods of distributing individuals to positions certainly do exist in our society,[3] for example the drawing of lots, a vote, the authoritarian decision of a supreme power, ordeal, examination or other competition, co-option, partnership, as well as descent. But it is competition (which in examinations is *formally* meritocratic) and recruitment by personal association with an existing holder of a position (in the particular form of descent, kinship or marriage), which are most widespread. And it is the coexistence of competition and recruitment and their opposition (or rather the fact that at times they occur in an offensive combination) which are the nub of most of the debates about the distribution of positions in our own society.[4]

People take it for granted, for example, that individuals pass their property to their children. Naming any other beneficiaries is regarded with suspicion and is seen as 'wronging one's children' and it has to be 'justified' (which shows that hereditary transmission requires no justification). It is also taken for granted in our class/hierarchical society, that class position is inherited. Both the actors and social analysts accept that the sons of workers 'normally' become workers and equally that the sons of owners normally become owners — though it is also accepted that the sons of workers do not *inevitably* become workers. However, the hereditary character of class is not always explicit — one might even say it is often disguised, even in academic definitions.

Studies of social mobility are frequently set up in such a way that inheritance equals no movement/no change. Hereditary transmission is taken as the null hypothesis, as the starting presumption, or the historical condition from which meritocracy has evolved, which means usually that only *other* situations are studied. Heredity is not treated as of the same order, as *as social*, as are the other forms of transmission mentioned above (election, appointment, co-option, etc.), because in the collective consciousness hereditary transmission is seen as arising not from culture but from nature. Studies of social mobility incorporate the transmission of position as an axiom, but this axiom is implicit and not recognized in their conceptualization, precisely because they adopt the views of a hereditary society. Their conceptualization prevents them looking at the very process which is at its base. They don't see hereditary transmission to the extent that they incorporate it.

Heredity is also disguised via the distinction often drawn between our own class society and caste societies, which suggests that while caste is determined by heredity, class is not;[5] or that while in non-Western societies, the social hierarchy is either mixed with or derived from lineage hierarchy, the social organization of our own society is economic in character. The principles of constitution of our classes and hierarchies, like the principles of organization between them, are declared to be external to kinship. This of course confuses two orders of phenomena: first, the principles concerning the *constitution of* groups (and the hierarchy between them); and secondly, the rules of *generation recruitment* to (and/or individual membership of) these groups. Groups or classes can be constituted on extra-kinship criteria at the same time as individual membership within them is ruled by kinship. We can see this in caste societies, where membership of groups (generational recruitment) is governed entirely by birth, while the groups themselves are occupational or religious — as is the hierarchy which orders them in relation to one another. Membership of the groups is familial in character, but the principles constituting and ordering the groups is extra-familial. In our society too, individual *class membership* is tied strongly to kinship, while the *relationship between classes* is non-familial/economic.

Sociology therefore in various ways fails to *see* hereditary transmission; it is taken for granted and simultaneously ignored because it is not considered a social phenomenon. We know about the ways in which hereditary transmission takes place in particular groups (which relatives are entitled to inherit, under what circumstances and the rituals surrounding the handing-over) — though we know more about this in 'primitive' societies than in our own. We also have large-scale surveys which show the extent to which hereditary transmission exists in a society (what mitigates it and what, eventually, replaces it). But the central study of hereditary transmission as such — *who* enters *which* groups and *how* — is curiously untouched. That is to say, class analysis doesn't actually look at heredity as an institution: it looks only at certain aspects of heredity, and presents these aspects as the whole. This means that large areas of heredity are neglected and the action within and between groups is represented inaccurately. For instance it is hypothesized, explicitly and implicitly, that in the reproduction of classes, heredity operates in the direction of stability (or 'reproduction'), and has no effect on the internal principles of constitution of social groups. Both these hypotheses are questionable and are illuminated by a study of gender.

Most studies of social mobility focus not only on mobility, but on *upward* mobility, i.e. on the degree of possibility of individuals entering a class higher than their class of birth, because the studies derive from a political concern with democratization. This has two consequences:

1 First, downward mobility is relatively ignored — it is not desirable, so it is neither admitted nor dealt with. It is assumed that the individuals born in a class stay within it — unless it is being suggested that they have *risen above* it.

2 Secondly, upward and downward mobility are seen as having a common cause: they are both supposedly due to meritocratic forces (of whose existence and efficiency mobility is both the sign and the consequence); while non-mobility is seen as the result of heredity (and even as the mark of the latter's existence). Hence the action of heredity is equated with the production of similarity and heredity is itself identified with and by such actions. All differentiation is held to be exterior to, and also in opposition to, heredity.

However, inheritance is part of the institution of the family — and this, as we stressed in the last section, is pre-eminently a hierarchical institution. Transmission is also related to family status, yet in studies of mobility and cultural transmission, all the children of a family are treated as if they are equals, as if they are all equal heirs and succeed equally to their father's position, inherit equal shares of similar property and are equal members of the wider social group. Yet the everyday experience of members of our society — especially (one would have thought) of those members who are sociologists — teaches us that these are three very different things. The fact that you are born into a family does not guarantee you will be an heir, still less that you will succeed your father. Inheritance is a system which can be, and very often is, based on inequality, on some being advantaged and others disadvantaged. For example, most inheritance systems in Western Europe are characterized by the more or less total exclusion of daughters from the inheritance of certain key forms of property, and many by an unequal inheritance by the oldest (or a favourite) son to the disadvantage of his male and female siblings — even when by law there is formally equal inheritance. Studies of mobility and cultural transmission however, treat the differences between children, and in particular the differences between sons and daughters (including differences of education among the professional classes where education is a key form of property), as being attributable solely to 'general' social processes such as 'sex-role stereotyping in schools'. Differences by order of birth are virtually ignored by sociology and are the domain of psychologists. We know of not one case where the differences between siblings by order of birth or by gender has been seen as the result of the logic of family transmission/inheritance (despite Bourdieu and Passeron's 1964 title).

The action of hierarchical inheritance is very clear in situations where inheritance of property is the main means of succession to the father's position — viz. in rural societies where the father's position as a farmer necessitates the inheritance of certain property (a farm, or the lease of a farm), where there is only one farm to hand on and where there are several children. The oldest son then gets the farm and other children inherit other property. They may even inherit property which is formally (by local accounting) of 'equal' status. For instance, daughters may inherit stock which their father has decided is worth as much as the farm their brother inherits; but it is not the same sort of property and it locates them very differently within the society. They do not receive their father's status, nor a status identical to his, nor even a status which is similar to his.

The action of differential inheritance is less clear where accession is at stake — not succession to the father's actual position, but rather to a status *similar* to his — and where this is tied not (as classically) to material inheritance, but to cultural inheritance. It is also less striking when there are few children in each family and the circumstances are those of general expansion of 'middle-class' jobs (such as we were experiencing until the last few years).

Evidence from rural situations, however, (see Delphy 1984b) leads us to put forward the hypotheses that in all families one son will succeed to the father's position and that among the others (potential non-successors) we must distinguish two categories, sons and daughters, who have quite different fates. Among the sons, depending upon the resources available, one or more will be located in positions which may be similar, *or* markedly inferior, to that of the brother who succeeds (and *ipso facto*, to that of their father). Such sons may slowly and painfully *acquire* the same status as was *given* to their brother from the start. But they start lower down on the ladder. This particular point on the ladder is therefore filled from two sources: by the inheriting sons of men at that point or slightly below, and by the non-inheriting sons of men at points above. The constituting principle in both cases is inheritance. *It produces differentiation as well as similarity,* since the non-succession of some is the price of the succession of another to the full estate of their father.

The situation of the non-successor sons varies a lot, depending on whether the successor gets all the property, or just enough to secure him the same position as his father. It is because one succeeds that it matters to the others whether or not they are *also* excluded from *any* inheritance. Non-successors are not simply disinherited and left for some outside mechanism to take over and place them. On the contrary, they are placed very precisely and by heredity. They are disadvantaged, but within certain limits and to a precise extent.

Inheritance cannot therefore be reduced to the reproduction of similarity between parent and child, to sons inheriting their father's position, because inheritance is responsible simultaneously for both similarity and difference between father and sons and between brothers. It is not only a stabilizing factor, but also and even more so a factor causing mobility, especially where large families are the norm. Substantial downward mobility can occur in large families with limited non-partible resources. It thus distributes related individuals into *different* classes and subclasses.

Inheritance also acts directly on the constitution of each class (in the broad sense), for it produces both holders of the positions which define the class, *and also non-holders*. It not only indicates who enters a given class, but also determines who does not. Non-holders are principally (but not exclusively) daughters, for, as we said above, although not all sons are successors, the preferred successor certainly is. Daughters are excluded totally and systematically from succession even when they are not excluded from inheritance.[6] Inheritance (one part of the institution of the family) refuses daughters the possibility of acquiring independent status, though it gives this even to non-succeeding sons. In farming communities, for example, daughters cannot 'set up in their own right'. They can stay on the land only by becoming dependants. This they share with non-succeeding sons in some communities (Bourdieu 1962). In such communities, young women cannot own anything when they are single and whatever property they acquire when they marry, they 'carry' to their husbands. This applies also to their own labour power. A girl cannot be a farmer *de facto* and a wife cannot be one *de jure*. Clearly, it is not just the quality of being a non-successor which makes daughters into wives, since some sons are in the same position (and they don't become wives). Rather inheritance (a diachronic aspect of the family) combines with the rules of marriage: the role of wife (a synchronic aspect of the same institution).

Looked at in this way, it is clear that the situation of father and mother and of husband and wife, which are often talked of as 'sex categories' or 'family roles', are in fact categories integral to the internal structure of classes (in the broad usage of 'class'). They are created by the differential passing on of family property, which produces a population of successors and non-successors, some of the latter being then transformed into non-holders within each class.

Sociology (and common sense) recognize this in attaching women to the class of their father/husband when the women don't work outside the home, and also often even when they do, because women do not hold a 'position' of their own. Wives are frequently non-holders in fact, and non-holders by status. Being a wife is synonymous with being a non-holder. (Note how differently adult sons living at home are treated by the same studies.)

But of course, sociology doesn't just 'attach' wives to their husbands — it actually subsumes them. Wives are treated as if their class membership was *identical to/of the same nature as* that of their husbands, even though the process of attachment presupposes precisely the contrary. Being a dependant is a specific, distinct form of class membership (see Delphy 1984a).

Hereditary transmission and gender roles are seen culturally as 'natural' phenomena. The adoption of their fathers' position by sons is qualified as 'stability'; and the difference between the social situation of girls and boys 'obvious' because the sexes are different. Both phenomena are identified with inertia; as nature i.e. non-social and as nothing changing. But inheritance is a social process and it involves not just the recruitment of sons to their father's position (which is not inertia/stability, but itself a process) but also, and antagonistically, the exclusion of other children, particularly daughters from their father's position. Recruitment and exclusion are linked, not just because both are due to inheritance, but also because *the second is the condition for the first*, in the 'classical' effect of inheritance.

Class analysis must therefore reject the restricted use of the term 'inheritance', and the use of the term 'stability' to describe the inheritance of positions. It must extend its scope to see inheritance as concerning the composition of classes *and* the movement of individuals between these classes *and* (especially if we also are concerned with gender) the constitution of classes (i.e. the existence and creation of different and antagonistic categories and statuses *within* classes).

CONCLUSION

The emphasis in class analyses on the labour process (or the occupational structure) as a primary source of systematic social inequalities does not enable such analyses to begin adequately to explain gender inequalities. They cannot therefore substantiate their claim that class divisions (in the narrow sense) are *the* most important social divisions. Class or stratification analyses, which forefront *a* particular form of inequality, cannot therefore be regarded as adequate representations of society as a whole, or even of social inequalities.

In addition, however, the indifference of stratification studies to the institution of the family (the core institution of gender division) has deleterious effects on the actual representation of classes (in the broad sense) which classical class analyses have themselves put forward. This indifference has weakened their accounts of differences in the standards of living between groups at any one point in time, and weakened, sometimes to the point of non-existence, their study of the reproduction of the social structure over time.

The refusal to acknowledge obvious inequalities in the family, and especially differences between holders and non-holders of class positions, results not only in the 'omission of women' (which classical theorists might not care too much about), but also in the misrepresentation of 'class' life-chances, life-styles, patterns of association and socio-political orientations, which they certainly do care about. It also results in gross misrepresentation of the mechanisms (notably the hereditary transmission of status) which account for the perpetuation of and change within classes and between classes over time. Full recognition of gender in stratification studies therefore seems to us well overdue.

# 6

## The Relations of Technology
### What Implications for Theories of Sex and Class?

### Cynthia Cockburn

*'Like class, sexual antagonism is not something which can be understood simply by living it: it needs to be analysed with concepts forged for that purpose.'*

Sally Alexander and Barbara Taylor, 1980.

INTRODUCTION

Shareholder, manager, professional engineer, a team of male technicians and craftsmen, some female 'unskilled' machine operators — these could be seen, from one point of view, as a social hierachy in which the occupational definitions are strata and are surrogates for class. We could observe the fact that the only women in the technical hierarchy are at the bottom. But this approach would tell us little more than that. It cannot say how the ranking evolved, how men and women got to be in their particular strata, or what we might expect to happen next.

In the research project 'Advanced technology: effects on sex-gender and class relations in work'[1] the intention has been to study the *relation* between occupational groups and the sexes as they are involved with particular technologies, in such a way as to detect the *processes* of investment and scrapping, skilling and de-skilling, recruitment and expulsion, and also the processes of mutual definition that occur between different groups, especially between women and men.

The three instances of technological change chosen for study were: the displacement of manual pattern processes by computer-aided design (CAD) in the clothing industry; the computerization and automation of goods handling (especially picking, or order filling) in the mail-order warehouse;

and the introduction of the computerized tomography (CT) scanner in hospital X-ray departments. It will be evident that one of these is in manufacturing; one in distribution and one in a public sector service. In each instance I carried out a case study of one firm or hospital using the old methods, one with the new. The three instances I hoped would constitute a 'panel' that might be interrogated. Much as a panel of discussants in a seminar, it might result in the raising of different points and throw different lights on the subject of interest: gains and losses in pay, status and prospects resulting from new technology, job segregation by sex, women's and men's differing relationship to technology, to employment and to each other.

In addition to the above, there was a fourth component in the study. Technologies such as these do not arrive out of the blue. Somewhere the new equipment is being designed, developed, marketed, serviced. It is here that one would expect new jobs to be created and new trends observable. So I traced the three technologies upstream to the engineering industry to see such aspects of their generation as were visible in Britain. A case study was made of a large electronic engineering firm producing CT scanners; of two import agencies marketing and servicing United States and European CAD systems among clothing manufacturers in Britain; a consultancy involved in the master-minding of warehouse innovations; and a small mechanical engineering workshop producing mechanized conveyor systems, including the one introduced in the mail-order study.

The empirical research was carried out over a period of eighteen months from 1982 to 1984. The case studies included observation combined with interview and postal questionnaires. In total approximately 200 interviews were carried out with a wide range of people, all involved in one way or another with the technologies. The interviews were structured but open-ended, and they were recorded on tape and transcribed. Some were as short as 20 minutes, others as long as three hours.

In this chapter I will do no more than sketch some of the main findings of the empirical work and then make use of this opportunity to discuss their implications for theories of sex and class.

## SOME RESEARCH FINDINGS

The case studies showed, among other things, the following. Investment in new technology is in general a response by the firm to crisis and competition, but it is directed in different situations to different aspects of the problem. Thus, in the mail-order warehouses the intention was quite straightforward: productivity gains, by speeding throughput of work and reducing the labour force. In the clothing pattern rooms, on the other hand, the main intention was not to shed workers but rather to increase the firm's capability to produce complex and rapidly changing garment styles the better to compete with Third World manufacturing for a particular sector of the UK market. In the case of hospitals venturing into CT, the impulse was again different. The National Health Service (NHS) is being driven on by sales pressure, by medical and scientific professional interests and by public appeals and private donations generated by the fear of cancer. It is being held back by government spending stringency. The professional organization of radiographers and the relatively sheltered situation of the NHS has ensured against job loss due to CT however. In fact a slight gain of radiographer and other jobs was detectable due to acquisition of the new imaging modalities.

In all three situations women were to be found operating the new equipment. In the mail-order warehouse the female unskilled manual workers, cheapest of cheap labour, who had been engaged in conventional order filling, continued as pickers in the new, static, push-button job — though in smaller numbers. It continued to be thought of as women's work. In clothing, the trend in pattern rooms prior to new technology had favoured a gradual replacement of skilled male craft cutters by women. This was being confirmed, if not hastened, by the new technology since women are considered adequate and desirable operators of the CAD systems. The change was accompanied by a levelling of wages between the sewing units and the formerly privileged cutting and pattern rooms, as one would perhaps expect with a wave of feminization. In radiography, though increasing numbers of men are entering the profession, there is no evidence that they are acquiring proportionately more experience on, or advantage from, CT scanners than women. Women are held in considerable respect as radiographers.

The nature of the new jobs, both in terms of skill demanded and control permitted, varies from good to very bad. Three further characteristics of these women-held operator jobs are significant however. First, in all three technologies employees reported noticeably increased pressure of work as employers sought to maximize the use of costly equipment.

Secondly, they are vulnerable to further technological change. It is clearly the aim of the manufacturers and suppliers of the equipment to render succeeding generations more 'idiot-proof' and 'labour-saving'. Thirdly, the operator jobs do not afford the operators knowledge concerning the structure or internal processes of the equipment. There appears to be a general 'law' that women are found in jobs where they may 'press the button' to achieve normal output, but not in jobs that 'meddle with the works', jobs where they could be called on to intervene in the mechanism itself.

Some relatively secure, adaptable and well-paid technological jobs *are* being created at this level. They can be grouped into two broad categories: the job of maintenance technician; and that of systems technologist.

Women are simply not acquiring these jobs — the changed nature of technology notwithstanding.

Similarly, rewarding jobs are also being created at the 'upstream' locations, where technologies originate and whence they are delivered to users. Women are not entering these jobs either. I will take as an instance the engineering firm producing CT scanners. Here, of 197 technical managers and engineers/engineering technicians in field service, repair and production, *none* was female. Twenty-two out of the 23 software engineers (a desk job) were men. Women feature as the majority of unskilled and semi-skilled assembly workers in this plant producing scanners and other imaging equipment. In addition, women are present in adminstrative, secretarial, sales, demonstration and training roles. But the one woman software engineer was the only woman professional engineer, engineering technician or craftworker I encountered in the entire study.

Why are there so strikingly few women in the skilled technological jobs afforded by 'new technology'? It is often supposed that electronics, being cleaner, lighter and safer than mechanical engineering, would afford an entry for women. Why is this promise not being kept? Employers claim to be open-minded about women. They observe however that few women appear to seek such jobs, few are qualified for them, and industry appears to be an unattractive environment to women. In fact, however, those in a position to recruit or work with women pointed to many aspects of technological jobs that were in practice felt to be unsuitable or difficult for women to do. It was emphasized continually that the kind of woman who might be able to succeed in such jobs would not be a *typical* woman. I also encountered some prejudiced attitudes among male managers and engineers that belied their formal commitment to equal opportunity.

It seems likely that there is discrimination against women, but that other explanations are needed of women's absence. Further light was thrown on this in the course of interviews with male technologists and technicians. Men form friendships through, and thrive upon, the mutual exchange of knowledge and a humorous competitiveness concerning technology. A great deal of their enjoyment of work derives from this style of relationship with colleagues and clients. Men continually define women as *not* technological. By this dual process they create a highly masculine-gendered social environment and a woman who cannot fit into it. Women are aware of the discomfort that would be involved for them in attempting to enter technological work and, in a sense, boycott it.

Technological work, besides, demands a career commitment. The knowledge is rapidly obsolescent. Men gave plentiful evidence of working hard at their careers. Women are defined by men as *not* career people. In practical terms of course employers seldom provide the support to enable women to have family responsibilities and continue careers, nor do they (or men) expect men to have such responsibilities. Women therefore feel they cannot have both home/family life and a successful career in technology. Many women resent having to choose — men don't have to.

It was evident that technological competence and incompetence entered into relations between men and women at home as well as at work. It is men, not women, who handle carpentry or mechanical tools at home. Some women in the study endorsed men's view on women's relationship to work and technology, but many other women expressed an unsatisfied appetite for technological knowledge and competence. Women frequently reported that the *presence* of men, both at home and at work, is a factor that impedes women in acquiring technological knowledge and skill. The evidence points to an appropriation of the technological sphere by men — both in a material way with material effects, and ideologically.

The technological sexual division of labour then is a material practice that has expression in and is supported by a cultural and ideological process of gender construction. Technological competence correlates strongly with masculinity and incompetence with femininity. Women who have attempted to enter the male technical sphere of work, or even to take up 'do-it-yourself' and technical hobbies, say they have to make an impoverishing choice: they may be competent but unfeminine (and therefore unlovable); or they may be feminine but by definition incompetent. They must either be socially mutilated or remain marginal to technology.

There are many practical corollaries to this. The sexual division of labour surrounding technology contributes to the fact that women earn less than men, have lower status and worse career prospects. But it also contributes to women's physical subordination. Technological competence gives control over matter and environment and to some extent over people. You do not need necessarily to own the means of production (capital does that) in order to deploy them to sexual advantage.

What was clarified by the study of technology is the extent to which, within a familiar system of class relations of employment, of production (at work) and consumption and reproduction (at home) *power relations of sex and gender* are also active and need to be theorized.

TECHNOLOGY AND THE PATRIARCHY DEBATE

I want now to try to locate these empirical data and the observations to which they give rise, within the debate — by now quite well developed — about theories of the relationship between capitalist class and male supremacy. The 'patriarchy' issue is perhaps the central debate in socialist-feminism.

Three of the more intractable problems in the development of socialist-feminist theory have been:

1 the possibility or impossibility of extrapolating or interpolating marxist theory to account for the oppression of women;
2 the thorny question of whether we should be working with a unitary theory (i.e. a theory of a capitalist-patriarchy) or with two theoretical analyses of two conceptually distinguishable (though obviously interrelated) systems: capitalism and patriarchy, class power and sex power;
3 the uses and interpretation of historical materialist method in analysing women's position.

I believe that a focus on technology in the relations of capital and labour, women and men, can in modest measure contribute something to each of these debates.

### Is Marxist Class Theory Enough to Account for Sex Oppression, or Do We Need — 'Patriarchy'?

A recent book by Lise Vogel (1983) can provide a springboard for this discussion. She helpfully cuts through the arguments surrounding Engels' and Marx's writing on 'the woman question' dismissing them as inadequate to explain women's subordination. She then, however, proceeds to argue that Marxist theory does, in a way its originators never foresaw, actually explain women's oppression. She suggests it does so through its identification of capitalist processes of reproduction, situating 'the problem of women's oppression in terms of the reproduction of labor power and the process of social reproduction'. She argues that the separation of wage labour from domestic labour and the payment of wages are materialized in the development of specialized sites and social units for the performance of domestic labour, i.e. the home. And that in capitalist societies, the burden of the domestic component of necessary labour rests disproportionately on women.

This is by now a familiar argument. It was an essay by Louis Althusser (1971) that sparked off a renewed interest in capitalist reproduction processes. It led to some feminist analysts identifying the family as a locus of the reproduction of labour power (e.g. Seccombe 1974); and others using this concept to understand the relationship of women to the state (McIntosh 1978; Cockburn 1977).

Vogel's is perhaps the most elaborated and certainly the most recent version of these arguments. There is clearly nothing erroneous in her suggestion that the class relations that partly determine women's experience embody the processes of capitalist reproduction. But the rendering necessarily has three serious omissions. First, it assumes that socialism will put right women's disadvantage. The painful evidence to the contrary is dismissed by Vogel with unforgivable celerity.

Secondly, Vogel's theory ignores entirely any advantage accruing to men as men from women's oppression and the evidence that men actively organize to perpetuate both the sexual division of labour and their unique grasp of technology (see for instance Cockburn 1981).

Thirdly, Vogel's argument overlooks the interaction between women and men *as workers*. It cannot explain the relations of women and men to production technology and to each other demonstrated by the research summarized above. It locates the site of male power in domestic life. 'Patriarchy is at home at home. The private family is its proper domain' (Kelly 1979 quoted by Vogel). Yet we have evidence that an important source of men's advantage over women — higher earnings, social status and skills, including technical skills — derive from work. As Veronica Beechey (1979) has put it, those Marxists that rely on reproduction arguments 'leave the Marxist analysis of production untouched and uncriticised'. It remains 'economistic, the labour process has been divorced from the social relations of production as a whole and female wage labour has frequently been left out'.

One could add that it leaves the question of male practices in the trades unions out of account too. Vogel and other reproduction theorists fail to pose or to answer the question of why, under pressure from capital as they undoubtedly were, male workers reacted historically not by fighting for women's right to work and their right to equal pay but rather against both. My earlier study of the printing industry showed that men identified (and indeed acquired) advantages as men in removing women from the labour market and simultaneously ensuring their personal services at home (Cockburn 1983a). Nor can theories of class alone explain why the electronic revolution has not brought more women into engineering (Cockburn 1983b).

To understand the continuing technological job segregation by sex we cannot do without a concept of long-term organized male self-interest, of systemic male dominance: patriarchy. The rejection of such a concept, implicit in Vogel's work, leaves us with a feminism that is not mainly about the liberation of women at all, but mainly about reforming the Left, and that with one hand tied behind us. It does not envisage a demolition of a system of male supremacy over and beyond that of class power, or a renegotiation of gender characterization and difference, because it does not see these as problems.

### One Theory or Two? One System or Two?

Having established a need for a theory of sex-gender systems, of (in our case) male supremacy, or patriarchy, the question then arises whether we can or should unify the theories of class and sex oppression. Have we a unitary system (capitalist-patriarchy) for which we require a unitary theory? Or is it more meaningful and productive to describe our world as a binary system (a system of class power and a system of male power) for which we need a dual theory?

This debate is as old as socialist-feminism itself. It has had expression in most of the languages and countries in which feminist theoretical work has been pursued in the last 20 years. In the British literature it is implicit, for instance, in many of the contributions to volumes such as *Feminism and Materialism* (Kuhn and Wolpe 1978) and *Women Take Issue* (Women's Studies Group 1978) and it surfaced in 1979—80 in the sharp little exchange in the *New Statesman* between Sheila Rowbotham and Sally Alexander with Barbara Taylor. In the United States, some of the material has been collected by Zillah Eisenstein (1979) and Lydia Sargent (1981).

In the Sargent collection, Iris Young (1971) made the case for unitary working: 'It seems reasonable . . . to admit that if patriarchy and capitalism are manifest in identical social and economic structures they belong to *one* system, not two.' The most cogent argument for working with dual theories has been that of Heidi Hartmann (1981):

> The 'marriage' of Marxism and feminism has been like the marriage of husband and wife depicted in English common law: Marxism and feminism are one, and that one is Marxism. Recent attempts to integrate Marxism and feminism are unsatisfactory to us as feminists because they subsume the feminist struggle into the 'larger' struggle against capital.

Many of those who feel the same problem as Hartmann have preferred a tactical detachment — 'a decent period of shacking up' as Roberta Hamilton (1978) had put it.

Years of attempts at unification have indeed continually foundered in one of two kinds of failure. On one hand, as Hartmann warned, male supremacy slips out of focus leaving class in the centre of the page. Thus Eisenstein (1981) in her quest for 'capitalist-patriarchy' subtly subordinates the power of patriarchy to that of capitalism: 'Capitalism *uses* patriarchy and patriarchy is *defined by the needs of* capital' (my emphasis). On the other hand there are those who proclaim themselves to be working with a unitary theory, and who, despite protestations, continue to talk about the two systems separately, to talk the language of 'interrelationship'. Thus Beechey (1979) denounces dual systems approaches but proceeds to write of two systems and to call (quite correctly) for 'more historically specific studies of patriarchy and consideration of forms of patriarchy that exist in specific institutions'. Unitary theory is, so far, self-deluding.

In the case of technology there are indeed two sets of 'interrelated relations', and these demand recognition if we are to understand the implications of technological change for women. On the one hand capital applies new technologies to class advantage, 'revolutionizing the forces of production' with the effect of wresting back control of production from skilled workers, increasing productivity and maximizing profit. On the other hand men *as men* appropriate and sequester the technological sphere, extending their tenure (not *control* — that remains with capital) over each new phase, at the expense of women.

## On Historical Materialism as Method

There have been two major criticisms of the use of patriarchy conceived as a relatively autonomous system, however. The first is that it is ahistorical. The second is that its rendering of patriarchy leaves the theory of capitalist class relations unreconstructed, that it abandons the economic sphere to Marxism. I will look briefly at each of these points in turn.

'The word patriarchy . . .' wrote Rowbotham (1979), 'implies a universal and historical form of oppression which returns us to biology'. She insists, in Marx's words, that we should regard 'every historically developed social form as in fluid movement' and take into account its 'transient nature not less than its momentary existence'. She complains that this dialectical unity of transience and moment is lacking in 'patriarchy'. 'There is no transience in it at all. It simply refuses to budge.'

Let's admit that the term patriarchy is now and always has been used by feminists not because it is ideal but for lack of another. Behind its use has always been the idea of a *sex-gender system* that has been and could be different from what it is today. Sex-gender systems have clearly changed over the millenia and male power itself is different in form now to its form in the eighteenth century or even in, say, 1910. Lack of historical perspective is also an odd claim considering that two feminist writers who have consciously adhered to 'dual systems' working, Hamilton (1978) and Hartmann (1979), both discuss changing relations of male supremacy in the shift from feudalism to capitalism.

It is in fact only by disarticulating sex-gender system from mode of production that one can conceive of them, as we need to, as changing at different paces and with different effects. Certainly a historical study of technology needs to ask questions not only about the ownership of the means of production in different periods but the engagement of men and women as sexes in the development and use of tools and techniques. If productive technologies confer power on their owners they also confer relative power and initiative on the sex that invents and has tenure of them.

The second criticism — that when the sex-gender system is considered in relative autonomy from mode of production, questions about sex and power are left out of theories about economy, production and work — has been due in my view not to the *separate* consideration of the two power systems but to the fact that each power system has tended to be conceived of in a *unidimensional* way. Hamilton (1978) for instance writes about the '*economic* mode of production' and the '*ideological* mode of patriarchy' (my emphasis). That this unidimensionality is not just a product of dual systems working is clear if we return to Eisenstein who read patriarchy as *political* and capitalism as *economic*. In many versions, patriarchy is reduced to questions of sexuality, marriage and domestic life, while capitalism is reduced to work.

The best renderings of the Marxist theory of class have of course shifted from 'economism', to place emphasis on capital as a *relation,* as much social and political as economic, and having ideological expression. Patriarchy theory needs to move the same way: towards wholeness. Much of this problem hinges on the interpretation of 'material' and 'materialism'. Of course a good deal of feminist analysis has been frankly immaterial, dealing with psychic relations, or representing 'sexism' as an ideological or cultural form. To deal with technology, by contrast, is to encounter something highly tangible. It compels a focus on 'the material'.

To date however, materialist method has been partial. Among feminists who have used it, Shulamith Firestone (1971) for instance has interpreted 'material' as biological: class difference arises from sex caste and women are doomed to inferiority by their biological functions. Conversely, Christine Delphy (1977), in a kind of feminist economism, has interpreted 'material' as economic: women's oppression is rooted in the domestic economic exploitation of women's labour power by men.

Delphy also sited men's power in the family. But a study of technology cannot ignore capitalist production. A feminist view of work could only begin when women began to ask delicate questions about the *male working class* and its role in women's oppression. Early instances of such questions were Taylor's article 'The men are as bad as their masters' (1979) and her subsequent article with Anne Phillips 'Sex and skill: notes towards a feminist economics' (1980).

To my mind the most definitive step in this direction was taken by Hartmann (1979) and it was on this that I built my own analysis of technological change and skilled print workers (Cockburn 1983a). Hartmann shifted the feminist perspective to the workplace while at the same time refusing to accept that Marxism had the complete story on work. She focused on relations of male supremacy at work, highlighting in particular male social and political organization. Hartmann for the first time approached a *whole* interpretation of patriarchy (or of sex-gender system if we are to speak more generally). She defines patriarchy as:

> A set of social relations which has a material base and in which there are hierarchical relations between men and solidarity among them, which enables them in turn to dominate women. The material base of patriarchy is men's control over women's labour power. That control is maintained by excluding women from access to necessary economically productive resources and by restricting women's sexuality. (1979)

A material patriarchy for Hartmann has a strongly economic component therefore, but also a socio-political one: men organize their power.

But Hartmann's thesis allows of development. For instance, she says 'just as economic crises serve a restorative function for capitalism by correcting imbalances, so they might serve patriarchy. The thirties put women back in their place' (1979). We can add a further thought. New technologies offer a way out of the class crisis for capital, by deskilling and dispossessing certain groups of workers (often male and skilled, but also female and unskilled). So too technological innovation continually enables the renewal of men's power over women. As women learn to operate certain kinds of machinery, that machinery is made redundant, swept away by the investment policies of capital. Some men also lose their competence or their job. But it is men who retain the engineering skills that design, market and maintain successive technologies. It may be that as women make successful challenges to male power in other spheres (financial independence, control of fertility) male tenure of the technological sphere becomes increasingly important to the male sex.

What we can add to Hartmann's schema in this way is that the material base of patriarchy has to be conceived not only as economic; not only as economic *and* socio-political — but as including also the *physical,* men's physical power and initiative relative to women's. Men's tenure of technology, their physical initiative, male violence and harassment of women, militarism — these are by no means unconnected and together they add up to a formidable source of oppression. In thinking of 'the physical' we are no longer reduced to crude biologism — we have a means of analysing many material practices.

I would want to carry Hartmann's conception of the sex-gender system a step further yet. Historical materialism has, in Marxist hands, enabled us to analyse ideology. Material practices gain expression in ideological terms. Ideology bears upon and influences material practice. There is sometimes contradiction between practices and ideas. There is change and development, at both levels, often at different paces.

My study of technology has produced a rich expression of gender ideology: what a man 'is', what a woman 'is', what is right and proper, what feminists disagree on this - e.c. Chodorow + ground see women + men as fundamentally different.

is possible and impossible, what should be hoped and what should be feared. The hegemonic ideology of masculism involves a definition of men and women as different, contrasted, complementary, unequal. It is powerful and it deforms both men and women. We need to have the tools to be able to examine its origin in material practices (the fact, say, that all the technicians in a certain workplace are men, all the cleaners, clerks and receptionists women) and its bearing on them (the prejudice that inhibits the personnel manager from appointing a woman technician).

Then we may begin to acquire a concept of sex-gender system that can throw light on not domestic life alone, not work alone, but all the institutions we inhabit from the disco to the army. And we will have a theory that is whole enough and sufficiently explanatory to cohabit with Marxist class theory without falling into the role of wife.

# 7

## Households, Labour Markets and the Position of Women

### Christopher C. Harris and Lydia D. Morris

The research[1] to which this chapter refers, and which has stimulated the argument which it presents, is not directed specifically to the study of either stratification or to the place of women in social hierarchy. Its focus is rather upon the labour-market experience of a sample of steelworkers made redundant from the British Steel Company plant at Port Talbot, South Wales, in the second half of 1980, and upon the relation between experience of labour-market behaviour and the domestic organization and local social networks of those made redundant. Nearly all redundants were male. The bulk of the survey data refers to redundants' labour-market behaviour and experience. The prime source of data on domestic organization and local networks is Morris's intensive study of a representative sample of the households of forty married redundant workers between the ages of 20 and 55, and it is to these data that the chapter refers primarily. It is not our purpose however to present the findings of this study, as this has been done elsewhere,[2] but rather to use the study to reflect upon the problems involved in considering the relation between 'gender' and 'stratification'.

CONCEPTUAL INTRODUCTION: LABOUR MARKETS, HOUSEHOLD
POSITION AND LOCAL SOCIAL STRUCTURE

The argument which we wish to put forward has two elements which can conveniently be expressed briefly at the outset. The first is that conventional class analyses are not defective because they fail to take account of gender differences, but rather their inability adequately to conceptualize the position of women is a sign which points to an inadequacy in conventional class analyses as such. The second strand concerns the nature of this postulated inadequacy. We suggest that it is mistaken to identify the position of persons in the social hierarchy solely with reference to their position in the occupational hierarchy, whether that is used as an index of their position in the technical division of labour, or in the social division of labour, or both. We wish to argue, rather, that position must be defined not only in terms of position *in the occupational structure* but also in terms of position *in the labour market,* and that these *two* types of position, closely related as they are, are none the less distinct analytically.

This second point requires some fuller elaboration. There is in the literature a tendency to use the term 'labour-market position' to refer to position in the occupational structure and to define segments of the market chiefly in terms of types of occupation and patterns of recruitment. This however merely gives the appearance of incorporating the market into the analysis without actually doing so. It is the essence of a market that it brings the buyers and sellers of a commodity into relation with one another. This relation can be expressed in neo-classical economic theory in terms of the intersection of the supply and demand schedules relating to the commodity concerned. However such formalizations would have no empirical reference were it not the case that a market existed in the sociological sense: were it not the case that there existed a plurality of buyers who were actually or potentially buyers of the commodity offered for sale by a plurality of sellers and vice versa. Given this conception of a labour market it is necessary to investigate by means of what institutions, practices and relationships these two pluralities come to constitute a market, come to stand in a market relation to one another (C. C. Harris 1984).

The members of each plurality will differ from one another in terms of their 'market position'. This term will be used in this paper to refer (on analogy with Weber's notion of 'class situation' [1968: p. 302]) to the *typical probability* of obtaining rewards. In the case of sellers of labour power in a labour-market, sellers will be differentiated in terms of their chances of obtaining different types of employment which will in turn determine their 'class situation' in the Weberian sense. The immediate reward in the labour-market, employment, must be seen as differentiated not only in respect of its terms and conditions, but also in respect of its degree of permanency, and hence in respect of the frequency with which the holders of such employment will come on to the market.

The essence of our argument is that position in the social hierarchy is determined, not merely by *occupational* position (or lack of it) but by *market* position (the typical probability of obtaining different types of employment). It is not being claimed that persons in the same or similar labour-market positions constitute classes. It is being claimed that market position is an enormously important determinant of the formations of

collectivities on the basis of common position in the productive process
(however defined) with their corresponding 'life styles and patterns of
association, socio-political orientations and modes of action' (Goldthorpe
1983). Labour-market position does not define class, but it is a determinant
of class formation. It follows that experience *in* the labour-market as well
as experience *of* the labour process, are vital determinants of worker
attitudes and behaviour, both in the workplace and in social life more
generally, and that labour-market processes as well as processes occurring
within the workplace are crucial determinants of worker biography,
occupational mobility and hence of consciousness and action.

It only remains to link these two threads together: conventional class
analysis, in failing to give a proper place to labour-market position and
concentrating on position in the occupational hierarchy, makes it impossible
to comprehend adequately the position of women, since women's distinctive
economic attribute is that they constitute a negatively privileged category
within the labour-market. It is the inferiority of their labour-market position
relative to men that is the immediate source of their relative disadvantage.
The exploration of the causes of that disadvantage requires an
understanding of their location in the labour-market in a different sense,
that of their location in 'local social structure'. The term 'local' is
appropriate in that all labour-markets are territorially based, since the
transformation of labour power into concrete labour normally[3] requires
the regular movement of labourers from their places of residence to their
places of work. By the term 'social structure' is meant the network of
specific relationships between specific persons resulting from the existence
of institutionalized types of social relation, of means of co-operation and
co-ordination and of social practice carried out under a set of determinate
material conditions, and the forms of consciousness (or if you prefer,
systems of beliefs and values) which inform these practices whence-so-ever
they originate.

It is important to note in this regard that labour-market location is just as
important a determinant of the labour-market position of men as it is of
women. It must also be regarded as an important determinant of *differences*
in labour-market position between members of the same gender category.
It may be argued, therefore, that from the standpoint of class analysis
labourers should be classified in terms of occupational *and* market positions
but without reference to gender, race, age or whatever. In one sense this is
correct. Any theoretical specification of occupation or market no more
requires reference to these other categories than specification of biological
sexual differentiation requires reference to gender. However, any
sociological study of sexual behaviour must take into account gender
definitions since those definitions affect that behaviour crucially. Any
sociological study of the operation of the labour-market must take into
account those attributes which affect its operation, whether or not those

attributes consciously structure the behaviour of the participants. Hence a sociological study of the labour-market seeks to understand labour-market phenomena by the identification of the participants in the social structure. It is in no way to deny the basal character of economic differentiation to assert that such differentiation does not exhaust what is meant by social structure and that non-economic attributes may affect the operation of basal processes vitally.

The recognition of the importance of non-economic attributes in conditioning processes which are economic by definition does not imply that all such attributes are equally important or affect a given process in the same way. For example, whereas chronological age is clearly of major importance as a determinant of labour-market position, it does not specify a specific structural location. Gender, on the other hand, is associated closely with position in the household and in the structure of the family, and it is a truism to assert that it is the differential location of the genders in the private sphere that conditions their participation in the public world of employment. The 'model' of the social structure of the labour-market which we have adopted is therefore of households the participation of whose members in paid work is determined by their position within the household and the character of their local social networks which link households with one another and their members with different types of employment opportunity. We regard position within the structure of the household and the articulation of household members through their social networks with employment opportunities, as major determinants of individuals' labour-market positions, i.e. of their chances of obtaining different types of employment.

## THE EXPERIENCE OF REDUNDANCY AND EMPLOYMENT OPPORTUNITY

The study of redundant Welsh steelworkers from which this chapter arises made a radical distinction between labour-market position and employment status. A person may be unemployed at point of interview but have a high probability of finding work, while another person may be employed and have a high probability of losing it and little chance of obtaining further employment once s/he is back in the market. That this is so may be seen by an examination of the labour-market histories of those made redundant, which show that redundancy may be followed by a wide variety of different experiences in the labour-market, and which defy any simple classification of redundants into those 'successful' and 'unsuccessful' in the search for employment. Some men had not been employed since redundancy, whilst others had found work which promised to be secure, within months. More common, however, was a pattern of spells of employment and/or retraining broken by periods out of work and, in some cases, employment in the informal sector of the economy.[4]

Under these variable circumstances it is not surprising that the response to redundancy at the level of domestic organization cannot be identified easily and clearly. The central questions — addressed specifically in an earlier paper (Morris 1985) — are: how is work outside the household distributed amongst its members; how is work within the household distributed amongst its members; and what is the relationship between these public and private divisions? To these must be added a further question: how does the position of the household in the local social structure affect the division of labour between household members in terms of both participation in paid work and the extent and nature of this participation in labour in the domestic sphere?

Although figures at the UK national level show female participation in economic activity to have risen throughout the seventies whilst male participation fell, the female rate also began to fall in 1978, though less steeply than that for men. It has commonly been assumed that these national trends suggest a renegotiation of traditional gender roles which have placed the main responsibility for earning the household income firmly in male hands. Data from the present study however, suggest that such an interpretation would be mistaken. Indeed UK national figures *also* indicate that the wife of a man who is in employment is almost twice as likely to be in employment as the wife of an unemployed man.[5] We have identified a number of possible reasons for this (Morris 1985).

1 There has been a fall in employment opportunities for women as a result of recession.
2 The rise in employment for *married* women throughout the seventies was predominantly in part-time work.
3 It is popularly believed that a woman, even in full-time employment, could not earn as much as a man could claim in state benefits.
4 The better part of a wife's earnings will be deducted from the amount her husband can claim in supplementary benefit.
5 Local gender roles emphasize a woman's domestic obligations, especially in the rearing of young children.

The accommodation of redundancy by the 'reversal of roles' was not contemplated by respondents. This was so for a number of reasons. In the first place it implies a recognition by both spouses that the loss of employment by the husband will be, if not permanent, at least of considerable duration. This was not apparent at the point of redundancy and was in any case an outcome unpalatable to both parties. In the second place there was no already existing knowledge of employment opportunities which wives considered suitable. Hence when wives did take employment it was not the result of a decision to seek employment followed by a process of formalized job search, but rather through opportunities which arose as the product of informal channels of communication along which both information and influence flowed. In 12 of the 13 cases in which a woman took on employment after her husband's redundancy, the job was obtained through informal means.

A network of friends, relatives and acquaintances relayed information which enabled women to identify and gain access to 'suitable' employment. Such a network also, in some cases, provided child care and/or other domestic services which made it possible for a woman to take up paid employment.

'Suitable' employment may mean a number of things:

1 The job must match the woman's skills and experience or possibly her lack of skill in anything other than domestic work. Many women take on employment as waitresses, cleaners, machinists, etc.

2 Where a woman's husband is claiming supplementary benefit she may need to be employed 'off the cards', to avoid the income which she earns being deducted from that benefit.

3 Employment opportunities may be accepted or rejected according to whether or not the job can be held without disruption of the domestic tasks to be completed within the home.

In South Wales the sexual division of labour traditional to the area leaves the woman largely responsible for child care and most of the labour performed daily in the domestic sphere. Hence, either her paid work must take account of her domestic obligations or her domestic obligations must somehow accommodate her paid employment. Broadly speaking, there are three possibilities:

1 Hours in paid employment must leave the woman free at the appropriate times for the fulfilment of domestic and child-care obligations.

2 An arrangement may be made with female kin or friends whereby they assume some of the domestic labour, either for financial reward or on a reciprocal basis.

3 A husband may assume a share of the activities previously defined as the responsibility of his wife.

It is apparent that the participation of married women in paid work cannot be understood with reference to a rational decision-making model. The wife's participation in paid work was in no case the result of a consideration by the couple of different strategies of household survival involving different patterns of participation in paid work. Nor was there a deliberate attempt to discover opportunities for the wife's employment followed by an evaluation of different strategies in terms of the costs involved in the reorganization of the division of domestic labour. Rather participation in paid work was the result of the exploitation of informally acquired knowledge of suitable work opportunities: 'suitable' being defined as opportunities which did not interfere too severely with traditional patterns of domestic organization. Wives' participation was structured by their position in the traditional family-household and the ability of their social networks to channel at least knowledge of 'suitable' work to them.

The nature of a man's participation in the domestic sphere will be affected not only by his own employment status and his *availability* to perform domestic labour and child care, it will also be influenced by norms which govern ideas about appropriate male and female behaviour.[6]

In an area where the sexual division of labour has been based historically on a rigid segregation of male and female spheres of activity, and where the man has carried the responsibility for earning the household income through work in heavy industry, then ideas about masculinity are likely to be bound up with employment. Unemployment will pose a threat to the man's gender identity which will be increased by any suggestion that he should assume labour within the home which has traditionally been viewed as the responsibility of the woman. Equally, a wife's entry into paid employment may challenge her husband's ability to maintain the household and therefore question his masculinity. The greater the extent to which a man's exposure to peer-group pressure reinforces these ideas, then the stronger his resistance to either assuming domestic responsibilities or to his wife's taking up employment.

Peer-group influence may be exerted through a man's network of social contacts; the *structure* of the network will be a critical factor in determining the strength of group norms (C. C. Harris 1969). Where there are multiple connections between the individuals who make up the network, and especially where some sense of a collective identity emerges, then a high degree of standardization in the content of gender roles is likely, while interaction between ego and his or her set-members provides the means by which conformity is maintained. In the present sample locally prescribed gender roles were adhered to most rigidly where the man belonged to an extensive, sexually homogeneous social network.

It follows that the participation of the wife in paid work is influenced by two *unrelated* factors: her position within the structure of domestic organization and the ability of her network to provide knowledge of suitable employment. The structure of the husband's network affects the degree to which the traditional division of domestic labour within the household is maintained, and the woman's network may also serve to preserve the low participation of males in domestic work by providing domestic services. The husband's network had a normative function in that, interaction within the relationships constituting it maintains conformity to traditional conceptions of male gender-roles, while the woman's network has an additional function in that it provides both domestic support and job opportunities.

In so far as informal access to chances of employment allows married women with dependent children who desire to 'work' to identify 'suitable' jobs, there is a certain narrow sense in which informal methods of recruitment operate to the advantage of the employer by allowing him to identify 'suitable' workers. Married women with domestic responsibilities often prefer part-time employment, provided the better part of their subsistence needs are met by their husband in exchange for domestic services. This arrangement between husband and wife, however, allows the employer to recruit women at fairly low levels of pay (and generally unfavourable conditions) whether the job be full-time or part-time.

Similar considerations also apply to the recruitment of male workers. Whatever the means of recruitment, employers are anxious to identify workers who (as well as being suitable technically) are also 'acceptable' personally (Jenkins 1983: pp. 101—5) and use networks of social contacts to obtain such information informally. When, however, a male worker is in receipt of an income which pays some part of his subsistence, he becomes a worker whose employment is advantageous to the employer in the same way as the employment of women. It would not be surprising therefore if, when such male workers existed, informal means were used to identify and recruit them.

Redundants who found new employment during the 18-month period covered by make-up provision could have their earnings made up to 90—100 per cent of their British Steel Company salary until the end of that time. The arrangement has operated to the benefit of particular kinds of employers — those not committed to national agreements on conditions of employment and operating with a non-unionized workforce.

Many firms working to short-term contracts appear to have kept their wage costs and therefore their tenders low by employing ex-steelworkers in receipt of make-up pay. Another way of reducing labour costs is to employ workers for minimal wages 'off the cards', leaving them to bring their wage to a viable level by claiming benefit. Between contracts, of course, these workers become totally dependent on the state.[7]

We have noted that because of domestic constraints a woman may wish to use informal channels to identify employment which might not otherwise be considered satisfactory, and the employer will in turn avail him/herself of informal information to recruit such workers. For a man, the only sense in which the kind of employment acquired informally suits his situation, is that it is better than no job at all and informal contacts may give him a competitive edge. The employer on the other hand, minimizes both recruitment and wage costs.

Within the sample however, there are clear contrasts between the types of employment opportunities available to different men. This is because of their contrasting positions in the local social structure. A man with an extensive network of contacts is more likely to have informal means of access to employment than a man with a restricted network. It is also the case that a man with an extensive sexually homogeneous social network is more likely to adhere rigidly to a traditional, sexual division of labour. A tendency to attract short spells of employment will additionally discourage any fundamental reappraisal of the way domestic life is organized.

Whilst a *woman* with an extensive network is more likely to be presented with opportunities for employment, she is also more likely to be married to a man with his own extensive social pattern, who is resistant to assuming domestic responsibilities. She will therefore turn to her female network to provide domestic back-up and restrict her job choice (in so far as there is a choice) to the kind of employment which can be fitted around her traditional, domestic responsibilities.

Both position in household structure and the character of a person's social network are major determinants of the nature and extent of their participation in paid work. Furthermore, these two characteristics interact so that the type of network affects the degree to which the traditional division of domestic labour is maintained. Moreover, there may also be an empirical association between a female network which increases the chances of a wife obtaining employment and a male network which both enforces traditional patterns of behaviour within the private sphere, while providing intermittent employment to the husband thus postponing the necessity for a consideration of any radical renegotiation of the responsibilities of the spouses as between the private and public spheres, and within the private sphere itself. Such employment also serves to postpone the point at which the wife's formal employment ceases to be beneficial because the husband has exhausted his entitlement to unemployment benefit.

We do not wish to claim any generality for the empirical association between types of male and female networks. We do wish to emphasize that the access of spouses of both genders to employment opportunities has to be understood *structurally*. That is to say that the persistence of traditional patterns of behaviour both within the domestic sphere and the market are the result of a concatenation of mutually reinforcing structural elements. We do not wish to argue that location in the 'private' sphere determines behaviour and outcomes in the 'public', or that 'formal' outcomes (employment in formal organizations) have to be understood as the result of 'informal' processes. Rather we seek to escape from a definition of the situation which we have been examining as a set of households composed of actual or potential sellers of labour and a set of employment opportunities (however limited), by postulating the existence of a middle ground: a set of interrelated social relations which comprises both domestic relationships and work relations. This set of relations not only articulates actual and potential buyers and sellers of labour power, thus making them members of the same market; the occupancy of different locations within it affects its members' labour-market position vitally: their chance of obtaining different types of employment or different types of employee.

## CONCLUSION

It is now possible to return to the argument sketched briefly in the first section of this chapter. The immediate source of women's relatively disadvantaged position in paid work is their inferior position in the labour-market. In the absence of any sociological conception of a labour market this is a truism. If however one not only understands position in the labour-market as the chance of obtaining different types of employment, but seeks to understand variations in such chances in terms of persons' differential locations in local social structures, then differences in labour-market position become a form of economic inequality which is structured socially.

Persons of whatever gender who are unable, for whatever reason, to obtain employment in response to public, formal methods of recruitment, will depend for their knowledge of such opportunities on information (if not invitations) flowing along networks of social relations. Persons who, for whatever reason, are able and willing to work for exceptionally low wages in conditions which are in some, if not all senses 'poor', will be attractive to certain sorts of employers who are likely to utilize networks to identify and recruit such workers. The employment of such persons will not therefore be the result of formal rational and public procedures on the part of either worker or employer. Rather each contract of employment will, from the point of view of each party, be adventitious, the exploitation of a chance opportunity arising out of their routine everyday activities in a common social location.

If the traditional sexual division of labour and the existence of the family-household are taken as given historical conditions of the operation of both labour-market and economic production, it is not difficult to see why women, because of their position in the household, constitute a form of cheap intermittent labour recruited informally[8] or why men who stand in a certain relation to the state occupy (in a loose labour-market) a similar labour-market position: i.e. have similar chances of obtaining low-paid insecure employment recruited by informal means. There is however an important distinction between the genders in the way that recruitment operates. The household is a closed bounded group, and the socially prescribed tasks and identities of women require that they spend the majority of their time within it. A woman is therefore unable to engage in active job search and is forced into the more passive role of snapping up passing chances of employment. Recruitment of males recognizes the greater participation of men in what it has recently become fashionable to call the 'public' sphere, their greater participation in 'society' in the eighteenth-century sense. While unemployed men are also forced to await passing chances of employment, those chances are likely to 'pass' in public settings such as pubs, clubs and other points of male congregation. Where lack of work, income and unfavourable residential location prevent men from going out into society, their social situation becomes similar to that of women and their labour-market position deteriorates accordingly.

We are moving as a society into a situation when, at any given time, large sectors of the population such as the young and older workers are out of employment but wish to obtain suitable employment, and a substantial percentage are without *permanent* employment but seeking suitable temporary work. That is to say that an increasing number of the male labour force is coming to share the typical labour-market situation of women. This makes it imperative that we conceive of the population as differentiated hierarchically in terms of labour-market position as well as in terms of occupation and investigate the structural determinants of that differentiation. Membership of a category of labour-market position does not however constitute the basis of the formation of collectivities and such categories are not the direct result of structural oppositions. However important labour-market position is as a determinant of class formation, labour-market categories are not classes. If stratification theory suffers from tunnel vision (Gamarnikow *et al.* 1983: p. 6), that myopia results from the ignorance of the market rather than the ignorance of women. Remedy it and the restoration of women to a proper place within the study of stratification becomes an objective possibility.

- interesting analysis.
- chance of finding work depends on local social network. but denser male network also increases traditional ideology, making it harder for ♀ to work, even if opportunity arises.
- methodological insight: examine local social networks + role in ① providing information + access to jobs and ② sustaining ideology

# 8

## Domestic Responsibilities and the Structuring of Employment

### Janet Siltanen

#### INTRODUCTION

The recent defence of the conventional view notwithstanding (Goldthorpe 1983), it is acknowledged generally that an adequate theory of inequality must be able to explain inequalities between women and men.[1] For those who accept the need for an inclusive theory, an important issue is the construction of theoretical categories which can be used to provide consistent statements of social processes. The problem raised here concerns whether current conceptions of 'gender' facilitate the production of an inclusive theory of inequality.[2]

In the literature on 'gender' and social stratification, there is a tension between, on the one hand, attempts to develop an explanation of aggregate-level inequalities between women and men and, on the other hand, the recognition that neither group is homogeneous in its characteristics. Time and again the point is made that the diversity of women's experience defies treating them as an undifferentiated social grouping. Yet, arguments for the integration of 'gender' into theories of inequality are premissed typically on a conception of 'gender' as constituting two social groupings — 'women' and 'men' — which have identifiable characteristics with some sort of general validity.

The argument to be presented here is that in order to develop an adequate explanation of inequality we must abandon the use of 'gender', 'sexual divisions', 'women' and 'men' as theoretical categories which have meaning over all aspects of social experience. This view is established through an examination of 'occupational segregation by sex'.

OCCUPATIONAL SEGREGATION BY SEX

Studies of occupational segregation by sex concentrate typically on the outcomes of social processes. That is, they are concerned with the distribution of women and men across occupations. From such studies (e.g. Hakim 1979), we can see a persistent differentiation between jobs in terms of their sex composition and a stark picture of the disadvantaged location of most women in waged work. While a patterning of distribution by sex clearly exists in employment, the precise nature of this patterning and the social processes giving rise to it, have yet to be specified sufficiently. Beyond establishing general associations between the sex ratio within jobs and levels of pay, status and so on, there has been no attempt to discover precisely who the women and men in different jobs are, or how the nature of their general social circumstances might be patterned in relation to their employment. In the absence of more complete information, the salient aspect of a person's circumstances, in the operation of social processes, has been assumed to be his/her sex. In this chapter I argue against characterizing patterns in the distribution of people to jobs in terms of an unspecified notion of segregation by sex, and hope to demonstrate the utility of locating occupations, and the relations of women and men to them, within a wider understanding of how employment is structured.

In response to the inability of theories of class and status to explain inequalities between women and men, there has emerged a number of theories focused specifically on gender/sexual divisions. It is indicative of the tension noted earlier that these specific theories are usually criticized for treating women as a homogeneous category — see, for example, Beechey (1978) on women as a secondary labour force; Beechey (1983a) on women's consciousness; Garnsey (1978) on gender as a separate dimension of stratification; and Rowbotham (1982) on patriarchy. Nevertheless, the fact that women and men are each concentrated in a limited number of jobs highly skewed in their sex composition, and the fact that the highly rewarded jobs are those in which men predominate, have led many to argue that 'gender' operates to shape the general features of occupations and labour-force distribution. Two suggestions as to how 'gender' is implicated in the distribution of people to jobs and in the structure of inequality between occupations, are discussed below. One approach concerns the effects of a sexual division of labour in domestic life. This approach was once quite prominent, but is now thought to be unable to account fully for employment patterns. Because of this limitation, another approach has currently gained more support and interest. This concerns the construction of 'gender' within employment itself, and has been studied recently, for example, as the relation between 'gender' and skill. In the view presented here, the approach which attempts to establish 'gender construction' within employment does not overcome the inadequacies of the previous approach in that both rest on an *a priori* assumption that 'gender' has general validity as a theoretical category, and both take 'sexual division' as an adequate statement of the general nature of the distribution of women and men to jobs.

The idea that attention must focus on 'gender construction' within employment is one which has been promoted recently as a promising direction for the development of a theory of occupational segregation (Beechey 1983a) and the sex-typing of jobs (Murgatroyd, 1982b). That occupational segregation by sex is a phenomenon which involves a matching of 'gender' characteristics with the attributes of jobs, is a notion which has appeared in a number of forms. Indeed, an early version concerned the coincidence of tasks women performed in the home and tasks they performed for wages. While this coincidence is still regarded as important, the basic point has been given a more general expression recently. The 'gender saturation' of work tasks has been argued to be a major dimension in the social definition of skill and a major factor in maintaining the identity of, and inequality between, 'women's work' and 'men's work'. There are three main reasons why this approach cannot provide an adequate understanding of employment experiences.

First, the analysis of differences between 'women's work' and 'men's work' in employment involves distortions similar to those identified in the study of 'sex differences'. Attributes associated, on average, with the paid work done by women and men, are reified as differences between two categories which are taken to be internally undifferentiated and mutually exclusive. These reified categories are then used to explain, or are assumed to correspond with, women's and men's employment experiences. As a result, insufficient attention is paid to important variations in the employment of both sexes and rarely are similarities between them considered. Attempting to understand variations in employment circumstances in terms of an opposition between 'women's work' and 'men's work' involves the use of categories which do not correspond adequately with the nature and complexity of either women's or men's employment experiences.

Secondly, it is not clear that characteristics which have been identified as distinctive of 'women's work' are important elements of the disadvantages in women's employment. It has been suggested, for instance, that as the traditional basis of skill distinctions become increasingly eroded, 'gender' is mobilized as a basis for differentiating job grades which would otherwise be indistinguishable. The association of 'women's work' with unskilled jobs is thought to be strong and potentially on the increase (Coyle 1982; Philips and Taylor 1980). However, the demarcations between skilled, semi-skilled and unskilled jobs are of little use in distinguishing between women with different returns to employment. In the UK, while men in skilled jobs have typically earned more, on average, than men in other manual jobs, the average earnings of women in skilled jobs have often been lower than those of women in semi-skilled jobs. In 1978, the average earnings of women in skilled manual jobs were below those of women in semi-skilled and unskilled jobs (Routh 1980: p. 121). Typically, the earnings of women in skilled manual jobs are above the earnings of women in unskilled manual jobs, but the difference has rarely been substantial. In 1979, the difference in average earnings between women in skilled and unskilled jobs was just over £100, compared to a difference of over £1,000 between men in the two types of jobs. Skill levels, in other words, do not appear to be a significant issue in understanding women's earnings and, speaking generally, the correspondence of conventional skill distinctions with significant differences in women's employment circumstances is highly questionable.

Thirdly, it is difficult to sustain a division between 'women's work' and 'men's work', either in the characteristics of jobs or those of incumbents. Despite differences in earnings, Stewart *et al.* (1985) found similar characteristics attributed to the quality of labour power and job tasks in jobs with skewed sex compositions. In the cases of occupational segregation and discrimination by sex to be reported in this chapter, we shall see also that a 'gender' identification of job tasks played no part in the creation of an official distinction between women's and men's employment. Further, although there are some jobs which employ men only, there are none in which men are not employed. Given this, one difficulty with the attempt to explain the distribution of women and men to jobs by a conception of the 'gender' appropriateness of an occupation, is providing an explanation for the presence of the minority sex. They are, from the outset, outside the territory on which the attempted explanation is based. That this is so reflects necessarily on the adequacy of the type of argument constructed to explain the employment of the majority sex.

Taking 'sex-typing' and 'gender construction' to be accurate statements of the major process giving rise to skewed sex distributions in occupations is problematic, and the search for an explanation of the configuration of women's and men's employment in terms of a division between 'women's work' and 'men's work' is bound to be unproductive. That some consider such an approach a positive one stems from the misunderstanding that a distinction by sex is the key feature of occupational segregation, and that the salient distinction to be made in relation to sex-skewed occupations is indeed between 'women's' and 'men's' jobs. Later in the chapter, more productive distinctions will be proposed.

The above discussion has concerned the argument that 'gender' is an intrinsic feature of waged work and that 'gender construction' is the major process underlying occupational segregation. It seems possible that the current appeal of this approach is due to the perceived failure of earlier attempts at explaining the configuration of women's and men's employment, particularly arguments concerning relations between sexual divisions in domestic responsibilities and their importance for employment experiences. Indeed, Beechey (1983a: p. 43) offers as an underlying rationale of the need to locate occupational segregation in processes internal to waged work, the point that women's 'position within the occupational structure cannot be simply 'read off' from an analysis of the sexual division of labour within the family, as a number of feminists . . . have suggested in the past.' In her earlier work, Beechey exerted a positive influence by stressing the importance of examining the relations between domestic life and employment, and I believe that the disinclination to give this examination prominence now is due to the lack of headway gained in earlier treatments. The fact that earlier discussions appear inadequate, however, is not because the attempt to examine the importance of domestic relations for women's and men's employment experiences lacks value. The reason lies, rather, in the limitations of the theoretical categories and data used to approach the issue. The attempt to conceptualize the employment of married women in terms of the reserve army of labour is a case in point, and the more general idea that there is need to establish a relation between 'gender' and 'class' is another.

Original attempts to explain the occupational distributions of women and men in terms of domestic circumstances focused on 'sexual divisions' in the home. It was assumed *a priori* that 'women' had relations to domestic circumstances and employment that were distinguished from the relations of 'men', and that 'sexual divisions' in households were definitive for women's and men's waged work. For 'women', the division entailed disadvantages in waged work in both the short term (for example, the accommodation of hours of waged work to domestic responsibilities) and the long term (for example, lower occupational attainment and income). For 'men', the division entailed advantages in waged work in terms of claims that could be made as wage-earners with domestic responsibilities as husbands and fathers.

In this form, we have an imprecise and insufficient statement of relations between domestic responsibilities and employment. It is insufficient because it considers marriage and parenting to be the only features of domestic life which may impinge on employment experience. It is imprecise because it takes 'sexual division' as the general form of relations between domestic circumstances and employment. In this context, it is important to note that it is precisely in the case of relations between domestic responsibilities and employment that women's and men's experiences are becoming less differentiated.

During the past few decades there have been substantial changes in the negotiation of relations of parenting and employment. As an indication of this, the proportion of women in employment has increased for all age-levels of dependent children and the profile of women's work-histories show shorter periods as full-time mothers (Stewart and Greenhalgh 1982). With women taking less time out of employment for full-time motherhood and with more women supporting households as single parents, a traditional and extended sexual division of labour between parenting and wage-earning is becoming much less prominent. To explore fully the importance of marriage and parenting for women's and men's employment, we would need to examine variations in domestic responsibilities and their connections with the structuring of employment. We shall see in the research presented in this chapter that gender/sexual division is a particular instance of a more general structuring of employment in relation to domestic responsibilities.

The problem of incorporating 'gender' into a theory of inequality heightens the necessity of constructing new theoretical categories which are consistent with social experience, so as to reconstruct the theory of inequality. The development of an adequate explanation of inequality has been hindered because of a concern to maintain conventional concepts of inequality in relation to women's employment. That such conventional concepts of inequality provide only limited understandings of women's employment must be taken as an indication of their general inadequacy as theoretical statements of inequality. With more adequate theoretical categories and more comprehensive data, an examination of relations between domestic responsibilities and employment may provide a better understanding of the social processes underlying the skewed distribution of women's and men's employment. The acceptance of 'gender' as a theoretical category with general validity is an obstruction to this project. While we need a theory of the distribution of people to jobs which can explain sexual divisions where they occur, this must be a theory which can account for those aspects of social processes which yield similar outcomes for women and men. Taking 'gender' or 'sexual divisions' as a general statement of social experience and the object of explanation, has had two deleterious consequences: the importance of similarity in women's and men's experiences has been neglected and social processes giving rise to sexual divisions have not been understood adequately.

These arguments flow from research material gathered on women and men employed full time for the British Post Office and British Telecommunications and the chapter now turns to a presentation of this material.

The research on which the chapter is based concerns women's and men's employment in 1979 in two jobs which have been regarded as sex-typed. The first is telephone operator, and the second is postal worker (postman/woman). As jobs in the Post Office and British Telecommunications, both are in the same 'manipulative' grade and, although located in different businesses, are organized by the same union — the Union of

Postal Workers (UPW).[3] Neither job requires any form of previous training or qualifications and, in both, new recruits pass through a short training period that takes place primarily on the job.

Although equally accessible in terms of pre-entry experience, the two jobs employ women and men in different numbers. Within the establishments where the interviews were conducted, the concentration of women and men in the jobs is typical. Ninety per cent of postal workers are men, and 73 per cent of telephonists are women.[4] However, there is an important distinction between telephonists on the day shift and telephonists on the night shift. While women form the majority of the day-shift workers (89 per cent), they are a minority on the night shift (23 per cent). Although the telephonist job is often regarded as a 'woman's job', it appears that in certain circumstances it is an occupation performed predominantly by men. In terms of the sex composition of jobs then, it may be more appropriate to distinguish three jobs: postal worker, night telephonist and day telephonist.

While today the official recruitment policy and employment conditions of the jobs do not distinguish between women and men, this lack of discrimination by sex has been in effect in Britain only since the passing of the Sex Discrimination Act in 1975. The history of both jobs includes a period of time when distinctions between the employment of women and men were official policy. Before 1975, men were designated officially as the preferred workers in the postal job. Although women were hired for the postal job, their employment was conditional on no men being available for the job. For telephonists, full-time employment was segregated by sex. Women were employed full time only on the day shift and men were employed full time only on the night shift.

THE STRUCTURING OF EMPLOYMENT:

*Discrimination by Sex*

There is nothing intrinsic in the tasks of the postal and telephonist jobs that explains why, prior to 1975, men were given priority in the postal job and employed full time exclusively on the night-telephonist shift. Aspects of the postal job require a capacity associated typically with 'men's work' — strength — and indeed some postmen tried (unsuccessfully) to propose that due to the manual tasks associated with the job, the legal requirements of the Sex Discrimination Act could be evaded. Yet, there are postwomen who find their current job no more demanding physically than some 'women's work' they have done in the past, and assessments of strength have never determined who is or is not hired for the postal job. In the telephonist job, the social and material circumstances of the day and night shifts vary substantially. On the day shift, the routine and pace is more exacting; social contact between telephonists is more restricted and regular earnings are less. However, the actual tasks performed on the two shifts are identical. It was, in fact, the recognition of this equivalence, along with the acknowledged advantages of the working environment and pay on the night shift, that led many of the night-shift men to fear they would be inundated by women from the day shift when access to both shifts was equalized. There is no evidence, in short, that the discrimination by sex in either of the jobs was based on 'sex-typing' or 'gender construction' in relation to the labour performed.

The introduction of formal segregation and discrimination between women's and men's employment in the postal and telephonist jobs was related mainly to recruitment problems occasioned by changes in employment conditions in the jobs. In both cases, changes in job conditions involved a strain on particular aspects of employment for the majority sex in each job — the hours of the women telephonists and the wages of the postmen.

A full-time night-telephonist shift came into being shortly after the Second World War. The creation of the night-telephonist job as a male job was due primarily to difficulties in recruiting sufficient women willing or able to work night hours on a full-time basis. The management tried various means of getting female day telephonists to accept employment during the evening, but by and large the women were very resistent to 'unsocial' hours being incorporated into their regular hours. The management also attempted to abolish the distinction between a day and night shift, and favoured hiring women and men to work an integrated 24-hour grade. This move was resisted by all telephonists. Both women and men objected to the fact that they could be called upon to work any hours 'in the interests of the service'. The attempt to recruit telephonists onto a 24-hour job grade resulted in severe recruitment shortages. Following the failed attempt to secure sufficient numbers of women for the night shift and the failed attempt to institute a sex-integrated 24-hour grade, permanent and sex-segregated day and night shifts were created as the solution to recruitment difficulties.

The sequence of events in the postal job is somewhat more complex, although here too recruitment of the majority labour force became problematic because of changes which placed the job in a different relationship to standard aspects of women's and men's employment. In this case, the issue was not hours, but wages.

The wages and recruitment of postwomen have been contested issues between the Post Office management and the UPW ever since the formation of the union in 1920. At its first conference, the UPW adopted the demand for equal pay — a policy opposed strongly by the Post Office until the mid-fifties. The Post Office management used a strategy of employing women at lower rates as a cheap answer to shortages of male labour. In these circumstances, the support from the union for equal pay should not be construed as indicating a favourable attitude toward the employment of women. At a number of conferences, postmen voiced objections to employing female labour in the postal job. The fact that demands for equal pay were often accompanied by demands to curb the recruitment and employment of women suggests that the UPW was interested in equal pay as a strategy to protect the interests of its male members against what they saw as the negative effects of cheaper female labour in their jobs.[5] By making female labour an equally costly labour, it was hoped that the interest in hiring women for the postal job would lessen and the postmen's leverage on wages would increase.

The issues of wages and recruitment, as far as the postmen were concerned, became increasingly acute. Their earnings position relative to other semi-skilled workers dropped dramatically during the first half of the century. In 1906, postmen in Britain were earning 119 per cent of the average earnings of semi-skilled male workers. Their position declined steadily until, by 1955, they reached a low point of 85 per cent of the average earnings of semi-skilled men (Routh 1980). As their income position degenerated, the job became less attractive to men and shortages of male labour for the job were a chronic problem.

In 1955 equal pay was introduced into the Civil Service and, consequently, into the postal job. A long-standing demand of the union was finally realized and management could no longer employ cheaper female labour. Nevertheless, the management interest in employing women did not lessen. With the relative decline in earnings and the resulting shortages of postmen, women were still an attractive source of labour since it was thought that their employment would avoid the need to increase the wage rate in order to attract sufficient numbers of men to the job. While the job paid wages that were relatively low for men in semi-skilled occupations, the wages were, at that time, approximately 60 per cent higher than the average for women in semi-skilled occupations (Routh 1980). In the face of a continuing threat to wages from the employment of female labour, sex was mobilized as a criterion of discrimination. In order to ensure the employment and wages of postmen, the union successfully negotiated an agreement which put limitations on the employment of postwomen and defined them as a supplement to the male labour force. This agreement came into effect in 1955, the same year that equal pay was introduced. For many postwomen, 1955 was the year they got equal pay shortly before losing their jobs.

Between 1955 and 1975, women were hired for the postal job as 'temporary' workers only. As temporary workers, the women had inferior sickness benefits, no pensions and no accumulation of seniority. Since seniority was the basis on which job duties and vacations were determined, postwomen usually found themselves with the most undesirable job tasks and holiday times. They also had only minimal job protection and could be fired with statutory notice. Coincident with their temporary status, women were designated a 'reserve labour force'. A vacancy quota was maintained in sorting offices in order to guarantee a supply of jobs for men. When the number of vacant jobs fell below quota level, an appropriate number of postwomen would be fired in order to restore the vacancy quota. These were the conditions of employment that obtained in the postal job until changes were brought about to comply with the Sex Discrimination Act.

In the case of the postal job, the Sex Discrimination Act enabled a positive change in the conditions of women's employment within circumstances where their disadvantaged position was a direct result of their union's policy and strategy. To counter the effects of a declining income position relative to other male employment, postmen pursued a strategy of social closure in order to protect their priority in the postal job and increase the strength of their wage claims. Support for equal pay for postwomen was one attempt to curb the demand for female labour. By restricting full access to the job on the basis of sex, the postmen sought to control the labour supply for the postal job as a means of guaranteeing men's employment and guarding wage rates.

To summarize, the creation of a division by sex as a meaningful component in both areas of employment was not due to the 'sex-typing' or 'gender' infusion of job tasks. Although the postal and telephonist jobs have been regarded as sex-typed, and while each has characteristics which fit gender stereotypes in employment (for example, the strength component of the postal job and the routine, sedentary nature of the telephonist job), the official distinctions that were drawn between the employment of women and men did not come about in relation to such characteristics. Sex-segregated day- and night-telephonist shifts were established as a solution to the problems encountered when the management tried to  extend women's employment to hours outside of those which are typical for the female labour force. The relative decline in income position experienced by postmen and resulting shortages of men applying for the job, were conditions which occasioned attempts to protect the wages and employment of men by modifying the demand for and supply of, female labour.

Since 1975 being female or male has been of no consequence for the formal conditions of employment within the postal and telephonist jobs. Why then, do the jobs continue to have a skewed distribution of female and male workers? It will be clear from information to be presented that while one of the main features of the telephonist and postal jobs is their skewed sex composition, the social circumstances of the women and men employed in the jobs vary strongly in particular ways and in a similar manner for women and men. The jobs continue to be characterized by sex segregation, but the processes underlying the distribution of women and men to the different jobs encompass a patterning of social circumstances that is both more extensive and specific than this simple characterization implies.

In order to explain the existing distribution of women and men in the day-telephonist, night-telephonist and postal jobs, we need both a more precise understanding of the general social circumstances of the female and male labour force in each of the jobs and an appreciation of how variations in social circumstances are located as processes structuring relations to employment. We shall see that there are very clear patterns in relations between social circumstances and employment experiences and that some patterns are coincident with differentiations in women's and men's experience, while others are not.

THE STRUCTURING OF EMPLOYMENT:

*Full-wage and Component-wage Jobs*

Employment in the telephonist and postal jobs is structured by opportunity and need, and relations between social circumstances and employment form coherent patterns in two major ways. The first is in terms of the social origins and resources of job incumbents, and in this case postal workers are distinguished from both day and night telephonists. The second involves relations to household financing, and here a distinction will be drawn between the day-telephonist job — as a component-wage job — and the postal and night-telephonist jobs — as full-wage jobs. Following a brief discussion of the first and more familiar pattern, this section of the chapter will focus on the second pattern: that is, the importance of domestic responsibilities for the structuring of employment and the distinction between component-wage and full-wage jobs.

Within the general structuring of employment opportunities and social resources, all of the jobs are poorly placed. They offer little in the way of career prospects and are not well paid. Nevertheless, there are significant differences between the postal job and both telephonist jobs in terms of the social origins and resources of incumbents. Considering the opportunities afforded by education and families of origin, the postal workers are the most disadvantaged. They come from non-skilled manual families of origin and low educational backgrounds. Seventy-six per cent of the postal labour force is unqualified (81 per cent of the women and 73 per cent of the men). Their employment experience has been almost entirely in non-skilled manual jobs. A high proportion of postwomen are black (46 per cent) and almost all of these women have emigrated from the West Indies.[6] The family backgrounds of the black postwomen are somewhat more advantaged than those of white postwomen. While the occupations of mothers are similar, the fathers of the black postwomen are more likely to be skilled, rather than non-skilled, workers. When age differences are taken into account, there are no significant differences in educational and occupational experiences between the white and black postwomen.

Compared with postal workers, all telephonists are better placed in relation to the structuring of opportunities. There are, however, important differences within the telephonist labour force and two main groups can be distinguished. One group is composed of the night telephonists (female and male) and older women on the day telephonist shift. They are only marginally more advantaged than postal workers in terms of education and previous employment. The main distinguishing feature between the postal workers and this group of telephonists is the social location of their families of origin. The families of origin of the night telephonists and older female day telephonists are more likely to include a parent in non-manual occupations. By virtue of their social origins, and in contrast to the postal workers, this group of telephonists possess one of the few 'qualifications' for the telephonist job — a relatively unaccented voice. The second distinctive group of telephonists is composed of the young day telephonists (female and male) and the older male day telephonists. This group is the most educationally qualified of all the sample. In addition, the men attained their qualifications at higher types of schools and are from the most advantaged families of origin. Close to 40 per cent of them are from families in which parental occupations include professional or managerial jobs.[7]

While aspects of social background and resources differentiate the postal workers from the telephonists, further clarification of patterns of experience in relation to employment requires consideration of the domestic circumstances of the women and men in the three jobs. The domestic circumstances of the women and men in the day-telephonist job are distinctive, and they contrast dramatically with those of the women and men in the postal and night-telephonist jobs. To characterize this contrast, the night-telephonist and postal jobs will be referred to as full-wage jobs, and the day-telephonist job as a component-wage job. Before discussing the relations between domestic circumstances and the distribution of people to full-wage and component-wage jobs, a brief justification for characterizing the distinction in these terms is presented.

The average weekly earnings of the three jobs are shown in table 8.1. Day telephonists are paid the lowest wages of all workers in the three jobs. However, it is important to note that the wages of the day telephonist job stand in a different relation to other female, compared to male, earnings. While wages as far as women are concerned are comparable to women's earnings in other routine clerical jobs, the day-telephonist job is very badly paid compared to men's average earnings in similar sorts of jobs. In 1979,

**Table 8.1   Average weekly earnings of telephonists, postal workers and other selected occupations** [a]

|  | Women (£) | | Men (£) | |
|---|---|---|---|---|
| Day telephonists [b] |  | 57.1  (54.3) |  |  |
| Night telephonists |  | 88.8  (67.2) |  |  |
| Postal workers | 70.6 | (61.1) | 83.5 | (64.9) |
| General clerks | 57.5 | (56.7) | 77.4 | (72.5) |
| All manual | 55.2 | (53.3) | 93.0 | (79.0) |

*Notes:*

a   Average gross weekly earnings of full-time employees in 1979 are presented. Figures in parentheses are average gross weekly earnings excluding overtime. Earnings for telephonists have been supplied by British Telecommunications and those of postal workers by the Post Office. Other earnings are from *New Earnings Survey* (HMSO, London, 1979), part D, tables 99, 100.

b   Earnings by sex for the telephonists are not available, but are unlikely to vary substantially from the amounts shown here. In each job, women and men are on the same pay scale. Earnings vary mainly by the number of overtime hours worked and differences in overtime hours are minimal.

male day telephonists were earning approximately £20 less per week than the average earnings of male general clerks. Some overtime is available in the day-telephonist job, but neither female nor male telephonists work overtime to any significant extent.

The earnings of night telephonists are substantially higher than earnings of day telephonists, in terms of both regular earnings and the overtime component. Without overtime, the night-telephonist job pays a wage which compares favourably with that of women's earnings in similar jobs. Considering total earnings, including overtime, the job provides women with a much higher average wage than is typical for women in this type of job.[8] For men, the regular earnings of the night-telephonist job are fairly low compared to the average for men in routine clerical jobs. The average earnings of male night telephonists inclusive of overtime, however, compare favourably with earnings of male routine clerical workers. In the postal job, the wages picture is similar to that for the night telephonists. Postwomen earn wages which, inclusive and exclusive of overtime, are highly placed in relation to women's earnings in similar jobs. In contrast, the earnings of postmen, exclusive of overtime, are poorly placed relative to men's earnings in other manual jobs and postmen can only approach the average earnings for male manual workers by putting in a large number of overtime hours.

To summarize the earnings profile of the three jobs, day telephonists earn wages which are typical for women's earnings in comparable routine non-manual jobs and which are very low compared to men's average earnings in such jobs. Despite such low earnings, male day telephonists do not attempt to adjust their wages upwards by putting in extensive overtime hours. In contrast to the day-telephonist job, earnings in the night-telephonist and postal jobs are high compared to women's earnings in similar types of jobs, although for men the average payment for regular hours is below the earnings of men in comparable jobs. In these cases, men do put in large amounts of overtime hours in order to boost their wages. This pattern in the earnings of women and men in the three jobs, and the relations of their earnings to the average earnings of women and men in comparable jobs, is an important aspect of the distinction between the day-telephonist job as a component-wage job, and the night-telephonist and postal jobs as full-wage jobs.

Although one of the main differences between the full-wage and component-wage jobs is the higher pay of the former, the distinction does not rest solely on a quantitative difference in wages. The distinction is based primarily on differences in relations to household maintenance. A full-wage job is one which enables its incumbents to take sole responsibility for maintaining an independent household, a responsibility which can include financial maintenance of other household members not in waged work. A job which provides a component wage is one which does not enable incumbents to be wholly responsible for the financial maintenance of a household. People in component-wage jobs contribute to the financial maintenance of households, but do not have the resources to maintain an independent household single-handedly.

The characterization of the day-telephonist job as a component-wage job and the night-telephonist and postal jobs as full-wage jobs is justified in that a substantial proportion of the night telephonists and postal workers are maintaining independent households, while the proportion doing so in the component-wage job is less. Fifty-one per cent of incumbents in the two full-wage jobs — 56 per cent of the women and 48 per cent of the men — are in such a position. In contrast, 29 per cent of both women and men in the component-wage job are solely responsible for the financial maintenance of their households.[9]

While the postal and night-telephonist jobs are full-wage jobs, they are marginal ones. The ability of their incumbents to provide the sole financial support in a household depends mainly on a large number of overtime hours as a regular component of employment. And, it is possible to use this information to interpret further the conflict between women's and men's employment in the postal job. The standard pattern of female and male employment is employment in component-wage and full-wage jobs respectively. With the decline in relative wages in the postal job, the job was becoming increasingly marginal as a source of full-wage employment and it is this that lay at the centre of the postmen's opposition to women's employment — employment which they assumed would hasten the transformation of the postal job from a full-wage to a component-wage job.

To reiterate, the day-telephonist job is distinguished from the night-telephonist and postal jobs in terms of the relations of incumbents to household maintenance. The component-wage and full-wage jobs employ women and men at particular stages of the domestic life cycle and in different domestic circumstances within these stages. The women and men in the two types of jobs stand in a different relation to standard employment patterns associated with women and men. Women and men in jobs typical for their sex have a profile of relations between domestic and employment experiences that approximates the aggregate pattern for each sex. Women and men in jobs atypical for their sex (the postwomen, female night telephonists, and male day telephonists) are in particular domestic circumstances and it is the particular nature of these circumstances that requires, or facilitates, their atypical employment. To elaborate these patterns of employment in relation to domestic circumstances, the age at which people are recruited to the two types of jobs, and a brief account of the variation in domestic circumstances at recruitment, are presented first. This is followed, finally, by a presentation of the aspects of social experience which structure the distribution of women and men to full-wage and component-wage jobs.

The distribution of women's age at recruitment to their current job is illustrated in figure 8.1. The difference in the pattern of recruitment age to the component-wage and full-wage jobs is striking. For women in the component-wage job, the distribution of recruitment age is similar in structure to that of the full-time economic activity rates of the female population generally: it is bimodal. The first peak in recruitment is in the under-twenty age-group. Twenty-nine per cent of female day telephonists are recruited at this age. Recruitment then diminishes in the twenties and drops sharply to the lowest point in the thirties. Only 8 per cent of female day telephonists were recruited in their thirties. Recruitment increases again in the forties (which is the second peak at 29 per cent) and then falls off in the older age-groups. This bimodal recruitment-age pattern for women in the component-wage job is in marked contrast to the recruitment-age pattern for women in full-wage jobs. It is precisely in the age category when recruitment to the component-wage job drops off — the thirties — that recruitment to the full-wage job is at its peak. Forty-seven per cent of the women in the full-wage jobs were recruited when in their thirties. Few women are recruited to the full-wage job under the age of thirty, and recruitment in the forties and fifties age-groups is similar for both types of jobs.

Variations in the age of recruitment to component-wage and full-wage

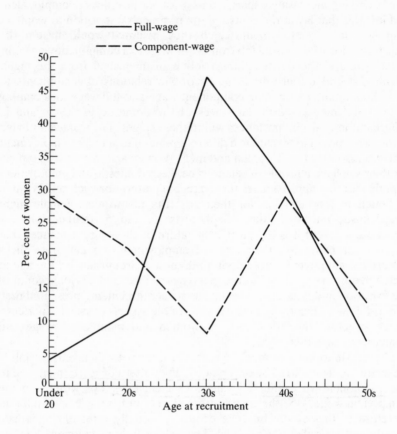

*Figure 8.1   Age at recruitment for women by type of job*

jobs are coincident with differences in women's marital and family circumstances at recruitment. Over two-thirds of the women in full-wage jobs had dependent children when they entered their current job. This was particularly the case for the black postwomen — sixteen of the eighteen with children had dependent children when recruited to the postal job. Only one quarter of the women day telephonists were in a similar family position when recruited. Further, although a similar proportion of women in the two types of jobs are recruited at age forty or over, over two-thirds of the women of this age who are recruited to the component-wage job are married, while just under two-thirds of women who are recruited to the full-wage jobs in their forties are divorced, separated or widowed. The white women predominate among the group who are previously married when recruited to the full-wage job.

The distribution of men's age at recruitment to component-wage and full-wage jobs is illustrated in figure 8.2. The distribution of recruitment age to the component-wage jobs is strongly skewed toward the younger ages. Recruitment to the component-wage job is highest for men in their twenties (44 per cent are recruited at this age) and is relatively negligible in other age groups. The distribution of men's ages at recruitment to the full-wage jobs is less skewed and there is a more gradual decline in recruitment among the older age-groups. As in the component-wage job, recruitment of men to the full-wage jobs is concentrated in the twenties age-group. However, there are marked differences in the domestic circumstances of men recruited to the two types of jobs at this age. For example, all of the men recruited to the day-telephonist job in their twenties were single at the time. Of the men in this age-group who began employment in the night-telephonist job, over half were married and over half of the married men

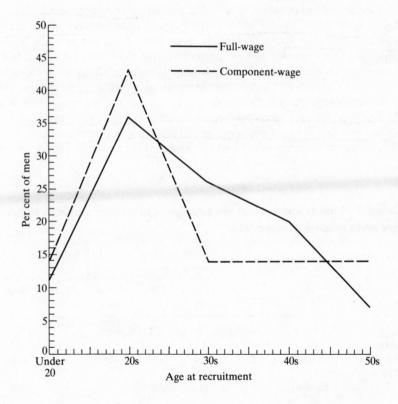

*Figure 8.2   Age at recruitment for men by type of job*

had pre-school-age children. Of the men in this age-group who began employment in the postal job, again over half were married, and in this case all of the married men had pre-school-age children.

For both women and men, family and marital circumstances are strongly related to the nature of employment, in particular in either a component-wage or full-wage job. To conclude this section, the key elements of the structuring of employment by domestic circumstances are presented. Table 8.2 shows the current family and marital circumstances of women and men in the two types of jobs. A clear patterning of domestic circumstances in relation to employment is present in these data. Understanding the importance of domestic experiences for the structuring of men's employment in the component-wage and full-wage jobs is relatively straightforward and the following presentation begins with the central feature in this process — marital status. We shall then move on to consider the more complex structuring of the women's domestic circumstances and their relations to employment.

It is evident from the data in table 8.2 that whether or not men have ever been married is the crucial factor in their distribution between component-wage and full-wage jobs. While just over half of the single men in the sample are in a full-wage job, 96 per cent of the men who have ever been married are in a full-wage job. A similar picture results from looking at the ratio of single men to ever married men in the two types of jobs. For the component-wage job the ratio is 6:1 and for the full-wage jobs it is 1:4. For men, the relationship between never married/ever married and employment in a component-wage or full-wage job is a strong one.[10]

The domestic circumstances of the married men in full-wage jobs are

**Table 8.2  Family and marital circumstances of women and men in full-wage and component-wage jobs**

|  | Component-wage jobs | | Full-wage jobs | | |
|---|---|---|---|---|---|
|  | Women | Men | White women | Black women | Men |
| Single | 9 | 12 | 6 | 0 | 13 |
| Married | 12 | 1 | 7 | 12 | 43 |
| (dependent children) | (2) | (0) | (1) | (7) | (22) |
| Previously married | 3 | 1 | 13 | 7 | 5 |
| (dependent children) | (1) | (0) | (4) | (3) | (0) |
| Total | 24 | 14 | 26 | 19 | 61 |

fairly standard when compared with those of employed married men generally. A roughly similar proportion of the married male labour force and the married men in full-wage jobs have dependent children (62 versus 50 per cent, respectively). Considering the employment activity of the wives of these men in the larger population, 46 per cent were not in paid work, 39 per cent were employed part time, and 15 per cent were employed full time.[11] In the full-wage jobs, the comparable percentages for married men with dependent children are 45, 36 and 18 per cent.

Being a single man appears to coincide with some flexibility in financial requirements — roughly half of the single men are in both types of jobs. It is likely, however, that older single men have financial obligations over and above those of younger single men (such as full responsibility for their own support, housing, support of aged parents and so on). Consistent with the differentiation that has been made between the component-wage and full-wage jobs, younger single men are concentrated in the former, while older single men are concentrated in the latter. Among older single men in the full-wage jobs, over three-quarters were independent householders paying commercial rents or mortgages. Among younger single men in the component-wage job, a slightly higher percentage were not independent householders and the majority were still living with their families of origin.

It is obvious from these data that men in the job atypical for their sex — the component-wage day-telephonist job — are also not typical of the range of domestic responsibilities found among the male labour force. The overwhelming majority of them are single, most are under the age of thirty, and many are still living with their families of origin. The men in jobs typical for their sex — the full-wage night telephonists and postmen — have domestic commitments which are much more extensive and which are representative of married men in the general labour force. As with the men, patterns of standard and non-standard relations between employment and domestic circumstances are present for the women.

It has already been established that women's age of recruitment to the day-telephonist component-wage job is patterned in a manner similar to the full-time employment activity of the general female population. The bimodal pattern of recruitment age to the component-wage job indicates a particular relationship between domestic commitments and employment which is the main pattern that this relationship takes among the female labour force. It is a pattern that is a minority one among the domestic and employment experiences of women in the full-wage jobs. In addition, black women have a pattern of employment in relation to domestic commitments which diverges from that typical for white women.

As table 8.2 indicates, variations in both marital status and job distribution between the white and black women are considerable. All of the black women have been married and all are employed in a full-wage job.[12] We have also established that the black women were more likely to have had dependent children when they entered their full-wage job and a high proportion of them are currently supporting dependent children. The domestic and employment circumstances of the black women in this study appear to be consistent with the general traditions of employment among women of West Indian origin in Britain. Generally, West Indian women have the highest employment activity rate of all racial minority women in Britain, and they have a higher rate than the white female labour force. Married West Indian and white women are especially different in terms of employment activity in relation to family circumstances. Married West Indian women are much more likely to be in employment when their children are dependent, particularly during pre-school years, and they are more likely to be employed full time (Smith 1977). They are, in short, full-time wage-earners supporting dependents to a greater extent than is the case for white women. And, it would appear from the data presented here, that, as married women, they are more likely to be full-wage earners as well.

For white women there is some variability in job distribution. As with the single men and for the same reasons, the distribution of single women to component-wage and full-wage jobs varies with age. Further, there is a relationship between marital status and the distribution of white women to component-wage and full-wage jobs. In contrast to the men and the black married women, the majority of the white married women are in the component-wage job. The relationship between never married/ever married and employment in the component-wage or full-wage job is much weaker for white women than it is for men because the distribution of single and married white women in component-wage and full-wage jobs is identical. Just under two thirds of both groups are in the component-wage job.[13] While there is no major difference in the distribution of single and married white women to the two types of jobs, the difference between these two marital groups and previously married white women is sizeable. Only 19 per cent of previously married white women are in a component-wage job. The termination of a marriage is, for white women, the key element of the process underlying their employment in a full-wage job and the association between a terminated marriage and employment in a full-wage job is a substantial one.[14]

Comparing the experiences of the white and black women, those who are previously married have fairly similar experiences. Their employment is concentrated in full-wage jobs and a roughly similar percentage of them are supporting dependent children as single parents (31 and 43 per cent for the white and black previously married women respectively). There is, on the other hand, a very large difference between the white and black married women. While all married black women are in full-wage jobs, the majority of married white women are in the component-wage job. In addition, the households of the married white women in the day-telephonist component-wage job are unlikely to include dependents (only 16 per cent include dependents), while those of the married black women in the full-wage jobs have the highest proportion (58 per cent include dependents). Note, however, that the married white women in the component-wage job are not distinguished from those in the full-wage job in terms of their current support of dependent children.

One final aspect of the women's domestic circumstances needs elaboration before relations to their current employment can be located completely. The domestic circumstances of the white married women in the component-wage job are distinguished from those of the white and black married women in the full-wage jobs by the financial resources of husbands. The average weekly take-home pay of day telephonists' husbands in full-time employment is £10 higher than that of the husbands of black postwomen, and £13 higher than the take-home pay of husbands of white postwomen. Considering potential claims on financial resources brought into a household by a spouse, the married white women in the component-wage day-telephonist job are better off than the married black and white women in the full-wage jobs.

To summarize the circumstances of the women, there is, in the first place, a differentiation between white and black married women in terms of typical patterns of employment experience in relation to domestic responsibilities. The married black women are more likely to be joint full-time wage-earners in households with extensive financial needs. In general, however, black women, whether married or previously married, are employed in the full-wage jobs. In the second place, there is a differentiation among the white women in terms of the relation between marital status and employment in a full-wage or component-wage job. Previously married white women, many of whom are single parents, are employed in the full-wage jobs, while single and married white women are employed mainly in the component-wage job. Thirdly, and finally, older single women are more likely than their younger counterparts to be employed in full-wage jobs. Generally speaking, women who are carrying domestic responsibilities which are more extensive than that typical for women in Britain, are in employment that is atypical for women in Britain — full-wage employment. Similarly, women who have experienced relations between domestic circumstances and employment in a manner that is standard for women in Britain, are in typical employment — component-wage employment.

## SUMMARY

There is a general patterning of relations to domestic circumstances and employment which is consistent with variations in and between women's and men's experiences. Financial need and relations to household maintenance structure the distribution of people to component-wage and full-wage jobs. The limited nature of the domestic financial obligations of women and men in the day-telephonist job is a crucial aspect of their ability to sustain employment in a job which provides a component wage. They are in circumstances where other household members are making financial contributions and where claims on the financial resources of the household are not extensive. In contrast, a substantial proportion of the women and men in the full-wage jobs are solely responsible for the financial maintenance of a household and in many cases this responsibility includes the financial support of dependent household members. This distinction, and the social processes giving rise to it, have been shown to be consistent with the patterning of women's and men's experiences in the component-wage job, where women are in the majority, and with women's and men's experiences in the full-wage jobs, where men predominate.

Rarely do occupations employ women and men in proportions equivalent to their representation in the labour force. The skewed sex composition of occupations has led many to believe that occupational segregation by sex is an adequate description of a general feature of employment, and has contributed to the idea that 'gender' is a generally valid category in relation to the structuring of employment and a theory of inequality. The main purpose of this chapter has been to demonstrate that 'occupational segregation by sex', and a distinction between 'women's work' and 'men's work', are inadequate understandings of the nature of the skewed sex composition of jobs. Not only are these categories unable to encompass variations within women's and men's employment, they mislead as to the social processes giving rise to the aggregate differences between women's and men's employment. The patterns in relations of domestic and employment experiences that have been presented could be discerned within the research process only by regarding the correspondence between social experiences and the categories 'women', 'men', 'gender' and 'sexual divisions' as issues to be addressed, rather than assuming each as an unlocated entity. It is hoped that any extension of explanation that has been gained speaks favourably for such an approach.

*[handwritten annotation:]* - d' relationship tween household structure and allocation to jobs is interesting. I fail to see, however, how these findings support the interest of the utility of a concept of "gender."

# 9

## Women and the 'Service Class'

### Rosemary Crompton

#### INTRODUCTION[1]

In a well-known article, Hartmann argues that Marxist class categories are
'gender-blind': 'Marx's theory of the development of capitalism is a theory
of the development of "empty places" . . . The categories of Marxism cannot tell us who will fill the empty places.' (Hartmann 1981: p. 10). Marxist
attempts at a solution to the 'woman question', she argues, have all suffered
from a basic and fundamental flaw in that ultimately, woman's oppression
has been conceptualized and understood as but a particular aspect of *class*
oppression (e.g. Engels, Zaretsky, Dalla Costa). Radical feminists, in
contrast, argue that 'the original and basic class division is between the
sexes, and . . . the motive force of history is the striving of men for power
and domination over women, the dialectic of sex' (Hartmann 1981: p. 13).
Hartmann accepts the radical feminist account of patriarchy as constituting
an independent system of domination, yet she is reluctant to abandon
Marxist class theory altogether. In Hartmann's account, Marxist analysis is
presented not as *incorrect*, but rather as incomplete. The way ahead, she
suggests, is to examine the partnership of patriarchy and capital — an
approach which has been described as 'dual systems theory' (Young 1980;
1981). Hartmann's 'dual systems' approach treats capitalism and patriarchy
as two separate, if interrelated, systems, each with its distinct material
base. The 'material base of patriarchy is men's control over women's
labour power. That control is maintained by excluding women from access
to necessary economically productive resources and by restricting women's
sexuality' (Hartmann 1981: p. 15). Thus: 'Capitalist development creates
the places for a hierarchy of workers, but traditional Marxist categories
cannot tell us who will fill which places. Gender and racial hierarchies
determine who fills the empty places' (p. 18).

Hartmann's discussion has been subjected to an extensive and wide-ranging critique.[2] However, she states in a clear and unambiguous fashion, some of the major problems to be confronted by sociologists attempting to face up to this important and difficult issue. Do class inequalities effectively overdetermine gender inequalities? Is the way ahead, as Hartmann argues, to regard class and gender as separate, albeit complementary, systems? Or are class theories flawed fundamentally and irretrievably in their omission of gender, requiring the development of a new body of theory?

Marxist class categories *are* 'gender-blind', in that they cannot specify who will 'fill the places'. Abstract theorists might retain a lofty indifference to the problem (Poulantzas 1975), but it simply cannot be avoided at the empirical level. As has been observed widely, the form assumed by the structure is not determined simply by the capitalist function, but is rather a product of the interaction between capital and labour. In determining the outcome, the characteristics of labour — whether skilled or unskilled, black or white, male or female — are obviously crucial. (Abercrombie and Urry 1983: Crompton and Jones 1984).

Class theories may be criticized legitimately therefore, for failing to give a satisfactory account of gender. However, it may also be suggested that they have suffered further at the hands of practitioners in that 'gender blindness' has been used as a justification for 'gender exclusion' in empirical research. I refer, of course, to the relatively common practice of excluding women from empirical investigations of the 'class structure' (Goldthorpe 1983).

I wish to emphasize, however, that there are no *theoretical* grounds for excluding women from consideration in empirical research. An exception may be argued for some versions of Weberian (or neo-Weberian) theory. For Weber, 'classes' are aggregates of *individuals* with similar 'life-chances' in the market. To quote directly 'the kind of chance in the *market* is the decisive moment which presents a common condition for the *individual's* fate' (Weber in Giddens and Held (ed) 1982 p. 62). Thus gender-based strategies of 'exclusion' (Parkin 1979) might debar women totally from 'market participation' and women rendered a particular, gender-based, 'status group'. Where no such exclusion exists, however, women 'in the market' must, logically, be seen to possess a 'class situation'. Similarly, there is nothing in the most abstract theory of 'empty places' to suggest grounds for the systematic 'declassing' of any of the occupants. However, in his recent defence of the 'conventional view', Goldthorpe wishes to assert that 'class analysis begins with a structure of *positions,* associated with a specific historical form of the social division of labour' (Goldthorpe 1983: p. 467; my italics), yet simultaneously deny the relevance of such 'positions' to over 40 per cent of those who occupy them (see West 1978; Stewart, Prandy and Blackburn 1980).

Goldthorpe argues that those researchers (including himself) who have excluded women from consideration have not done so because of a wilful ignorance of gender inequality, rather 'the argument for so doing . . . in fact *stems from* a clear recognition of major sexual inequalities, especially in regard to opportunities for labour-market participation, and of the consequent relationship of dependence that generally prevails between married women and their husbands' (1983: p. 469–70 italics in original). However, we should surely move beyond the mere 'recognition' of major sexual inequalities towards an *understanding* of the reciprocal relationship between class inequality and gender inequality. This understanding is certainly *not* going to be achieved by excluding women from empirical research.

Indeed, it may be suggested that implicit in the strategy of the 'conventional view' is the assumption that major sexual inequalities are a permanent and relatively unchanging feature of society — they are simply taken as 'givens'. (Paradoxically, it may be argued that this stance has much in common with the radical feminist perspective.) It is my contention that this assumption is unwarranted, and that recent changes in the structure of gender inequality — which admittedly fall far short of the complete dismantling of patriarchal structures — may prove to have a significant impact on class practices.

My strategy will be to examine systematically the gender division of labour which underpins the occupational division of labour within which the putative 'service class' has been identified (Abercrombie and Urry 1983: Goldthorpe 1982). It is important to extend 'the brief of stratification analysis . . . beyond the task of mapping inequalities of position and person to the investigation of the formation and reproduction of the positions' (Garnsey 1982: p. 427), and the systematic consideration of gender relations is an essential part of this task.

The burgeoning literature in the United States and Europe on the 'labour process debate' (Braverman 1974; and for a useful summary see Thompson 1983), together with the closely related work of 'dual' and 'radical' labour-market theorists (e.g. Edwards 1979), has made a significant contribution to our understanding of the 'formation and reproduction' of occupations. Such writers have certainly not ignored the 'woman question'; however, their discussion of 'women's work' has been confined largely to women's participation in the 'public sphere' — that is in employment. Women have been viewed as an essential element of the 'secondary' labour force or as contributing to the 'reserve army of labour'. It is recognized that the extent and nature of women's 'economic activity' is massively constrained by the requirements of their roles in the private, or domestic, sphere, and as we have seen, these constraints have been a major rationale for the exclusion of women from studies of the 'class structure' (Goldthorpe

1983; Giddens 1973). It would seem logical therefore, that an examination of the gender division of labour should cut across the public/private distinction to encompass 'work' in both the public and private spheres.

## THE 'SERVICE CLASS'

The concept of the 'service class'[3] was developed to describe and analyse changes in the class structure following upon the separation of *de facto* control from *de jure* ownership. As formulated originally by Renner (trans. Bottomore and Goode 1978) it describes those who are appointed/ employed to carry out the functions which are no longer carried out personally by the capitalist — not only in private corporations, but also, indirectly, in public bodies. For Renner, the fact that the service class are salary (rather than wage) workers reflects the crucially different nature of their employment contract. They are employed in positions of trust, and, in return for the trust which is placed in them, they are rewarded with better employment conditions, job security and access to a bureaucratic career hierarchy.

Renner's formulation has been adapted extensively by a range of authors, (Bain and Price 1972; Dahrendorf 1959). My present discussion, however, will focus on two recent contributions to the service-class debate: Goldthorpe (1982) and Abercrombie and Urry (1983). Although the conclusions and interpretations offered by these writers differ in many respects, there are important areas of similarity in their identification of the service class itself.

Goldthorpe applies the 'service-class' description to the first two classes of the seven-fold class schema developed in the course of his work on male occupational mobility (Goldthorpe *et al.* 1980: p. 40–1). Class I — 'Higher-grade professionals, self-employed or salaried; higher-grade administrators and officials in central and local government and in public and private enterprises; managers in large industrial establishments; and large proprietors . . . may be taken as very largely corresponding to the higher and intermediate levels of . . . the "service class".' Class II — 'lower-grade professionals and higher-grade technicians; lower-grade administrators and officials; managers in small businesses and industrial establishments and services; and supervisors of non manual employees' complement 'Class I of our schema in representing the subaltern or *cadet* levels of the service class.' There are some problems with Goldthorpe's formulation — a 'class' is being identified as an agglomeration of occupations which includes employers and the self-employed — but it is worth describing at some length to make clear his intention, carried over into his more recent account, of clearly distinguishing the service class from routine white-collar employees. Abercrombie and Urry also emphasize this distinction.

The 'market' and 'work' situations of the service class, they argue, are very different from the proletarianized places occupied by lower-grade clerks. In my discussions of the 'service class' therefore, I shall follow these authors in including only professional, administrative and managerial levels of white-collar employment.

Both authors are similar to Renner in that they stress the central place of a *career* in their identification of the service class. 'What is yet more central to the logic of the service relationship . . . is the part played by rewards that are of an essentially *prospective* kind above all, on career opportunities' (Goldthorpe 1982; p. 169). Similarly, Abercrombie and Urry emphasize the importance of a career to the service-class market and work situations (1983: p. 119).

As defined above, the 'service class', together with its 'cadet or subaltern divisions', includes just under a quarter of the employed population in Britain. It is also overwhelmingly *male*. For example, the 1981 Census reveals that 80 per cent of Socio-economic Group I (employers and managers: large establishments); 77 per cent of SEG 2 (employers and managers: small establishments); and 90 per cent of professionals were male; conversely, 69 per cent of SEG 6 (junior non-manual workers) were female (*Economic Activity Tables* table 16A).

These facts are well known and their background requires little explanation. Although the proportion of women of working age in employment in Britain has increased from 38 per cent to 55 per cent since the Second World War, this increase (which has largely been an increase in the employment of married women) has not been distributed evenly through the occupational structure (Hakim 1979; Martin and Roberts 1984). There still exists a considerable degree of horizontal gender-segregation of occupations — that is, women tend to be concentrated in occupations which reflect their gender-assigned roles — cooking, cleaning, nursing, child care and so on. Horizontal segregation is accompanied by vertical segregation — men work most commonly in higher-grade occupations and women work most commonly in lower-grade occupations. Economic activity rates in Britain are high for women in their teens and early twenties, decline as women leave the labour force to bear and rear children, then rise from the late twenties to reach a level equal to that of younger women by the mid-forties.

The occupational data demonstrates therefore, that women, even when employed by large-scale white-collar bureaucracies within which careers are technically possible, do not progress through the career hierarchy. Our empirical research has demonstrated that women have not gained promotion because of (a) broken work experience — most characteristically, leaving work in order to rear a family; (b) difficulties caused by being geographically immobile — again because of family commitments; and (c) the failure to acquire vocational post-entry qualifications such as banking and insurance examinations — perhaps as a consequence of (a) and (b). (Crompton and Jones 1984.) In short, the explanation for the women's lack of success in career terms may be sought in the near-impossibility of combining the demands and requirements of a successful career with the gender-assigned responsibilities of the domestic role. Thus, as Abercrombie and Urry have noted: 'The division between the service class and deskilled white-collar workers is increasingly a division between males and females' (1983: p. 139).

As developed so far, my argument is neither new nor contentious.[4] It rests upon the fact — which many other authors have noted — that when women enter the public sphere their activities are massively constrained, in particular by their 'private' domestic responsibilities. However, it is equally important to emphasize the *contribution* of women, in the public *and* private spheres, to the creation and maintenance of the (largely male) 'service class'.

— what about this public/private distinction?

## WOMEN'S CONTRIBUTION TO THE 'SERVICE CLASS'

In developing my argument I would not wish to give the impression that the 'service class' is the only area in which gender has a crucial 'impact' on the class structure. A major objective of the overall strategy I advocate would be the systematic investigation of the reciprocal relationship between 'gender' and 'class' as a whole. This is clearly a substantial undertaking and my present focus is defined more narrowly. Initially, I would suggest that there are two, rather different, ways in which the 'service class' may be seen as resting upon a foundation provided by women. First, women's work in the private sphere (or more precisely, that of 'service-class' wives), provides, through domestic labour in the household, the conditions under which men may embark on service-class careers and may also make a direct contribution to these careers. Secondly, women's employment in the public sphere is concentrated heavily in occupations supplying the raw material or essential 'back-up' services for 'service-class' occupations; as, for example, clerks, typists, secretaries and punchgirls, and as nurses, teachers, occupational therapists and basic-grade social workers.

The observation that the domestic responsibilities assumed by middle-class wives 'liberate' their husbands to pursue a 'service-class' career is paralleled by the Marxist argument that women's labour in the sphere of reproduction contributes to the intensification of the exploitation of men's labour in the sphere of production.[5] It can be suggested, however, that the 'service class' provides a particularly extreme example of this tendency. 'Service-class' work often requires its incumbents to work unusual hours, to be absent from home and be geographically mobile. In these circumstances, the wife's role in maintaining the home is clearly essential

(Cohen 1977). Additionally, successful male careerists require considerable preparation for public participation (suits, clean shirts, etc.), and the standards achieved within the home (comfort, cleanliness, well-behaved children, capacity for business entertaining, etc.) contribute to the 'public' evaluation of the individual. It could be argued, therefore, that the service-class wives' 'role in reproduction' is particularly crucial. To add another dimension to the argument, some wives are also incorporated into mens' work.

The 'two-person career' (Papenek 1973) pinpoints the 'vicarious achievement' of the wife in making an active contribution to her husband's career. Wives act as unacknowledged and unpaid secretaries, researchers and personnel officers to their husbands — in short, within this model the wives' contribution is not confined to the domestic realm, but carried over into the public realm and appropriated by her husband's employer — or her husband. (Finch 1983; D. E. Smith 1983.) Although therefore, such women make a direct contribution to 'public sphere' production, this contribution is obscured effectively by the ideological construction of the home and work as separate spheres and the assumption that a woman who is not formally 'economically active' works only in the domestic sphere.

It may be suggested that the relative importance of these two different aspects of wives' contribution may vary within the service class. That is, the 'spiralists' — individuals pursuing 'occupational' career strategies — may in practice rely most heavily on their wives' domestic inputs, whereas the 'burgesses' — independent professionals, managers of small-scale enterprises, etc. — may derive proportionately greater benefits from their wives' inputs into vicarious careers (Watson 1964; Delphy 1977; Brown 1982).

Some debate exists as to whether the 'two-person' career is exclusively or mainly a middle-class phenomenon — Finch, for example, argues that vicarious careers are not restricted solely to the middle class (1983). Smith, however, argues that the significance of middle-class wives' labour is that they manage their families in a subcontractual relationship to corporate capitalism (Smith 1973; 1983). She argues that in the early stages of capitalist development, the middle-class family, as represented by the husband and father, was a major agent in the transmission of capital. Because of the central importance of 'the family', the nineteenth-century patriarch controlled the property and rights to the sexuality of 'his' women (see also Abercrombie and Turner 1980; 1982).

However, with the separation of ownership and control and the emergence of corporate capitalism, the bourgeois family lost its crucial role in capital formation. The corporate employee now owes his allegiance to the corporation rather than to his family. 'The individual man becomes the enterprise as far as the family is concerned. . . . It becomes general as the career rather than individual ownership structures the entry and activity of the individual as economic agent' (D. Smith 1983; p. 14). The middle-class wife's role becomes one of active creation and sustenance of the moral status required by the corporation and thus is her work incorporated into her husband's.

I have also suggested that women (and not just 'service-class' wives) provide a material underpinning for the service class as a source of low-grade white-collar employees. Such employment often, but not invariably, mirrors in the public sphere the wider private/public female/male assignment of gender roles — as in the secretarial 'office wife' (Davies 1974; McNally 1979). Women's contribution to the service class, therefore, cuts across the public/private distinction; from their labour of reproduction in the home, and incorporation into mens' careers to formal employment in the public sphere. It may thus be argued that the very existence of the 'service class' depends, to a considerable extent, on a particular set of 'arrangements' relating to the gender division of labour. In the next sections of this chapter therefore, I will explore both existing, and possible future, tensions in these gender 'arrangements'.


WOMEN AND EMPLOYMENT

In Britain, women became increasingly available for employment during a period of economic expansion (the 1960s) when jobs were readily obtainable. Indeed, it has been suggested that women constitute an important element in the 'reserve army' of labour required during such an expansion (Braverman 1974; Siltanen 1981). For women, the most rapidly expanding area of employment since the Second World War has been in routine white-collar work. Economic recession, however, has not pushed women back into the domestic sphere, perhaps because both increased rates of marital breakdown and declining family living standards have enhanced the necessary contribution of female wage labour to the household.

The increasing participation of women in the formal economy has been accompanied by important legislative and ideological changes. The ideology of bourgeois liberalism proclaims the equality of 'man' in the public sphere — 'all "men" are equal before the law'. Such equality may be exposed as a sham and indeed, has only been achieved formally during this century, but it does not follow that its impact can be disregarded. Historically, liberal feminism has fought for equal rights for women in the public realm — the right to vote, to enter the professions, to participate in public life without legal hindrance. Despite these formal freedoms however, the 'in practice' relationship between the 'private' and the 'public' appears as unchanged, as patriarchal structures in both public and private constrain women's capacity to participate in the public realm on anything like equal terms with men

(Stacey and Price 1981). However, even though the formal equality of women may appear to have had very little impact, its presence is not without significance.

Eisenstein has argued that in capitalist societies, the ideology of liberal individualism and patriarchal relations are in fundamental tension:

> At present the cohesion (i.e. between the 'public' and 'private') is weakened by conflicts between the relations of patriarchy and the ideology of liberalism, which is to say that the narrowly restricted sexually dependent role of women in patriarchy in the family and in the market is contradicted by the ideology of equal opportunity. On the other hand, the relations of capitalism and the ideology of patriarchy, which is to say the need for women wage workers, is contradicted by the patriarchal ideology that woman belongs in the home. The two ideologies of patriarchy and liberalism come into conflict as the idea of woman's inequality contradicts and is contradicted by the image of equal opportunity. (Eisenstein 1981: p. 205)

Thus as more women enter employment, they experience daily the tension between their subordinate role in the sexual hierarchy and the ideology of equal opportunity which extends to women the promise of equality — a promise which has been reinforced by equal opportunities legislation in Britain in the recent past. This tension can be illustrated by quotes taken verbatim from our recent research, (Crompton and Jones 1984) but first I should emphasize that our questionnaire was not designed to explore the topic of gender relationships at the workplace. These comments made by the women we interviewed, therefore, emerged spontaneously in the course of questioning on other issues. 'If you play football and you're in the cricket team, and you're a young man with A levels you're going to get on. I noticed when I first came, the man I was with got all the encouragement (to take the insurance examinations) — it made me even more determined to take them' (insurance clerk). 'They reckon that men and women are equal but we're not'; 'Well, men get priority, they're looked after first . . . The Bank say they're not biased but they are. We're not dim, we can see it around us' (bank clerks).

I would not suggest that the very real resentment expressed by many of the young women we interviewed will have immediate consequences. Three possible responses to the tension I have described may be suggested: Firstly, as Prandy *et al.* (1982) have demonstrated, many of the strategies employed by individuals to resolve tensions in their working lives simply serve to reproduce the existing situation — as when, for example, dissatisfaction with work and promotion prospects is 'resolved' by apathy and retreatism — no *change* occurs. It would be surprising if many — perhaps even the majority — of women did not adopt a similar strategy. Given the pressures on women to accept 'the family' as their most important area of activity, a lack of stimulus and/or opportunity at work may be

countered psychologically by a woman's *own* definition of that role as
'secondary' and the subsequent absence of any response which might
change her situation.

Secondly, working women may hold 'internally inconsistent values
concerning work and family relations' (Costello 1983). That is, they may
hold feminist attitudes about working women's rights — equal pay,
promotion opportunities and so on — at the same time as maintaining
conventional attitudes regarding women's role in the family. Such views
were expressed frequently during our recent research. Young women —
particularly those in their late twenties — were often extremely angry and
articulate regarding their lack of promotion prospects compared to those
of men, but their other comments indicated that they expected nevertheless
to leave employment at the birth of their first child.

Finally, women may seek actively to realize their career potential fully,
either through collective trade-union and/or feminist struggles, or
individually by competing with men, gaining qualifications, an unbroken
employment record and so on. (Both strategies may, of course, be employed
simultaneously). Although the evidence I can produce in the next section is
far from comprehensive, there do seem to be a number of recent indications
that more women *are* adopting this last strategy and taking steps to pursue
a career systematically.

### FEMALE CLERKS

During the course of our recent research, we collected background data on
over 400 female employees working for three large, bureaucratic white-
collar organizations (the classic locus of the 'service class'); in local
government, banking and insurance. No restriction on grade level was
applied when the data was collected, but nevertheless 82 per cent of the
women were on basic clerical grades. The age profile of the sample
reflected the 'two-phase' work profile characteristic of the female labour
force, although, as few part-time employees were included in our research,
older women were relatively less well represented (300 women under 35,
124 over 35 years old). The older women we interviewed[6] most of whom
had returned to employment after rearing a family — were much less likely
to express an interest in promotion than the younger women. For example,
only 29 per cent of older women with a break in employment wished to be
promoted, as compared to 79 per cent of young, unmarried women without
a break in employment. Marriage itself would seem to bring about some
diminution of aspirations, as the proportion of young married women
wanting to be promoted dropped to 65 per cent. (This difference was not,
however, statistically significant.)

The reasons the older women gave for their lack of interest in promotion clearly reflected their domestic roles — 30 per cent said that they were not willing to take on more responsibility — 'With a family and home to run I feel I'm doing enough' — and a further 24 per cent that they were simply 'not interested' in a career. Older women were also less likely than younger women to complain of gender discrimination in respect of promotion. It might seem plausible to argue, therefore, that the level of resentment at the lack of promotion opportunities which we found among the younger women is not particularly significant. Attitudes to work and promotion clearly vary according to the stage reached in the domestic life cycle; and, as the young women begin to have children — and most likely leave work — they may simply 'adapt' to the lack of promotion opportunities available to women as the older women have apparently done (Martin and Roberts 1984). There are a number of other reasons however, which suggest that this interpretation should not be accepted too easily. First, it should be remembered that the two-phase female work profile was not *firmly* established for women until the early 1970s. A woman of 35 who re-entered the labour force at this time (and who would still be working, aged 49), would *first* have gone out to work in the early 1950s. It is most unlikely that such a woman, when she first went out to work, would have had any notion of a career — or even a job — extending much beyond marriage. Her attitudes would have been massively reinforced by the prevailing milieu. For example, in the 1950s, the major clearing banks required their female employees to resign formally on marriage. Young women today, however, are entering the labour force with the *expectation* — if they leave at all — of returning to work after completing a family: 'I'm leaving anyway. But I hope to come back and make section clerk before I retire.'

Secondly, there were, in our sample, marked differences between the younger and older women in respect of formal educational qualifications. Sixty-three per cent of the women aged over 35 possessed no formal academic qualifications whatsoever — in marked contrast to the older men, only 16 per cent of whom had no qualifications. However, only 10 per cent of the younger women were totally unqualified. Post-entry, vocational qualifications (for example banking and insurance diplomas, accountancy qualifications) also demonstrated some interesting trends.

At first sight, the pattern of post-entry qualifications might, on the contrary, appear to reinforce conventional expectations that women do not seek to add to their 'human capital' whilst in employment. Seventy nine per cent of women under 35, as compared to 56 per cent of men in the same age group, had not acquired any formal, vocational qualifications. However, more detailed analysis by age suggested that there had been a recent, and relatively substantial, increase in the rate of acquisition of post-entry qualifications amongst the very youngest age group. Of the 37 people under 25 years old with vocational qualifications, 14 — nearly 40 per cent were women.

Subsequent examination of national figures confirmed these trends. In the first place, girls have been steadily improving their academic qualifications relative to boys. Fewer girls than boys leave school with no formal qualifications whatsoever, and, at the aggregate level, girls' performance in 0 level examinations is rather better than boys'.[7] Girls are also narrowing the A level gap; more girls than boys leave school with at least one A level, and in 1981–2, 9.2 per cent of girls and 10.7 per cent of boys left school with three A level passes (*Statistics of Education 1982*. table C22). These improvements have been reflected in university entrance, between 1970–1 and 1981–2, for example, there was a 14 per cent increase in male university enrolments; the comparable increase for women was 74 per cent.

There has also been a substantial improvement in the extent and level of qualifications gained by women after leaving school. With considerable over-simplication, qualifications gained after leaving school may be classified into two broad categories; (a) 'organizational' — where the qualification is acquired in respect of an organizational career, and is often acquired by part-time or day-release study, for example banking, insurance, etc. and (b) 'occupational' — where the qualification represents a licence to practise and is more usually obtained through full-time study, for example teaching, medicine. Tables 9.1 and 9.2 reveal quite conclusively that there has been a recent and substantial increase in the rate of acquisition of both types of qualification amongst women.[8]

A recent review of male/female earnings differentials has concluded that most of the variation in male and female earnings can be explained in 'human capital' terms — that is, the labour offered on the market by women is simply less skilled, qualified or experienced. Thus 'If all . . . discrimination were to be removed overnight the improvement in average female earnings would be substantial, but the average would still be likely to remain around 80 per cent of male earnings' (Chiplin and Sloane 1982: p. 122). I would certainly not accept uncritically the validity of 'human capital' arguments in respect of gender differentials, but they provide a useful framework through which questions may be raised concerning male *and* female careers (Breughel 1978; Crompton and Jones 1984; Siltanen 1981). In particular, if an increasing proportion of younger women take systematic steps to augment their 'human capital', will this have a substantial impact on gender differentials in the future? To repeat the same point with a slightly different emphasis, will the increasing proportion of young women gaining formal qualifications be reflected in increasing rates of promotion amongst women?

Chiplin and Sloane conclude: 'If women are to approach the earnings and occupational levels of men, it is necessary for a complete reappraisal of social attitudes to take place' (p. 132). This statement may be accepted as broadly correct if a situation is envisaged where *all* women compete on

**Table 9.1  Women as a percentage of total passes in examinations of the Institute of Bankers (IOB), the Chartered Insurance Institute (FCII), and the Chartered Building Societies Institute (CBSI)**

|        | IOB  | FCII | CBSI |
|--------|------|------|------|
| 1970   | 1.9  | 0.4  | 0    |
| 1975   | 4.2  | 3.5  | 1    |
| 1980   | 11.6 | 11.8 | 7.9  |
| 1981   | 12.2 | 17.1 | 12.7 |
| 1982   | 19.2 | 16.1 | 14.0 |
| 1983   | 20.6 | 18.3 | 14.2 |

*Note:*  The data is derived from the examination pass lists of the awarding bodies, which print forenames and surnames in full. The IOB data refers to the major clearing banks only, the CII and CBSI data to all passes.

**Table 9.2  University first-year enrolments: selected subjects (percentages)**

|                        | 1970  | 1978  | 1983  |
|------------------------|-------|-------|-------|
| Medicine               | 29    | 38    | 45    |
| (Total numbers)        | 2,870 | 3,646 | 3,770 |
| Dentistry              | 27    | 30    | 42    |
| (Total numbers)        | 772   | 922   | 885   |
| Business management    | 10    | 27    | 37    |
| (Total numbers)        | 578   | 1,123 | 1,126 |
| Accountancy            | 8     | 24    | 30    |
| (Total numbers)        | 319   | 792   | 777   |
| Law                    | 24    | 39    | 46    |
| (Total numbers)        | 2,240 | 3,255 | 3,012 |

*Source: UCCA Annual Reports.*

equal terms with *all* men. Changes falling far short of 'a complete reappraisal of social attitudes' however, may have a substantial interim effect. For example, we estimate on the basis of our research data that if only 10 per cent of the young female clerks we studied eventually achieved some form of promotion, then *male* promotion opportunities would be cut by a third.

Qualifications alone of course, provide no sure guarantee of career success and indeed there is substantial evidence available that, even when qualified, women are less successful than their male counterparts — this evidence conflicts clearly with 'human capital' arguments (Benenson 1984; Chisholm and Woodward 1980; Crow 1981). Our research demonstrated that a willingness to be geographically mobile, and long, unbroken work experience, were also extremely important factors affecting promotion. To these must be added the essentially unquantifiable factors such as 'fitting in with the company' and, as our research demonstrates, 'fitting in' may be subtly — or not so subtly — biased towards male activities (Crompton and Jones 1984: ch. 4, 5). Qualified women who are unable to be geographically mobile, or who leave work in order to rear a family, will still find their promotion prospects curtailed. It would not be sensible, therefore, to predict that the increase in qualified young women will be reflected, in exact proportion, in the numbers eventually achieving 'service-class' positions, but nevertheless, the increase has been so substantial that it would be surprising if it has no impact.

DISCUSSION

Goldthorpe argues that the 'service class' which 'emerges from the relevant data' is 'far from being threatened with any kind of decomposition, is rather at one and the same time expanding *and* consolidating' (1982: p. 178). What significance, therefore, might the evidence I have reviewed in this paper have for this prediction? Given the time taken for careers to develop and the fact that the increase in the proportion of suitably qualified women appears to be a relatively recent phenomenon, it may be ten years before any changes are revealed by the raw data, but the following suggestions may be made with regard to possible future developments. First, let us assume that the increase in qualifications amongst young women *will* be reflected in increased levels of promotion.

If more women achieve promotion, fewer men will be promoted — unless, of course, the number of 'service-class' positions increases at the same rate as the proportion of potential 'service-class' women available to take them up. This possibility, however, cannot be predicted confidently and at the moment appears positively unlikely. Our empirical research suggests that the combined impact of technological change and economic recession may actually be reducing the number of such positions (Crompton and Jones 1984). Within the 'service class', it may well prove to be the case that women will predominate in the middle and lower ranges and men will continue to occupy the most senior positions. This possibility does not, however, invalidate the major thrust of my argument. Using Goldthorpe's classification, the size of the 'cadet' or 'subaltern' group is greater than that of 'service class' proper and our evidence suggests that only a minority of *men* embarking on white-collar careers reach these higher levels (ibid. p. 99). If the positions in which a substantial proportion of men work out their 'service-class' careers are filled by women, then my original argument still holds. Thus the possibility must be raised that an increasing proportion (men and women) of qualified 'service-class' aspirants will fail to achieve their aims. Such a situation would clearly threaten the supposed 'trust' relationship *vis-à-vis* the employer. Indeed, it may reasonably be suggested that promotion difficulties might lead to an increase in collective action amongst the 'service class'.

Secondly, if the increase in the proportion of young women gaining qualifications is reflected in promotion, then the likelihood of such women remaining in the labour force, or only withdrawing for a very short period, will be further enhanced. For example, Daniel's survey of the take-up of maternity-leave provision revealed that 'one-third of qualified non-manual women returned to work compared with 14 per cent of more junior non-manual women. Twenty-six per cent of the higher grades remained with the same employer compared with only six per cent of the lower grade', and he concludes that 'the chief influence upon rates of return to work were the degree of involvement and investment in work' (Daniel 1981: pp. 76–7).

Thirdly, my discussion so far has focused on the possibility that women might displace men from service-class occupations. However, I have argued that women's contribution to the service class occurs not only in the public sphere, but also originates in the domestic realm through women's labour in the home and their incorporation into men's careers. There can be little doubt that the majority of women, even when they work, nevertheless still assume the major share of domestic responsibilities. In our research, for example, 18 per cent of women interviewed — all with full-time jobs — approved of 'flexitime' because it helped them to fit their work around the demands of domesticity, while only 7 per cent of the men made this point. Thus many women work what is effectively a 'double day' (Eisenstein 1981; see also Finch 1983; and Edgell 1980). Women who work may, by intensifying their efforts, still be able to provide the 'labour of reproduction' for service-class men; it may be more difficult however, for them to be 'incorporated' into their husbands' work via the 'two-person career'.

There is however, a further dimension to many 'service-class' careers which simply cannot be over-emphasized in the context of this discussion. This is the need to be geographically mobile — an explicit requirement in some organizations such as banking, but also so common as to be counted a necessity for many individuals pursuing 'occupational' career strategies. The need for mobility required of 'spiralists' is not, in contrast, particularly important for 'burgesses' (Watson 1964). Although class endogamy is far from total, women with the kinds of qualifications under discussion in this chapter are likely to marry aspiring (or arrived) service-class husbands. Such husbands — and the women themselves — may be either 'burgesses' or 'spiralists'. Of the four possible combinations: burgess/burgess, spiralist/spiralist, spiralist/burgess, burgess/spiralist, in only one — the burgess/burgess combination — is it possible for both partners to be unaffected by geographic mobility requirements. Indeed, the burgess/

burgess combination may be beneficial to both partners who may take advantage of each other's professional contacts, etc. Historically however, there can be little doubt that many middle-class wives' jobs and careers have been sacrificed to the optimal career strategy of the male — 'dual career' families prove, on closer inspection, to be households where the man has a 'career' and the wife has a 'job' (Handy 1978). If the wife's career/income however, is seen as sufficiently important/lucrative, then increasing numbers of middle-class couples may 'choose' to sacrifice the long-term objectives of one partner to the medium-term objectives of both — that is, decide *not* to be occupationally mobile. Those service-class men (and women) with working wives (and husbands) will therefore, be handicapped in their careers compared to those with non-working partners. The interesting possibility therefore arises that the 'service class' may be internally differentiated according to the domestic arrangements prevailing in individual service-class households. Bailyn has already noted that 'It is unlikely . . . that any of the highest occupational position will soon be held by an accomodative person' where 'accommodation' is defined as 'the degree to which work demands are fitted into family requirements' (ibid. p. 159). Thus those in the most senior positions might, as compared to those in junior and middle-ranking positions, be drawn increasingly from single (or 'two-person') career households. (Some dual-career households might choose to combine childlessness with a split-site marriage, but they are likely to be a minority).

If therefore, an increasing proportion of women begin to achieve a measure of career success, then it could have a considerable impact on the future development of the service class. I have made my argument without even raising the further question as to the more general impact that an increasing number of women in higher-level positions might have on attitudes to priorities, power and authority in society as a whole. Women who have currently 'made it' to the top have frequently done so as surrogate men, relatively isolated from other women. More women in positions of authority — even only middle-ranking positions — might have very different consequences.

The possibility must be raised however, that women, despite gaining more in the way of formal qualifications, will still be confined in the lowest grades of white-collar employment. Two consequences can be suggested. First, if qualified women fail to gain suitable rewards then it is likely that resentment will be expressed as a feminist struggle against patriarchal structures. Such educated women will have considerable resources for organization and mobilization, which is likely to be organized on a cross-class basis (Abercrombie and Urry 1983: p. 139). This scenario may be contrasted briefly with that of the first possibility described above; that is, an increasing pressure on positions to be promoted to. Declining mobility chances for men *and* women in the white-collar field may be expected to result in more active and militant *collective* organization, whereas if only women are excluded, wholly or partially, conflict will be manifest along gender divisions. Secondly, there will be a serious risk that the legitimacy of 'credentialism' itself will be called into question. Although recent analyses of the 'service class' by Goldthorpe, Abercrombie and Urry, differ in a number of important respects, they are united in their emphasis on the ever-growing significance of credentials to service-class formation (Goldthorpe 1982: p. 181; Abercrombie and Urry 1983: p. 150). Indeed, Abercrombie and Urry argue that the emergence of the service class itself 'is made to seem legitimate precisely because many such places are acquired as a consequence of achieved educational credentials' (p. 150). Were a significant minority of women to acquire such qualifications, but not the occupational places commonly associated with them, then it is difficult to see how the ideological functions of 'credentialism' could be sustained.

### CONCLUSIONS

I would accept the feminist criticism that class theory in the Marx/Weber tradition was developed initially with respect to a range of activities associated with production and the market in the male-dominated, public sphere. Thus, from the very first, such theories lacked the concepts to accommodate work and other activities taking place in the private, or domestic sphere. Classical theory may be judged as being seriously incomplete in this respect, but in my opinion, it would not be particularly useful to reject it out of hand because of this failing. However, perhaps because of this original theoretical weakness — compounded, perhaps, by the male-dominated nature of sociology as a discipline (Stacey 1981) — researchers have tended to exclude women from both empirical investigation and theoretical consideration even when they have worked in the public realm.

The resulting gaps in our knowledge and understanding of women's role in the class and occupational structure are too obvious to bear further repetition. In this chapter, however, I have emphasized further that our understanding of *men's* work cannot be grasped adequately unless women's contribution in both the public and the private spheres is also taken into account. Work carried out within both is essential to the reproduction of society as a whole. Although it has not been a major topic of this chapter, it is obvious that the relationship of interdependence between the public and private spheres is not fixed and immutable, but in continual flux. I would argue that class analysis should seek to systematically acquire both an understanding of the interdependence of these two spheres of social life and a sensitivity to the changing nature of the relationship between them.

I have attempted to make my case via the strategy of a 'worked example'

— i.e. the implications that a systematic consideration of the gender division of labour might have for the currently revived theoretical debate concerning the 'service class'. At the time of writing, the 'service class' is populated overwhelmingly by males. I have argued that this gender imbalance is by no means accidental, but is a direct consequence of gender-assigned roles in our society in both the 'private' and 'public' spheres. Middle-class women's work in the family and marriage both liberates the husband/father to pursue a career and often makes a direct contribution to that career.

This arrangement may appear convenient — Finch for example, points out that 'Being married to the job makes perfect sense for most wives' (1983: p. 168). It is not, however, necessarily stable or without inbuilt tensions. In particular, as Eisenstein has argued, the ideology of bourgeois liberalism which proclaims individual equality in the public sphere is contradicted daily for women, by their experiences within it. These conflicts must become the more acute once gender discrimination has been legally abolished. It would seem that an increasing minority of young women are attempting to resolve such conflicts by acquiring 'service-class' qualifications which, in theory at any rate, should place them on an equal competitive footing with men. Were increasing numbers of women to begin to undertake — even at a relatively modest level — 'service-class' careers, then this could have a very substantial impact on the internal cohesion of the service class.

In my concluding remarks, I would wish to make it quite explicit that I am in no way complacent with regard to the position of women in British society. Given the sheer magnitude of the difficulties faced by women, it is not surprising that much current feminist research and theorizing should have been devoted to the exposition and explanation of the nature of gender oppression. Nevertheless, I feel that it is also important to recognize that liberal feminism has not been without an impact and has indeed made gains which perhaps only now are beginning to have an effect.

Class theorists, to the extent that they have acknowledged the relevance of gender, seem to have been overwhelmed by the size of the task at hand. Allen has recently argued that 'those who endeavour to analyse women's position in the class structure enter a workshop which is lamentably ill-equipped for the task. There are few tools but, more important, little recognition that the task requires even burnished tools let alone freshly fashioned ones' (Allen 1982). Other chapters in this volume will contribute to the fashioning of 'new tools'; my major objective has been to argue that substantial advances in our understanding of this problem might also be achieved by making better use of those which are already available.

# 10

# Similarities of Life-style and the Occupations of Women

## Ken Prandy

On the face of it the question of gender and occupational classifications is not one to quicken the pulse with the prospect of intellectual stimulation. Rather, the topic would appear to belong to that class of worthy activities which are necessary if one is to deal with data but which are somewhat removed from the really important issues of theoretical analysis. To use a provocative analogy, these activities are often seen as a form of 'good housekeeping' — useful, but essentially supportive of real work.

However, just as the substance of the analogy has been misconceived, so also is this view of classification. It reflects a positivist distinction between objects of enquiry and theoretical analysis in which the former are assumed to be relatively unproblematic. In contrast, this chapter attempts to show that a thorough-going inquiry into the nature of 'objects' of analysis involves central theoretical issues, and conversely that theoretical analysis involves a full understanding of objects. The two aspects cannot be distinguished, and the furtherance of explanation and understanding concerns both 'objects' and 'relations' between them.

Classification is both a simple form of measurement and the basis for more complex forms. At its simplest it is a procedure for dividing up a set of 'objects' in such a way that groups within the set are both homogeneous and distinguished from all other groups. Clearly this requires differentiation that is both consistent and, in some sense, useful. 'Common sense' and its associated language often provides an early basis, as in, say, the distinction between trees and flowers, or between clerks and personnel managers. These categories however, are refined and changed in the development of the classification, with consistency and usefulness again playing a central part. This development proceeds together with empirical investigation and theoretical understanding — a process clearly visible in the natural sciences but somewhat veiled in the case of social scientific categories such as occupations.

The criteria of similarity and difference for one purpose are not necessarily the same as those for other purposes. Occupational classification at its simplest level may be useful for descriptive statements of the different forms of employment in different regions, but of only limited relevance for, say, the distribution of income or experience of other areas of inequality. Decisions about differentiation are made in the light of theoretical considerations. The process suggests the existence of a particular structure of relationships among the objects, at which point the classification takes the form of a more complex form of measurement.

Use of the term 'measurement' immediately summons up in most minds the idea of quantity, of there being more or less of something. This is undoubtedly its more important association, but it is necessary to emphasize that order, which is what is involved in quantity, is only one kind of structure of relationships and that there may be other kinds suggested by one's theory. Bearing this in mind also helps in our understanding of quantity, since the usual tendency here is to begin with a reified view of an abstract concept and to see measurement as a problem of finding the appropriate instrument to gauge, with reliability and *validity*, what is actually there. Objects, individuals, or whatever, are seen as possessing intrinsic qualities which the correct measuring device will be able to record. In contrast, a more satisfactory approach is to see that it is the structure of order among objects which defines a quantity. On this view objects and relations are created and change together and analysis of the action which creates relations among objects is crucial.

The development of occupational classification in the direction of measurement has taken two partially related forms. One is the quantity approach, where occupations have been seen as possessing a given amount of prestige, standing or something similar which has to be measured by expert judges or a sample of the population at large. The other is the attempt to tie in occupational classification with theories of social class. Since the idea of status has usually been involved in some form in this attempt, there is a frequent tendency for the two forms of development to converge. This is true, for example, of the UK Registrar-General's social classes, which were originally seen as groupings of occupations sharing a similar social position and life-style, with strong hierarchical overtones. More recently this has been modified to groupings of occupations of similar standing and, now, to those of similar levels of skill (Leete and Fox 1977). The groupings, though, remain much the same.

The Registrar-General's and similar social classes do suggest a hierarchical structure of order. However we should bear in mind that the Marxist tradition presents an alternative account of classes where there are certainly relations between classes, but not of an ordered kind. Wright's (1978) class schema provides a recent example, while the Hope-Goldthorpe social classes (Goldthorpe and Hope 1974; Goldthorpe et al. 1980) are a case of an attempt to merge both traditions, with property ownership cross-cutting hierarchy.

The important difference in the social class tradition as against the quantity approach is of course the idea that occupations, or the occupational/employment status combination, are not the primary units of analysis but can be grouped together into broader homogeneous units. Marxists and non-Marxists alike tend to see economic relations as the real basis of class, locating social classes in what is seen as the 'economic' sphere, primarily the ownership of productive property and the possession of 'market power' in the form of skills and qualifications. At the same time almost all approaches want to recognize the social nature of classes and the way in which they are maintained and created through, for example, mobility and other forms of social closure. Such recognition is necessary because 'classes', as defined by economic relations, do not coincide with perceived actual differentiations of the population. The attempt to deal with this problem is clear in the work of Parkin (1979) and Giddens (1981); amongst Marxists it tends to take the form of a debate (e.g. Wright, 1978; 1979; Carchedi 1977; Poulantzas 1973).

Regarding both the 'economic' and the 'social' aspects, there is an assumption — for it is little more than this — that the processes of differentiation lead to homogeneous, integrated class groupings. However, the opposition of differentiation on the one hand and integration on the other necessarily leads to problems. Thus the integrity of 'social' groupings may be threatened by internal inequalities created by differences in market capacity. Similarly, while traditional theories of class differentiate the population on grounds of opposition, or at least competition, no such divisions are required by most theories of 'social' differentiation. For example, men and women may tend to marry those who are in some sense socially similar to themselves, without this involving clear breaks which could be identified as the boundaries between classes. Certainly 'class' has been used in many studies and relationships shown between it and other aspects of social life, but such studies have demonstrated no more than a more or less hierarchical ordering of the 'class' categories. They have not demonstrated the integrity and validity of particular class schemes — that is, that the groupings used are both internally homogeneous and clearly differentiated one from another. The fact that all current theories of class allow for variations which cross 'class' boundaries or make divisions within them surely necessitates a critical approach to the question of their constitution which is actually prevented by accepting their facticity.

In fact we have very little evidence for the homogeneity of, say, the

Registrar-General's social classes. We may recognize the skill of an engine driver, but what determines that a train guard is at the same level, as is the person issuing the tickets (albeit non-manual and therefore superior); while bus conductors, packers and postmen are partly skilled; messengers, stevedores and porters unskilled? Some may see these as reasonable distinctions, others may wish to replace them with preferred schemes of their own, but the point remains that by jumping to a limited number of classes — to an extent constituted arbitrarily — we lose the chance of determining what relations exist within such classes and between more closely defined occupational groups.

However this is not the only problem with the use of class schemes, although it is involved in the others. If classes are to be used as basic units then as I suggested earlier, it is important to examine relationships between the classes in order to determine the form of the structure which links them. Theories which suggest a structure on only the vaguest of empirical material obviously require more rigorous examination, the discipline of which will point up their weaknesses. This is the case when one looks at the two most important instances (social mobility and patterns of marriage) where an attempt has been made to look at the relations between classes, even though that is not necessarily the way in which the task has been conceived. Studies of social mobility have tended to be large-scale prestigious projects, while studies of intermarriage have been considerably less so. Thus development has proceeded rather further in the former case than in the latter, but the parallel between them is very close. In particular, both are important elements in any study of an issue which is central to class analysis, that of social closure. However, as I have suggested, because they both try to deal with relations between classes, both bring out the difficulties and problems in the underlying conceptualizations which can only be solved by moving beyond them. It is not that in either case the findings are worthless or even that their implications may be ignored. It is simply that the conceptualizations set a limit to and distort our understanding — a point that will become clearer in the discussion of marriage patterns.

CLASS CATEGORIES AND SOCIAL HOMOGENEITY

Table 10.1 is typical of the kind that is produced when looking at the relation between husbands' and wives' occupations. It shows the cross-tabulation of the wife's social class at marriage (as defined by the Registrar-General and obviously only for those in employment) with that of the husband's social class as determined by his job at the time of our interview. The different bases for occupation and the fact that this is not a random national sample but one designed for our own purposes, make this an atypical table as regards the marginal distributions, but the points to be made are very little affected by that.

Without at present questioning the Registrar-General's scheme, what kind of information can be gleaned from this table? Formally it is identical to a standard social mobility table, and traditionally mobility analysis has concentrated on the main diagonal — inheritance — or, in this case, homogamous marriage. Given the concern with the social aspects of class the main diagonal was seen to be crucial because there could be found social stability or rigidity. In a sense this rigidity was seen as defining the social, as distinct from or additional to the economic, aspects of class. Looked at in this way the table gives only limited support for the idea of social rigidity as regards marriage, since only 28 per cent of marriages are made up of people from the same class. However, rigidity is not completely absent because this figure is 53 per cent higher than one would expect by chance.

It is not uncommon to deduce from tables such as these that women tend to be 'upwardly mobile' through marriage — for example, Leete and Fox (1977: note to table 5) refer to 'women marrying above their social class'. Thus there is a direct link with the analysis of social mobility. Here, though, analysts fairly soon came to see the importance of the marginal distributions — the fact that the structure of employment, and therefore occupations and classes, changed between one generation and the next. Given that the economic definition of classes was not questioned seriously, attempts were made to look at the social aspects in terms of distinctions such as that between structural and exchange mobility. The former was seen as a necessary consequence of economic processes, the latter as social. Looking at the very different marginal distributions in table 10.1 it

**Table 10.1  Social class of husbands and wives**

| Husband | | I | II | III N-M | III M | IV | V | Total |
|---|---|---|---|---|---|---|---|---|
| Wife | I | 48 | 28 | 2 | 6 | 3 | 0 | 87 |
| | II | 261 | 328 | 71 | 92 | 62 | 7 | 821 |
| | III N-M | 203 | 536 | 263 | 457 | 170 | 25 | 1654 |
| | III M | 16 | 120 | 46 | 212 | 150 | 25 | 569 |
| | IV | 20 | 113 | 54 | 243 | 219 | 34 | 683 |
| | V | 1 | 12 | 4 | 15 | 15 | 6 | 53 |
| | Total | 549 | 1137 | 440 | 1025 | 619 | 97 | 3867 |

*Notes*:
Gamma = 0.49     Somers' D = 0.38
*Source:* General sample — see Stewart *et al.*, 1980

would appear that something similar is called for here. For the husband-seeking females in a given class there may be a severe shortage or an excess of males in the same class, and similarly for the wife-seeking males. Taking the figures from the 1971 British Census as an illustration, and ignoring age, there are five times as many men in Class I as there are women, and in Class III M four times as many. On the other hand, women in Class III N-M outnumber men by more than three to one. In fact, given the national distributions the maximum possible share of class-homogamous marriages is only 65 per cent. In table 10.1 the comparable figure is 67 per cent, which makes the earlier 28 per cent look rather more impressive. If one adds to the main diagonal those adjacent cells from which there is, as it were, forced or necessary intermarriage caused by relative surpluses and shortages, this leaves only 32 per cent of marriages not accounted for by either social rigidity or structural necessity.

In fact the structural/exchange distinction has led to theoretical and methodological difficulties (Goldthorpe et al. 1980: p. 74), which is one reason why the idea of relative chances and odds ratios has been introduced in an attempt to provide a satisfactory alternative. For each pair of classes we can calculate the likelihood that a person in one class will have a spouse in that class rather than another. For example a wife in Class I is $48/28 = 1.7$ more likely to have a husband in Class I rather than in Class II, while a wife in Class II is $261/328 = 0.80$ less likely. The ratio of these two odds $(1.7/0.80 = 2.15$ — see top left hand cell, Table 10.2) tells us how much more likely a Class I wife is to have a Class I rather than a Class II husband, than is a Class II wife. By a different arithmetical route the same ratio is obtained by starting with husbands, so it is symmetric. The matrix of all such odds ratios is shown in table 10.2. It may be seen, from the fact that the ratios are close to one, that the manual groups are not very sharply divided. (Classes III M and IV being particularly close). The non-manual groups are more clearly differentiated. Class I in particular shows a high degree of relative within-class marriage.

The use of odds ratios, however, is a neat way of side-stepping issues to avoid confronting them head-on. There is a conceptual symmetry between the rows and columns of a table showing father's class by son's class or husband's class by that of his wife which ought to force one to think through the meaning of class, to look for evidence of stability and structure where there appears to be change and differentiation. Symmetry of that sort is not necessary with odds ratios because the rows and columns do not need to be the same kind of objects. For example, a similar table could have been produced if the columns of the original had been which daily paper was read (assuming that six were specified). The odds ratios enable us to make comparisons among the wives' classes, or conversely among those of the husbands, but not to compare wives' and husbands' classes directly. That is, at one and the same time, a single concept is being used

**Table 10.2   Odds ratios of intermarriage between social classes**

| Class | II | III N-M | III M | IV | V |
|---|---|---|---|---|---|
| I | 2.15 | 31.09 | 106.00 | 175.20 | — * |
| II | | 2.27 | 6.30 | 10.25 | 23.43 |
| III N-M | | | 2.65 | 6.27 | 15.78 |
| III M | | | | 1.27 | 3.39 |
| IV | | | | | 2.58 |

*Note*:
\* Probably very large — one of the cells involved was zero.

for both husbands (or fathers) and wives (or sons), but the two are treated as separate entities. The use of the single concept reflects the purposes of the analyses — to examine the extent of social rigidity — but the separation contradicts this. Surely it would be more consistent in both cases to look for structured patterns indicating the existence of social similarity?

Before pursuing that idea however, two more tables can be introduced to illustrate the problems that have arisen in incorporating gender into occupational classifications of a theoretically structured kind — in the present case, class categories. Class is not only a matter of social closure it is also a strong influence on other forms of social behaviour. Significant among these is political action, and we have chosen to use as illustration data from the 1979 British General Election study (Crewe *et al.* 1981; cf. also Britten and Heath 1983). All of the arguments made above could have been based equally well on similar tables derived from this data set. However, the relationship between wives' and husbands' classes is weaker, as it is also with correlations based on Hope-Goldthorpe scale scores, which fall from 0.38 in our data to 0.33 in this one. The greater consistency between wives' jobs at marriage and husbands' present jobs, compared with husbands' and wives' current jobs is a point to bear in mind when we return to the comparison with social mobility.

In order to keep the numbers high we shall use not actual voting but political party identification, including also those who needed to be prompted before committing themselves to a general preference one way or another. For simplicity Labour Party supporters have been taken against supporters of all other parties, and this ratio, for various groupings, is shown in table 10.3. The first column shows the figures for all females, classified according to their own social class (where they were employed), the third those for all males. The relationship between social class and Labour identification is shown to be much the same in both cases, although it is slightly stronger for men than for women. The other two columns show the figures for wives and husbands, classified not according to their own,

**Table 10.3   Ratio of those identifying with the Labour Party to the
remainder, by social class**

|          | Own class: Female | Spouses' class: Wife | Own class: Male | Spouses' class: Husband |
|----------|-------------------|----------------------|-----------------|-------------------------|
| I        | 0.38              | 0.32                 | 0.33            | 1.50                    |
| II       | 0.42              | 0.25                 | 0.32            | 0.32                    |
| III N-M  | 0.41              | 0.33                 | 0.47            | 0.59                    |
| III M    | 1.08              | 1.16                 | 1.13            | 1.00                    |
| IV       | 1.16              | 0.84                 | 1.16            | 1.10                    |
| V        | 1.70              | 3.42                 | 1.50            | 0.88                    |
| Number   | 519               | 723                  | 807             | 395                     |
| Somers' D | 0.17             | 0.21                 | 0.19            | 0.14                    |

but to their spouse's, social class. From these it is clear that while the
husband's party identification is not very strongly affected by his wife's
social class, the wife's identification is influenced by the husband's class. In
fact this is actually the strongest relationship of the four.

One response to a result of this kind is to conclude that it demonstrates
the standard argument that the family has to be taken as a single unit of
stratification, with its position in the class structure indicated by the
occupation of the head of the household, normally the husband (Goldthorpe
1983). The unsatisfactory nature of this response is illustrated clearly by
table 10.4. For simplicity, and little if any loss of information, the classes
have been dichotomized into manual and non-manual, giving four possible
combinations. Within each of these is shown the percentage of Labour
support among male and female respondents in a household of that kind.
(Note that these are separate respondents, not husband-and-wife couples.)
In homogeneous households male and female support is very similar, but in
mixed households not only do males and females differ, they both fall
somewhere between the extremes marked by the homogeneous cases.
Thus the class position of the spouse as well as that of the respondent has
an influence on his or her party identification.

The doubts raised earlier with reference to mobility and marriage patterns
should by this point have been strengthened. Social classes, as they have
been considered here, are groupings of occupations on the basis of a
criterion of internal homogeneity. The source of this homogeneity is seen
to lie in the realm of the economic, with classes exhibiting a similarity of
economic experience. In the case of political party identification however,
we can see that behaviour cannot simply be read off from class position as
determined by economic location. The wife's behaviour appears to be

**Table 10.4 Percentage identifying with the Labour Party by household composition**

| Household composition: | | | |
| --- | --- | --- | --- |
| *Wife* | *Husband* | *Female* | *Male* |
| N-M | N-M | 23.5 | 23.8 |
| M | N-M | 27.3 | 36.8 |
| N-M | M | 26.2 | 46.3 |
| M | M | 60.7 | 56.6 |

*Note:*
N-M = Non-manual
M = Manual

predicted best by her husband's social class, while at the same time the class of each spouse, where different, also affects the actions of the other.

Thus the idea of the internal homogeneity of these class groupings seems very doubtful. Nor is there likely to be a solution in devising some different class scheme as an alternative, at least as long as the commitment to the purely economic determination of class is maintained. Rather, what is needed is a representation of what we can see to be happening, but which our current class schemes actually prevent us from understanding properly.

Although there are likely to be deviations from the normal position, which our methods and analyses must allow for, it is also clear that husbands and wives share many general aspects of social experience. Even allowing for different positions within the household, there is much in common, including most of the more significant aspects of both of their lives. Once this point is recognized then the absurdity of the problem of intermarriage that we considered earlier soon presents itself. If class boundaries are formed to include shared common life-styles then how can husbands and wives be in different social classes? There is good evidence, for example from other chapters in this volume, that the occupations available to and pursued by women (and hence also their class positions) reflect, in part at least, relations within the household. Despite this, dependence is maintained upon social-class categories which limit the possibility of marriage between those of similar social experience. Surely, then, there is something wrong with the theoretical basis for those categories?

SOCIAL HOMOGENEITY AND OCCUPATIONAL CLASSIFICATION

Working with these categories indicates that there is a high degree of structuring of social relationships, taking marriage as an example. They are not worthless, but they are flawed and need to be superseded. My colleagues and I have argued previously (Stewart *et al.* 1980) that we should look for units of stratification that are homogeneous in terms of life-style and social experience and which cut across occupation and economically-based class divisions. In the case of social mobility, rather than seeing individuals as moving between positions in a fixed structure, crossing and re-crossing class boundaries as they change occupations, we need to look at occupations and incumbents together. It is not a matter of one's position at a given time, but of that position in relation to past and anticipated future experience. Thus, typical patterns of occupational movement represent not change, but stability. The apparent phenomenon of counter-mobility — of sons moving down from their father's class position and then working their way back up — is no more than a typical form of occupational reproduction for which the term 'mobility' is quite inappropriate. We have suggested that apparently different occupations, clerk and manager for example, may often be part of a single, typical career trajectory, and that it is such trajectories which constitute the units within which similar life-styles, allowing for life-cycle position, may be found. Conversely, ostensibly similar occupations may be held by individuals at different stages in their working life, whose total actual and anticipated life-experiences may well differ considerably.

We believe, on the basis of the earlier arguments, that we need to look for similar regularities of experience and structured patterns of social interaction in the case of households. The only way of finding these is to go back to fine occupational groupings and to build up from these. The regularities and patterns will only emerge at their clearest if we start at a very detailed level. Analysis may show that some distinctions are unnecessary and that sub groups distinguished appear to be part of a larger homogeneous group, but it is always more fruitful to combine groups on the basis of clear evidence that they are equivalent in some relevant aspect, than to begin with larger groups within which all potential information on diversity is lost.

However, occupation alone is not a sufficient basis for distinguishing the primary units of analysis; one also needs to take into account the characteristics of incumbents of occupational positions. This requires us to distinguish typical incumbents and to consider incumbent/occupation groups as the units. While in some cases this is difficult it is relatively uncomplicated in the case of gender, and we can easily distinguish male and female incumbents of occupations. In practice this might be achieved simply by considering sufficiently detailed sub groups, since there is usually a clear difference between the actual tasks typically performed by male and female workers, except that information in such detail is difficult to obtain from respondents. Elsewhere, even though there may be a formal similarity in terms of jobs performed, there is typically a difference in the way in which the occupation fits into an overall career pattern. So, for example, male bank clerks are seen as being on the bottom rung of a promotion ladder which will lead through supervisory positions, perhaps to bank manager. The same ladder may in principle exist for women, but in practice is climbed by them much less frequently — or even seen to exist. In professional jobs such as teaching it is again more likely that men will expect to, will be expected to, and will actually be promoted into senior positions.

Of course there are women following lucrative careers, as there are men in marginal occupations, and it is likely that if we could establish the bases of social expectations more accurately then we could abandon 'gender' as the direct basis for distinction (Siltanen, in chapter 8 in this volume, is particularly instructive in this respect). For the present however, it does serve as a valuable indicator. Our starting units, then, are occupations distinguished by the gender of incumbents and our purpose must be to discover the relations among them. In our earlier analysis of occupations held by males, the distributions of the occupations of respondents' friends were used to create a matrix of dissimilarity indices, which were taken as indicating distances between respondents' occupational groups. (Similarly we also obtained distances between the occupational groups of friends.) Friendship choices, aggregated in this way, served as the relation between units which could be used to determine the nature of the structure within which they were located and their relative placements within it. In that case we found that the structure had one overwhelming dimension, so that a scale, and the scores of occupations on it, could be established (for more details see Stewart *et al.* 1980: pp. 36—9).

Ideally, in introducing gender it would be desirable to start again with the friendship choices of women, but the only data set where we have such information is really too small (166 female respondents) to be adequate for that purpose. There would also be a problem, if one considered only friendships between women, of how to relate together scales of jobs with female and with male incumbents. This is overcome if we combine men and women into a single analysis, but treating females (or males) in a particular occupational category as if they were, in effect, a separate 'occupation'. The emphasis is still on similarities of life-style as indicated by levels of social interaction, but in introducing female incumbents of occupations we rely less on friendship choice as an indicator than on marriage. The analysis is performed using all data sets on which we have friendship information, i.e. the Peterborough survey (Blackburn and Mann 1979), the 'white-collar' survey (Prandy et al. 1982), the 'general' survey (Stewart et al., 1980), and the most recent, smaller survey referred to earlier, which also includes 215 male respondents. This last is the only source of information on friendships among women, or on male friends chosen by women (it also has information on the occupations of the spouses of friends). For the most part, therefore, information on social interaction between the sexes is on female friends chosen by men (although gender was not recorded explicitly in all cases) and, predominantly, on wives' occupations (at marriage, for the most part, since the largest source is the 'general' survey).

Our earlier work has established that there is a unidimensional scale of occupations, or rather of similarities of life-style as indicated by occupation. Given this, it is acceptable to adopt a simpler method for the new, extended analysis. On the basis of the same assumption, that individuals interact on the basis of social equality with those of similar life-style, we would argue that a better estimate of the score for each occupational group can be obtained by calculating the mean score of all those with whom its members interact. The extent of improvement will be indicated by the increase in correlation between members of an interacting pair (friends or spouses). The new set of scores can in turn be used to calculate new estimates and the process repeated until no additional improvement is obtained.

Another aspect of the new analysis is the use of more refined occupational categories. The Office of Population Censuses and Surveys (OPCS) schemes have been criticized for applying primarily to men and for not dealing satisfactorily with women's occupations, but in our view there is room for improvement in current classification schemes regardless of the gender of incumbents. This applies to the UK Registrar-General's 1980 Classification of Occupations almost as much as the 1970 version that our data are coded to. It applies less to CODOT (Classification of Occupations and Directory of Occupational Titles), but this tends to make distinctions that are too fine for most purposes. Whether these schemes are even worse for classifying female occupations is in our view doubtful, and it seems more likely that the relative homogeneity of certain occupational groups overwhelmingly held by women is real. Even CODOT only manages to distinguish seven clear subgroups within the 'shorthand, typewriting and related secretarial' group.

Nevertheless there do seem to us to be good grounds for dividing up many of the Registrar-General's OUGs (Occupation Unit Groups). At any point one has to beware of reifying groupings; the process of theoretical development is one in which entities are treated as if they were real, but with the possibility of their dissolution and replacement by other entities always in mind. The point has already been argued in relation to classes, but it applies equally at the level of detailed occupational categories. Indeed, it is doubtful if the two can be separated, and at both levels one needs a theoretical criterion — an empirically testable one — to serve as a basis for division and combination. While it is not the only basis, we do believe that our choice of social interaction patterns as a means of determining similarities of life-style does provide a more secure grounding than most, from both a philosophical and a practical point of view.

Distinctions that are made then, have to justify themselves in some theoretically meaningful way, a point that can be illustrated by looking at some of the OUGs in which the largest numbers of women are employed. The largest of these are the categories of clerks and cashiers (this is true also for men, incidentally) and typists, shorthand writers and secretaries. Within these we have been able to distinguish twelve subgroups for which the numbers, in the case of females, were sufficient for analysis (see table 10.5). Originally the subgroups of the clerical category were used in developing scores for male-incumbent occupations and the results are confirmed, using the new analysis, in the first column of the table. Bank clerks and civil service clerks emerge with scores well above average for the whole OUG, while wages clerks, routine clerks, cashiers and a residual category including meter readers and progress chasers have scores below average. Taken on its own this is evidence that, among males, these subgroups differ in life-style, as indicated by the mean scores of those with whom they interact. The relevance of the distinctions in other respects is something that we are only just beginning to study, but it is interesting that when we look at these same occupation subgroups with female incumbents we find that the ordering of the subgroups is almost identical. The main exception is the residual category of other clerks, but here there is almost certainly a major difference in the actual jobs being covered in the two cases. In particular, among the men are a large number of 'industrial' clerks — progress chasers and similar people engaged in production control — while amongst the women these jobs are rare and those such as receptionist are much more common. Although a scale value is shown for male secretaries (the whole of the OUG), we are not entirely confident that this group does not include a number of women who were not explicitly identified as such. In the case of typists (shorthand- and copy-) we decided to treat all of them as women, so that here there may be some very minor errors in the opposite direction. What is worth noting, in any event, is that this OUG can also be usefully subdivided, with secretaries, shorthand- and copy-typists being hierarchically distinguished.

We can get a more direct idea of the utility of these subdivisions by looking at marriage patterns. The third column of table 10.5 shows the ratios of husbands in each of the Registrar-General's Classes IV and V to those in Class I. The value of the subdivisions is fairly clear. For example we can see that female bank and civil service clerks are three to four times

**Table 10.5  Sub groups of occupation unit groups 139 (clerks and cashiers) and 141 (typists, shorthand writers, secretaries)**

| | Males | Females | |
| --- | --- | --- | --- |
| | | | Ratio of husbands in social classes IV and V: I ** |
| Occupation | Scale value * | Scale value * | |
| Secretaries | 50 | 62 | 4.35 |
| Bank clerks | 56 | 60 | 2.78 |
| Civil service clerks | 54 | 58 | 2.78 |
| Shorthand-typists | — | 54 | — |
| Other clerks etc. | 41 | 53 | 1.33 |
| Money records clerks | 53 | 52 | 1.12 |
| Insurance | 57 | — | — |
| Other | 51 | — | — |
| Typists | — | — | 1.47 |
| Other office clerks nec. | 50 | 50 | 0.54 |
| Local government clerks | 49 | 50 | 0.33 |
| Copy-typists | — | 49 | — |
| General/routine clerks | 48 | 41 | 0.25 |
| Wages clerks | 43 | 41 | 0.22 |
| Cashiers | 47 | 39 | 0.29 |

*Notes*:

\* On a range 1—100
\*\* General sample only

more likely to have a husband in Class I than in Classes IV or V while for wages clerks, cashiers and routine clerks the ratios are of a similar order in the other direction. Although there is no doubt a good deal of overlap in the middle, there is a clear tendency for some women, in identifiable parts of these two OUGs, to be more likely to interact with professional and managerial men and for others to be more likely to interact with non-skilled manual workers.

Looking in detail at particular occupational subgroups in this way suggests that a more meaningful structuring can still be uncovered. Somewhat extreme examples are the OUG categories of 'maids, valets and related service workers n.e.c.' and 'painters, sculptors and related creative artists'. Within the former, airline stewardesses, 56 per cent of whom are married to airline pilots, emerge with a scale value of 91 (among the top 2 per cent), while maids and so on have scores of 27 (among the lowest 10 per cent). Within the latter, creative artists proper, combined with creative writers, have a score of 81, compared with a value of 49 for window-dressers — that is, the former are among the top 5 per cent, while the latter are just above the middle of the range.

As was pointed out earlier, the overall success of the method that we have used for improving on the values of the original Cambridge scale is indicated by the improvement in correlation between members of interacting occupational groups, in terms either of friendship or of marriage. As a baseline, in the 'general' sample, which provides the greater part of the data, the average correlation between the occupations of (male) respondents' and those of their friends was 0.61. After the re-estimation procedure described, this value increased to 0.71, an improvement in variance explained from 37 per cent to 50 per cent. Since each respondent could name up to four friends in all, it is possible to take out the variation within individuals by looking at the mean score for each respondent's friends (up to four). The correlation then increases to 0.82. The great majority of these friends are male, partly perhaps because our questions made no explicit reference to gender. However, even in our most recent survey, where we asked for the sex of each friend, 89 per cent of the friends given by male respondents were also men (ranging from 94 per cent of first friends to 85 per cent of fourth). Excluding female friends and using all four samples, the correlations given above are improved very slightly, to an average of 0.72 and to 0.83 using the mean.

Amongst our more limited number of female respondents friends are much less likely to be limited to the same sex. Overall only 66 per cent are women, ranging from 74 per cent of first friends to 57 per cent of third. The correlations between respondents and friends are less impressive than among males, except for the first-chosen friend (perhaps because this is more likely to be a colleague at work, doing the same job). Here the correlation is 0.73, but this drops to 0.43 for the fourth friend. Again, taking the mean of (female) friends gets rid of variation within individuals and the correlation in this case is as good as that for the first friend (0.73).

Although there is a little more individual variation among women respondents it would appear that we have not been much less successful in scoring occupations with female incumbents than those with males. This is particularly true when one considers that, even using our fine subdivisions of occupations, women do seem to be concentrated much more highly in certain jobs than are men. (Because of this it is also true that we had insufficient numbers to allow us to differentiate other occupational groups adequately.) However there seems to be a lower degree of structuring of relations when friendships between men and women are considered. The best of the correlations for the cross-gender friendship is 0.65, and the lowest 0.38. Even taking the mean (of male friends of female respondents and vice versa) does not give any improvement (0.51). In comparison with these figures then, the correlation of 0.62 between spouses' occupations is satisfactorily high. It may indicate that while social interaction with people of the opposite sex is not as structured as friendship with those of same sex, nevertheless choice of a spouse shows less of such random variation (though it is not the case that only unmarried respondents named friends of the opposite sex). In any event this correlation is a marked improvement over the starting value of 0.49, obtained using the same scores as for male incumbents of each occupation. The increase in variance explained is from 24 to 38 per cent. It indicates a far higher degree of consistency in marriage patterns than previous results have suggested.

The work reported here is not complete, but we believe that the results are sufficient to indicate the validity and the potential of our approach. One of the underlying concerns in this is the reintegration of the 'economic' sphere into the more general area of the social or, more correctly, to demonstrate the invalidity of any such distinction. Most class schemes locate the constitution of classes in employment characteristics, from Marx (ownership of the means of production and sale of labour power) through the UK Registrar-General (level of skill) and Goldthorpe (work and market situation) to Wright (location of some groups in the negation of Marxist economic relations). These schemes are patently deficient as statements of social groupings based upon male employment experience, but are at their most absurd when applied to women and the relations between men and women. Such schemes accept the autonomy of the economic, with concepts like those of 'market capacity' or 'reproduction cost of labour power', and result in an unfortunate cutting off of certain issues from sociological inquiry. These issues are purged of all content and occur in economic explanations as 'givens' and 'assumptions'.

In fact though, because the division is an artificial one, the problems that seem to have been cut off constantly reappear, perhaps in disguised form. A main argument of this chapter is that the disguised form cannot be penetrated, nor the problem understood, while we continue to cling to the existing conceptualizations which are components of the flawed understandings. In particular we have to recognize that our concern with class is necessarily a concern with the 'social' and the attempt to locate it in the 'economic' illustrates contradictions of various kinds. For example, there can be no problem of social mobility in the traditional sense if one accepts the facticity of market capacity, because that concept is contradicted by anything short of a perfect market. Thus the sociological analysis of rigidities in social groupings denies the assumptions of the economic constitution of such groupings that it sets out with.

The study of marriage patterns in relation to social differentiation shows up the problems of the economic/social division with particular clarity. If choice of a marriage partner were random, at least with respect to social stratification, there might be no problem, but the use of existing categories demonstrates that this is not the case. Nor, from a variety of theoretical perspectives, would one expect it to be. Theories involving the concept of social closure especially, but also weaker versions incorporating stratification criteria, would predict the social similarity of marriage partners with respect not only to their current situation but also to their own social origins and their expectations regarding children. However when it comes to examining data on marriage patterns this clear social view of classes is clouded by the adherence to economically-based categories, so that level of skill, work and market situation or, conceivably, the particular mix of contradictory class locations, are accepted implicitly as the bases of social similarity.

The problem is compounded when such class categories are maintained despite the fact that there are two apparently different structures of stratification, one for male and one for female employment, which cannot be brought into correspondence. Worse, the distinctness of the two structures is maintained even while it is argued that the two are intimately connected, and that the structures of male and female employment are a consequence of, for example, men appropriating skilled jobs (or manipulating social definitions in their favour). It would seem most remarkable if at the same time such men regarded as socially similar for purposes of friendship and marriage only those women doing comparably skilled jobs.

We believe that our approach provides a consistent and coherent alternative that solves these problems because it accepts the social (which includes the 'economic') nature of stratification arrangements. The general aim is to look for regularities in social relations and to use these as the basis for conceptual development. This is what is fundamental to all processes of measurement. Our previous work (largely on males) has shown that there is a consistent structure underlying friendship choice, and we have used this as a means of relating occupational groups, of a fairly detailed kind, to one another in terms of life-style. We believe that the work so far indicates that marriage provides an equivalent means of relating the occupations of women to those of men, demonstrating greater consistency between them than is achievable with other current conceptualizations.

# 11

## Industrialization, Gender Segregation and Stratification Theory

### Alison MacEwen Scott

Whatever their theoretical orientation, few sociologists would dispute the centrality of the division of labour in stratification theory. It is the major determinant of social, economic and political inequality and a fundamental source of social conflict. Whether class is deemed to originate in relations of production, market capacities or life chances and status, the work people do, the conditions under which they do it and the rewards they receive for it are the major variables in class formation and action.

Despite the universally pronounced segregation of men and women in the division of labour — a segregation that is strongly associated with inequality — gender has not been considered an important aspect of stratification. There are two main reasons for this. First, gender segregation is viewed as an *outcome* of market processes that are considered to be sex-neutral and which merely reflect pre-market differences between male and female labour. Therefore gender has no *causal* role as a mechanism of economic inequality. Second, differences between male and female labour are reduced to a narrow naturalistic conception of gender, i.e. women's role in biological reproduction. The concentration of women into low-status occupations is seen as an effect of 'preferences and endowments' which derive from their position in the domestic division of labour. Gender segregation thus appears an incidental aspect of the division of labour, a reflection of family structure rather than of stratification itself.

The contention that 'gender matters' for stratification theory requires a fundamental questioning of these assumptions. It depends on demonstrating that gender, like property, power or institutionalized privilege is a major element in the *construction* of inequality and that political consequences follow. This involves challenging the assumed sex-neutrality of economic processes and showing how gender as a system of social and political inequality is incorporated into the division of labour as a mechanism of stratification. This in turn requires an analysis of gender that goes far beyond the question of biological reproduction.

The assumption of sex neutrality rests on certain notions about the ways in which economic structures emerge and are transformed in the process of industrialization. Two principal ones are the increasing autonomy and dominance of the economy *vis-à-vis* other structures, and the development of an impersonal, instrumental market rationality as the basis for economic transactions. Undeniably, the process of industrialization has shifted the form of economic transactions away from customary status relationships towards individual contracts and there has also been a trend towards more formal mechanisms of labour recruitment. However, it is important to see these as tendencies rather than states and to understand that other structures constrain these tendencies. 'Pure' economic forces are modified by ideological and political pressures. This is because (a) economic institutions are articulated with other institutions that sustain gender inequality, and (b) gender relations are interwoven with production relations at the level of the labour process itself.

This chapter aims to demonstrate the 'gender embeddedness' of the division of labour in contrast to its sex-neutrality.[1] There are two parts to the argument: the first points out that even in advanced industrial societies, the market is subject to political and ideological influences. The distinction between these terms is arbitrary since the economy *is* both political and ideological. However, for the purpose of exposition, I shall assume 'economic' to refer to conventional notions of resource allocation through the market (supply, demand, prices); 'political' to refer to formal politico-legal rights and organized exclusionary mechanisms; and 'ideological' to refer to informal normative influences deriving from the value system. It is not intended that 'ideology' should refer only to the realm of norms and values, but to a series of institutions and practices which embody these factors.

The second part of the argument seeks to demonstrate that political and ideological influences on the market derive from the high degree of linkage between economic and non-economic structures and institutions. It shows how, as a result of these linkages, gender is incorporated into the division of labour and manifests itself in gender segregation and the structure of gendered occupations. Patterns of gender segregation are therefore constructed socially and historically and cannot be deduced from a universal economic or biological logic. Historical and comparative analysis is necessary to support this argument, first to demonstrate the process of historical causation within particular societies, and secondly, to illustrate the variability in patterns of segregation across societies. In the latter part of this chapter four contrasting societies will be examined for these purposes.

## THEORETICAL CONSIDERATIONS

First, let us consider in more detail the role of the assumed sex-neutrality of the economy in stratification theory. This is expressed in the conceptualization of the division of labour, the way the pattern of inequality is derived from the division of labour via the labour-market, and the theoretical premises which link both of these to consciousness and action. Underlying each aspect is a conceptual separation between jobs and people, or rather, between economically determined occupational categories and socially determined attributes of labour.

The division of labour is conceived as a hierarchical structure of occupational positions, statuses or relations of production, whose characteristics are defined by technical or contractual criteria. These criteria are derived from an internal logic of the economic system such as the profit motive or technology. Although it is recognized that this logic may be modified through political pressure,[2] it remains the dominant determinant of the division of labour (cf. Garnsey 1981). The conception of occupational placement also relies on this notion. Labour is allocated to jobs on the basis of economically relevant factors such as skill, price and job commitment, rather than social attributes such as age, gender or ethnicity. Such attributes are only important where they act as proxies for economic 'endowments'. The rewards attached to occupations are also determined by forces internal to the economy such as the interplay of the demand for and supply of labour.

The forms of consciousness and conflict that arises from the division of labour are based on these occupational categories. It is assumed that all other roles occupied by individuals are suspended while at work and have no influence on workplace interaction or organization. Since the social characteristics of workers are deemed irrelevant for the construction of occupational categories, it follows that they are also irrelevant to consciousness and conflict. Where political conflict is thought to be determined by workplace relations the causal variables are all gender-neutral (for example the capital-labour contradiction, market capacities, alienation, authority etc).

The irrelevance of gender in this schema implies that the political attitudes and behaviour of men and women working under the same conditions should be the same. The lesser militancy of women compared with men is therefore a reflection of structures outside the work situation, rather than an effect of the action of gender within it. Undeniably gender ideologies in the wider society have played a powerful role in demobilizing women workers, and this has been used by entrepreneurs as a mechanism of social control and as a means of cheapening the cost of labour. However, the influence of gender on workplace conflict is more complex than this since it affects the behaviour and consciousness of men as well as women. Not only has gender varied the availability of men and women for action, it has strengthened their solidarity within conflict and influenced the forms of action themselves (see for example James 1962).

Even if it is accepted that gender should be investigated as a mechanism of stratification, it is not clear that this can be done within existing conventions of analysis. The major problem is the reliance on a single classification of occupations consisting of highly grouped data. This disguises the full extent and function of gender segregation since two of its major aspects — workplace and industrial segregation — are lost from view. It is no accident that recent additions to our knowledge have arisen out of enterprise-based studies. Not only is gender segregation more visible at this level, it is easier to establish the relationship between economic and gender hierarchies directly.

Microlevel research in Britain and elsewhere indicates that gender is highly salient to workplace interaction and can affect the construction of occupational categories and forms of consciousness and action:

1 Gender influences the skill categorization of job tasks (Cavendish 1982, Coyle 1982, Phillips and Taylor 1980). It also affects technological designs that are based on assumptions about the skill composition of the workforce (Berg 1984; McGaw 1982).
2 Gender plays a role in determining the forms of authority and supervision in the workplace (Lown 1983; 1984).
3 It affects the status, income and forms of contract of certain jobs (Beechey 1983b; Berg 1984; Taylor 1983).
4 Men's and women's experience of work differs substantially despite similar structural situations. This means that they experience both gender and class relations while at work (Armstrong 1982; Cavendish 1982; Cockburn 1983b; Pollert, 1981, 1983).
5 This affects their consciousness and political disposition quite apart from any differences in domestic responsibilities (Armstrong 1982; Cavendish 1982; James 1962; Pollert 1981).
6 Gender plays a role in dividing the work-force, both structurally and politically (Armstrong 1982; Barrett 1980; Coyle 1982).

No one knows yet how generalized these findings may be, but they illustrate the role of gender in shaping the structures that determine class formation and action. Since its influence is greatest where jobs are most segregated, occupational segregation may be the major mechanism through which gender affects stratification. It should therefore be considered a central rather than an incidental aspect of economic inequality.

Let us now examine the role of 'pure economic forces' in producing gender segregation in advanced industrial economies and the ways in which they are constrained by political and ideological pressure. A variety of theories range from narrowly defined micro-level models (for reviews see Blau and Jusenius 1976; Amsden 1980) to broad theories about the 'fit' between the hierarchical structure of capitalism and the subordination of women within the family. In most of these the labour-market is the mechanism which integrates the two systems of inequality. On the supply side, it is argued that the divorce between the home and workplace, together with the division between economic and domestic responsibilities in the family has meant that men and women participate in the labour-market under different conditions. Women have acquired a status as 'secondary workers' which is translated into price and efficiency characteristics. They are assumed to have low labour-force and career commitment, high job instability, low educational aspirations and achievements, a lack of accumulated work experience, and a lower supply price, relative to men. On the other hand, the increasing hierarchization of work and the differentiation in the demand for labour, has led to a specific need for 'secondary workers', so that women are allocated to jobs which are compatible with their 'endowments'.

Whether gender segregation is explained in terms of dual labour-market theory or neo-classical discrimination models, and whether the demand or supply side of the equation is stressed, the *mechanism* of segregation remains the market, and its mode of rationality is assumed to be 'purely' economic, i.e. based on preferences, price and efficiency. However, the market is also a vehicle for the exercise of political pressure and the expression of cultural values. These two factors are normally invisible because the market incorporates social values and political pressure into its pricing system and institutions.

Occasionally, discrepancies emerge between economic, political and ideological forces, revealing the deficiency of the sex-neutrality assumption. In contemporary industrial societies this is occurring increasingly as a result of divergencies from conventional family structure and a reduction in the differences between male and female 'endowments'. Research is showing increasingly that the image of women as 'secondary workers' can be contradicted by fact. But this deviation from the norm is not reflected in desegregation. In particular sectors of the labour-market, women change jobs less frequently than men and comparable levels of qualification and career commitment (Curran 1984; Scott 1979). Also many men show high rates of job instability and a lack of job and career identification, particularly in the lower skilled manual occupations. There is variation amongst men and amongst women with respect to these factors, and these are not just minor deviations from a statistical norm, but general within particular occupations. At the very least therefore, we would expect less segregation in those occupations where men's and women's labour-force attachment and skills were similar. Yet these are the *most* segregated occupations (unskilled manual and professional/managerial occupations). The market therefore appears to be guided by stereotypes rather than actual behaviour — a curious contradiction of the principles of rationality and efficiency!

The assumptions of economic rationality allow the theoretical possibility of flexibility in the recruitment of men and women. If gender differences are constructed socially rather than genetically,[3] a non-discriminatory, non-ideological market should respond to changes in the supply characteristics of women. Thus, if women were to increase their skills, work commitment and career motivation, they should compete more effectively with men and achieve a more random distribution in the occupational structure. While differences still exist between the endowments of men and women, these differences have decreased significantly in Britain in recent years. Smaller families, closer childspacing, increasing nursery provision and maternity benefit, and the extension of public education have been reflected in a greater willingness of women to raise their qualifications and to work over most of their adult lives. Yet this reduction in supply constraints has not produced any significant decrease in segregation (Hakim 1979; Gross 1968; Oppenheimer 1970). It has led to a less efficient allocation of labour in the market: overly qualified women in many jobs, and higher unemployment for women than men, at particular levels of qualification. Longitudinal analysis shows that there has been relatively little *direct* substitution of one sex by the other (the major exception being teaching). Indeed gender segregation has protected men and women from competition with each other in spite of market pressure (Milkman 1976). Any substitution that has occurred, has been accompanied by substantial changes in the character and status of the jobs concerned (cf. Murgatroyd 1982b).

In searching for alternative explanations of gender segregation, many writers have pointed to political exclusion by male-dominated professional associations, guilds, unions etc. (For example Hartmann 1976; Kenrick 1981; Murgatroyd 1982b). Gender segregation in the work-force may also be the result of strategies of management control rather than efficiency or price considerations. However these practices themselves have to be explained. If men have organized to protect their jobs from the lowering of wage rates and status that would result from the inclusion of women, we need to ask why gender has the power to affect wages and status in this way? If gender is viable as an element of control in the workplace, why should the behaviour of women be different from men when they work in the same objective situation? And why are supervisory relations more effective when they are gendered in one way (i.e. if the supervisor is a man and the worker a woman) but not in the other?

These questions suggest that the social relations of gender are intertwined with the social relations of production. The clearest manifestation of this is the sex-typing of jobs which occurs once gender segregation has crystallized in an occupation. Thereafter it exerts a strong normative pressure on the market: there is resistance to substitution even when supply and price conditions change. Sex-typing affects recruitment normatively by stressing the 'appropriateness' of men or women for a job rather than their actual abilities to do it. This is backed up with the usual sanctions that accompany normative influences for example gossip and ridicule (Moser 1981; Murgatroyd 1982b). It endows occupations with notions of femininity and masculinity which are not technically part of the job but become part of its occupational culture (cf. Clarke *et al.* 1979; Cockburn 1983; Willis 1977). The stronger the influence of sex-labelling on particular occupations, the more occupational identities merge with sexual identities. Thus women in 'male' jobs are expected to be aggressive and 'butch', and men in 'female' jobs to be sensitive, caring and possibly gay. The resistance of men and women to crossing the boundaries of sex-typed occupations arises from taboos on sex-role reversal in the wider society.

These examples illustrate that even in an advanced industrial economy where instrumental rationality is the accepted basis for economic transactions, the market is subject to political and ideological pressures. Occasionally these pressures contradict economic forces and they then appear as 'non-rational'. However, this is a false opposition. Precisely *because* the economy has been shaped by the wider society in the course of its development, political and ideological forces become incorporated into the economic mechanisms themselves. Indeed even the notion of 'pure market competition' may be said to be ideological.

The incorporation of gender into the division of labour thus occurs through the combination of political, ideological and economic forces *in* the market. This affects the ways in which both labour *and* occupations are constructed socially. As discussed previously, male and female labour is differentiated not only by virtue of specific 'preferences and endowments' but also by general gender roles which are incorporated into workplace interaction. As this incorporation is routinized over time, gender enters into the definition of the job, both through the visible aspects of sex-typing as well as the invisible influences on forms of contract and levels of skill, income and status. These historically produced outcomes are carried forward in time to affect the market behaviour of future actors. Thus although industrialization did produce a gradual erosion of kinship statuses as the basis for labour allocation and a shift towards more flexible 'economic' criteria, the jobs to which the new 'freely negotiating individuals' were recruited were already in some sense 'gendered'.

Ironically, the onset of industrialization has usually been accompanied by a polarization of gender roles in the wider society. There are a variety of reasons for this: increasing economic inequality within the family, religious changes and the incorporation of gender into the wider processes of class consolidation and social control. Ideologies of domesticity have surfaced in different societies at different times and for different reasons, but they have usually been strongly associated with the dominant social class, which has played a major role in shaping social, political and economic institutions. The association between domesticity and industrialization is not just the product of the separation between the home and the workplace, but of the wider system of class relations. As the State and the educational system took over from the family as the institutions which would promote competitive individualism in the labour-market, those same institutions were perpetuating gender divisions for other reasons. The ambiguity between market equality and gender inequality was thus carried into the heart of the division of labour. It was then exported to other parts of the world through the political institutions of colonialism, the educational systems implanted there and the new enterprise forms associated with dependent industrialization, all of which were 'saturated with gender'.

In the pages which follow, I shall analyse the patterns of gender segregation which emerged within the urban-industrial labour force in four different societies, Britain, Peru, Egypt and Ghana. The purpose of this analysis is to illustrate different types of institutional influence on the division of labour and the ways they are reflected in patterns of gender segregation. These countries have been selected because they show the relativity of the economic and kinship structures that emerged in the Britain, which are often assumed to be universal. The contrasting patterns in other societies demonstrate the importance of political and cultural factors in shaping the division of labour. I hope this will justify the contention that the economic processes which create the division of labour are not sex-neutral and that stratification theory must accordingly be modified.

Table 11.1 (see appendix to this chapter) gives summary data on the levels of industrialization of the four societies, in terms of the relative importance of the manufacturing sector, the size of the work-force in non-agricultural activities and in wage and salaried labour. Tables 11.2 and 11.3 give data on educational levels. Tables 11.4–11.8 describe the structure of female employment in each society. Together these tables show that neither the levels of female labour-force participation nor the distribution of women between occupational classes correlate well with the structure of the economy or the skill levels of the work-force. Details from these tables will be discussed in the text below.

### Britain

Within the Western world, Britain has one of the most gender-segregated occupational structures. In 1971, 83 per cent of women in Britain were in disproportionately female occupations and 51 per cent in occupations with over 70 per cent female workers. The degree of concentration of men in male-dominated occupations was even greater; over 75 per cent of them worked in occupations that were over 70 per cent male. Nearly 75 per cent of all occupations were 'male' compared with only a quarter 'female' (Hakim 1979).

Gender segregation is even higher at workplace level. In 1980 63 per cent of women worked in 'women only' jobs in their place of work (Martin and Roberts 1984). Both workplace segregation and female concentration were highest at the bottom of skill hierarchies within manual and non-manual employment, and the levels were highest of all amongst manual occupations.

This pattern has remained remarkably stable over time despite occupational diversification, sectoral shifts and a redistribution of women between 'female' jobs (Hakim 1979). The main reason is that structural changes in the economy have replaced traditional female occupations such as domestic service, with new ones such as clerical work. Although desegregation occurred in the early stages of the development of new occupations or the transformation of old ones, their gender composition polarized rapidly and then stabilized. Since the rates of growth of 'female' occupations have been far higher than that of less segregated ones, the overall index of segregation has remained the same.

The influence of gender roles on the pattern of female employment in Britain is evident in the characteristics of labour-force participation and in the kinds of jobs women do. Despite the recent increase in the numbers of women in paid employment there is still a marked discrepancy between male and female participation rates which arises from women's domestic roles. Most women still withdraw from the labour-market after childbearing, although for shorter periods than before, and a preference for part-time employment is shown by married women (Martin and Roberts 1984). There remains a strong normative pressure on women to subordinate the interests of their work to their family.

Although women's occupations have changed in the course of this century, the characteristics of these occupations have remained remarkably similar. Most have a strong welfare or 'service' element or they reflect domestic functions directly.[4] Gender roles have a specific relevance to the content of these jobs independently of the particular educational levels or labour-force commitment of the women involved. A subsidiary group of occupations such as light-assembly workers have come to be dominated by women, although their job tasks are less obviously 'feminine'. These jobs are said to be 'appropriate' for women because of their 'secondary-worker' characteristics. Overall, women are excluded from occupations which involve the execution of power, scientific knowledge, control over capital or technology. Women are above all ancillary and routine workers, the executors of others' decisions and the providers of welfare and domestic services.

This situation is the product of a historically specific relationship between the economy and other social structures. A long view of the progressive changes in women's status within the family and the economy indicates that the pattern outlined above has been a relatively recent development in British history. It has however been a logical outcome of the interplay between economic, political, legal and kinship structures whose roots reach back into feudalism. The leitmotif of this story has been the specific character of the kinship system which gave women secondary and dependent status within the family, at the same time as allocating them primary responsibility for day to day and generational reproduction. This structure has been incorporated into the economy in different ways in different periods, but the general principle that women's labour was dependent on, subsidiary to, and of lesser value than that of their husbands or fathers has been relatively constant. The effect of the rise of capitalism has been to restructure and deepen the differential between male and female labour, and this came about not only through economic changes but through political and ideological ones too. The division of labour which emerged in this process was both a cause and an effect of these changes.

The kinship system played a crucial role in this development. Its main features were an emphasis on monogamy, the indissolubility of marriage, patrilineal property and inheritance rights, and a nuclear household structure. Up until the end of the nineteenth century, marriage laws deprived women of the right to personal property and independent legal status, while they also gave men the rights to women's domestic and economic labour (Clark 1982; Kenrick 1981). Women had no right to separate domicile, and until 1875 divorce was only available by Act of Parliament. This legal and political structure was accompanied by a dual sexual morality and authoritarian power relations between male heads of family and their wives and children.[5]

Household structure was strongly nuclear as far back as the fifteenth century. Although extended family links were important in a number of ways, and may have increased with the growing reliance on an uncertain labour-market (Anderson 1971; Levine 1977), composite household structures did not develop which might have permitted the collective organization of day to day reproductive activities (cf. Ghana below).[6] Since feudal times, the provision of food and child-care have been the responsibility of wives and mothers (Middleton 1983). However, the content of these activities and the values placed on them changed as standards of living and concepts of childhood and mothering altered. In the eighteenth century women's economic roles were given greater priority over mothering

(Tilly and Scott 1978). Domestic responsibilities did not prevent women from working, even when work was taking place outside the home. Various writers report the use of servants, wet-nurses, hired baby-sitters or extended kin to ease the burden of domestic responsibilities (Clark 1982; Lown 1984; Pinchbeck 1981; Tilly and Scott 1978). However, these services were organized on the basis of mother-substitution, and did not alter the fact that legally and ideologically the ultimate responsibility for the home lay in the hands of the wife or mother.

Women's economic dependency within the family increased through the process of industrialization. Although women's productive activities were always mediated by their marital status and were therefore structured within a situation of dependency, their activities were transformed from full-time participation in a complex range of activities, many of which were unsegregated, [7] to casual employment in a narrow range of highly segregated activities. These changes *appear* to have occurred primarily through economic forces; for example, the decline of female subsistence production, the disappearance of certain female occupations in textile production and domestic service, and the failure of women to participate in the expanding occupations of the nineteenth and twentieth century as a result of lack of skills or 'preferences'. However, these economic changes have been sustained politically and ideologically in a variety of ways. Let us examine the nature of these economic changes more closely.

Initially women's labour, both in subsistence and market-based production, was crucial to the survival of rural and urban enterprises. On pre-enclosure farms women produced many of the family's subsistence commodities, they discharged labour rents and undertook wage labour (Clark 1982; Pinchbeck 1981; Middleton 1979). They were active in manufacturing and trading activities, and were present in most of the guilds that were dominated by men. There were also some all-female guilds mainly in the field of textiles (Clark 1982; Tilly and Scott 1978). However, women could only engage in these activities and thereby gain access to productive resources and skills through marriage.[8] They were therefore unable to accumulate capital in their own right or to establish their own rules for access to productive resources and skills.

Women's role in subsistence production declined with the onset of industrialization as a result of the expropriation of the peasantry, and later as a result of competition from cheaper factory made goods.[9] Also, with the increased subcontracting of production to outworkers and the weakening of the guilds, women lost their 'protected' access to craft skills (i.e. as wives) and were transformed into semi-skilled homeworkers. The intensification of work which was induced by economic pressure from merchants made the labour of women and children crucial to this new form of production.[10] It increased fragmentation and segregation of productive processes within the home. These divisions were transferred directly into the factories and mines, especially where family labour was incorporated within these establishments.

Wage differentials between men and women became more common as these transformations occurred, although the pattern was uneven. Throughout the period there was a tension between wages that were determined by market forces and those set by status within the family.[11] In both cases women's incomes were determined by their domestic role and tended to be lower than men's.[12] As long as the unit of labour was the household and wages took the form of a collective piece-rate paid to the male head, or where the tasks were clearly segregated, there was little competitive conflict between men and women. However, this changed as recruitment and wages were individualized and subjected to the pressure of the market. The political conflicts which ensued have been well documented (e.g. Hartmann 1976; Lewenhak 1977; Rose 1984). The results were the exclusion of women from particular areas of production, and from the political organizations which endeavoured to control recruitment and wages.[13]

By the early nineteenth century, women's participation in household and factory production was severely limited. The concentration in textile and clothing production, and commercial and service activities, which today characterizes women's employment, was already established. Their participation in non-domestic wage work was small and dominated by unmarried women (Tilly and Scott 1978). Most other women were confined to outwork, domestic service and the street (Alexander 1983). This work was casual and the work patterns of the women who did it became increasingly irregular and correlated with the domestic cycle (Tilly and Scott 1978).

The ideology of domesticity provided a moral justification for the forms of segregation which emerged in the labour-market. It polarized sex roles and legitimized a more total economic dependency of women on men than had hitherto been customary. Its influence was strongest in the middle class, so the occupations which developed at this time through the spread of finance, commerce and the professions were dominated by men and heavily imbued with masculinity. Any work that was undertaken by women in this class, had to be defined as voluntary work.

The casual and irregular nature of working-class women's labour and the voluntary character of middle-class women's contrasted strongly with men's jobs which at this time were beginning to crystallize as full-time market-based occupations. The latter process was occurring through the increasing institutionalization of the male labour-market via unionization, professional associations and apprenticeships. Such institutionalization was an important factor in the construction of occupational status. Women were disadvantaged not only because they were excluded by these institutions, but because they were unable to institutionalize their own occupations and thereby raise their status.

Political and ideological interventions in the labour-market in Britain have always appeared implicit or non-existent, partly because of the indirect nature of the interventions and partly because of the *laissez-faire* ideology which since the time of Adam Smith has been the lens through which historical development has been viewed. Orthodoxy maintains that the British industrialization process took place without an interventionist State. Its action in the nineteenth century was confined to liberalizing measures which freed the market from the monopolistic restrictions on mobility of capital and labour.

Up to the nineteenth century Parliament had a direct influence on the economy since it was the main instrument for regulating property, labour and commercial rights. Although many of these rights had become diluted by the market in the preceding century, the 'liberalizing' measures of the early industrialization period were in fact forcible interventions in the economy with profound effects on production relations and the distribution of income. They were also selective, being more concerned with the rights of capital, and of capital over labour, than with the rights of labour. Enfranchisement issues lagged far behind other measures, racial and sexual monopolies were only confronted a century later. The State was conspicuously absent in other areas of liberalization too; in contrast with almost all other societies, Britain industrialized without a national educational system. However, from the 1830s on, the State intervened increasingly in the economy through controls and inspection, and a State bureaucracy was developing with an 'inbuilt tendency to grow and multiply' (Deane 1979). Protective legislation, poor-law reform and the regulation of industrial relations all played a role in structuring the emerging labour-market.

The State was supported by the system of common law which had an inbuilt reactionary tendency in that it relied on judicial precedent rather than general philosophical principles. Legal changes had to take place through Acts of Parliament, rather than through reinterpretation of legal principles. In the absence of such Acts, the legal system has remained the guardian of tradition. Sachs and Wilson (1978) show how judicial precedent was used to perpetuate gender discrimination in this century and the last.

In any case, the ideological effects of earlier structures tended to survive long after formal liberalization. One of the reasons for this was the strong influence of religion, which underpinned the politico-legal institutions that regulated relations within the family and economy. It also exerted strong normative pressure on gender relations outside the action of the State. Goody has demonstrated how the link between the Church, the State and property relations in feudal times moulded the early modern kinship system in Britain and Europe (Goody 1983). There were dramatic changes in the forms of these linkages after the Reformation, with the monarchy and the Established Church being subordinated to Parliament, and religion itself becoming more diversified by sectarianism. However, prior to and during the industrialization process, religion played an important part in structuring class relations in Britain and influenced the ways in which the State intervened in those relations. In the nineteenth century, religion was an important basis for social solidarity in the local community and played a pivotal role in the elaboration and diffusion of the domestic ideology. This ideology united morality, social order and economic worth in the sanctification of the home, with the middle-class leisured wife as the high priestess. The home became separated from the market not only geographically but ideologically (Davidoff *et al.* 1976). Within the middle class, domestic functions were divided further by status through the use of servants (Davidoff 1973; 1974). This middle-class domestic ideology influenced the actions of the State, voluntary agencies and employer practices, through which it was imposed on the working class. It was also assimilated by the latter through the process of social mobility, as manifested in their support for a male 'family wage' (see Land 1980; Barrett and McIntosh 1980).

Significantly, the earliest forms of protective legislation — which did constrain the freedom of market forces — were produced in defence of women and children and were influenced strongly by the domestic ideology.[14] The absence of women from the home because of long hours of work, and fears of sexual immorality in the workplace were seen as a threat to the family and social order. The Poor Law reform of 1834, and its later administration, which was intended to 'free' the labour-market of wage subsidies and discourage the work-shy, was premissed on the primacy of the male wage and women's status as non-wage-earning dependants. Poor Law relief to women, who were the majority of beneficiaries, was dependent on moral character and cleanliness (Thane 1978). Stability of marriage was encouraged by the withdrawal of relief upon separation, and the generally inadequate provision for single women, wives separated from their husbands, and unmarried mothers. This idealized family structure has also underpinned the twentieth-century Welfare State, dissuading married women from employment even to the present day (Ginsburg 1979).

Educational provision in the nineteenth century was limited and patchy, largely supplied by religious voluntary agencies and private endowments and run by clerics. State involvement in education was restricted by sectarian conflict and consisted mainly of financial support to private institutions. Free compulsory schooling was only provided in 1891 at elementary level and in 1944 at secondary level.[15] The educational system originated as a mechanism of class reproduction with a strong emphasis on religious instruction and symbolic aspects of status (Simon 1960). It was never geared to the labour-market and throughout the nineteenth century industrial and professional skills were transmitted through the workplace. The predominant emphasis in middle-class schools was on classical languages. In working-class schools it was on reading and Bible instruction. The concern in both was on 'character formation' and social placement.[16] Schools tended to be sex-segregated, especially amongst the middle classes, and educational provision for girls lagged far behind that for boys.[17] The curriculum in girls schools was highly influenced by domestic ideology, with an emphasis on social graces in the case of middle-class girls and domestic skills in the case of working-class girls (Marks 1976; Dyhouse 1981). Access to higher education was severely restricted for both boys and girls. As late as the mid 1930s only 0.4 per cent of elementary-school leavers went on to university (Thane 1982). Amongst this privileged elite, the proportion of women was infinitesimal. Even though the educational system is now more open and State control is firmly established, the legacy of elitism, class divisions and private-sector influence remains. Gender divisions have also survived, less in physical segregation and the content of the curriculum, than in enduring expectations that education provides a different function for girls than it does for boys.

During the second half of the nineteenth century and early twentieth, service occupations had begun to grow as a result of bureaucratization and professionalization. In particular, the Civil Service expanded at home and abroad. All these tendencies stimulated a demand for educated labour which the educational system was ill-equipped to provide especially during and after the First World War. Accordingly women were drafted in, but their inclusion was accompanied by the marriage bar — a formal or informal agreement that employment would terminate on marriage (Lewis 1984). The gradual re-entry of middle-class women into the labour-market made possible by their increased education was thus tied to marital status and remained so until the Second World War.

In modern-day Britain, the State and the legal and educational systems have enfranchised women so they have similar rights as men in access to education, to jobs and to pay. Political and ideological influences on the labour-market are thus formally absent, so sex segregation appears to be the result of 'pure' economic forces. However, these forces have been shaped historically by a number of non-economic institutions. All of these influences were discriminatory as far as women workers were concerned. The structure and ideology of the family has influenced and been influenced by the State, religion, the economy and the class system. The high degree of integration between these different structures accounts for the amazing stability of gender segregation over time, despite quite dramatic economic changes.

*Peru*

What is remarkable about Peru, and more particularly Lima,[18] is that the pattern of gender segregation is so similar to that in Britain despite being a much less industrialized society and having a different indigenous culture. Since the Second World War, Peru has had a dynamic pattern of economic growth involving high rates of industrialization and urbanization.[19] Yet Peru is still an agrarian society with a large peasantry, and most urban workers can trace their roots to an Indian culture within one or two generations. As far as we know this peasantry had a relatively egalitarian structure of gender relations and an ideology which stressed parallel and complementary gender relations rather than hierarchical ones (Bolton and Mayer 1977; O. Harris 1981). Yet even within the traditional sectors of the economy forms of segregation have appeared which indicate an increasing marginalization and social devaluation of women. In modern enterprises gender segregation replicates European and North American patterns. Both trends are legitimized by the dominant class ideology which appears more Victorian than modern. The reason for the similarity between Britain and Peru is that the gender ideology implicit in the economic processes that accompanied the development of capitalism in Peru was compatible with the gender ideology of the dominant classes there. This compatibility was the product of a common European heritage transported to Peru in Spanish colonial times. It persisted in post-independence institutions and came to form part of the ruling-class culture. It was imposed on indigenous groups through colonization, proselytism, education, miscegegation and the status order.

The pattern of female participation in the labour force in Lima resembles that of Britain at the turn of this century. The rates are low (22 per cent in 1972), there is a high concentration of single women and there is little part-time work. The degree of segregation and the types of jobs that women do are also strikingly similar, (see table 11.9). In 1974 80 per cent of the metropolitan labour force was employed in occupations which were heavily dominated by one sex or the other, and about 66 per cent were in occupations that were over 90 per cent male or female. Over 75 per cent of the men were in disproportionately male occupations and 94 per cent were in occupations in which they had a simple majority. Of women, 85 per cent were employed in disproportionately female occupations (compared with 83 per cent in Britain). Almost 66 per cent of all employed women were in just 13 out of a possible 107 occupations and they were the familiar ones of clothing, sales and clerical work, and personal and welfare services.

The metropolitan economy is polarized between large-scale modern capitalist enterprises (including the State apparatus) and small-scale activities such as outwork, independent craft production, petty trading and domestic service. It therefore presents aspects of various forms of production which have been present in different periods of British industrialization. Incredibly, the patterns of gender segregation within these different forms of production are also similar. Within the small-scale sector, women are confined to domestic service, dressmaking, outwork and petty commerce. In the large-scale sector, secretarial and shop work, teaching and nursing are the main occupations.

Economic development between 1940—72 truncated into thirty years the changes which in Britain took over a hundred. The aggregate female labour-market was transformed internally by the expansion of white-collar service work and the relative decline of domestic service and casual home and street work. However, some transitional processes whereby women were excluded progressively from craft and factory work (with the exception of textiles and clothing) and gradually took over white-collar work from men, were missed out in Peru.

How far is this pattern to be explained by economic factors, i.e. skills, prices and preferences? In the large-scale sector, educational qualifications do play an important screening function in recruitment. However, due to massive State investment in education and a high commitment within the society to mobility through education for girls as well as boys, levels of formal qualification have risen in recent years and the sex differential has fallen. Lack of formal qualifications does not constitute the barrier to male jobs *within* occupational classes; indeed the rise in female qualifications has meant that on average the women who cluster at the bottom of the manual and non-manual hierarchies have more education than men, not less (Scott 1984).

It has been said that the price of women's labour has risen relative to men's because of protective labour legislation, which is more extensive in large enterprises, especially in white-collar work. However, female employment has continued to rise despite this, so that sex segregation has protected women from market pressure in this case. Within this sector, therefore, the explanation would have to rely on 'preferences'. Both employers and employees are influenced heavily by an ideology of domesticity. The participation rates of married women are extremely low in Peru despite the availability of maternity benefit, domestic service and active extended kin networks. The rates are lowest amongst the middle-class and they are low amongst young, relatively well-educated single women as well as married women. As far as the preferences of employers are concerned, not only is the Peruvian domestic ideology important but so is that of the United States and Europe. This arises from the predominance of foreign companies in Peru and the gender assumptions implicit in their technology and management practices. Such practices are also common in national companies and State bureaucracies whose managers and technicians have been trained abroad and who use foreign technology.

As far as small-scale production is concerned, neither the separation between home and work, nor formal qualifications are of particular relevance since skills are transmitted within the workplace which is linked to the home. Furthermore, long traditions of women working in peasant production, domestic service or in family enterprises mean that segregation cannot be attributed to women's unwillingness to work. The explanation has to be sought in the historical forces which have excluded women from craft work and pushed them into domestic service.

During the colonial period in South America, the Spanish Crown and the Roman Catholic Church laid down the basis for a monogamous, Christian, patrilineal kinship system, and a gender ideology which stressed chastity, marital fidelity and domesticity for women. The legal framework for marriage, property rights and inheritance was transferred directly from Spain through a highly centralized politico-religious apparatus. Even today family law in Peru remains highly patriarchal. There is an emphasis on the separation of male and female roles, the submission of women to male authority and the legal and economic dependency of women on men. Married women are not allowed to own property in their own right (although they can inherit it, it becomes part of male patrimony), they are not legally responsible for their children and officially they require the permission of their husbands before undertaking work outside the home.

Religion played a crucial part in the establishment of social control in the initial conquest situation and the Church was granted special privileges in order for it to carry out this function. This included special responsibilities for the moral welfare of the Indians, access to property and political decision-making and control over education. Educational institutions were run by priests and nuns and were sex-segregated. This facilitated a bifurcation in the ideological content of boys' and girls' education, with a heavy emphasis on moral control and social skills in the latter. Even during the expansion of public education during this century these features have been retained, and a large proportion of upper-and middle-class girls are still educated in convents.

The domesticity of Peruvian elite women therefore developed earlier than that of their British counterparts and prior to the industrialization process. It was supported not only by religion and family law, but by the status system of the conquering elites which disdained manual labour.[20] It was enhanced greatly by ethnicity, which permitted the consolidation of the imported culture by providing Indian labour for work which was considered beneath the status of the colonizers.[21] The continuation of a strong interrelationship between the Church and State and the ethnic and class homogeneity of the Peruvian bourgeoisie accounts for the persistence of a Victorian-type gender ideology today.

The colonial empire was highly centralized economically, politically and geographically. However, it permitted a certain cultural autonomy within the Indian communities and even on the quasi-feudal estates. For centuries caste-like ethnic divisions separated white urban culture and institutions from the indigenous society. Gender ideologies amongst the two differed considerably. Women's economic role in the indigenous communities was highly participant and although segregated, was of recognized value socially. Although originally land was owned communally, when usufruct and property rights were privatized, women were able to inherit and own land in their own right. There was far less control over the sexuality of women (Bourque and Warren 1976). However, their participation in the local political system was restricted.[22]

The incorporation of Peru into the international economy set in motion a number of economic, political and social changes which gradually incorporated the Indian population into the dominant ex-colonial society. The large estates encroached progressively upon peasant agriculture, seriously undermining its viability, but not destroying it altogether. Peasants were drawn into the expanding capitalist labour-markets in order to subsidize their farms. These labour markets were sex-segregated, with the men going into the mines, plantations and urban factory or construction work and the women going into domestic service. The political institutions which arose around the urban workplace such as unions, guilds and voluntary associations[23] were exclusively male. Over time, upward social mobility and miscegenation gave rise to the formation of a mestizo class which absorbed urban middle-class values, including their gender ideology, and acted as a cultural broker *vis-à-vis* the lower classes. Today many poor urban women are forced to withdraw from the labour-market upon marriage due to pressure from their husbands (Chueca 1982).

In rural areas, gender relations changed as a result of increased economic and political articulation with the wider society. Peasant women were concentrated into subsistence activities while the men went off to work for wages. However, these activities were eroded increasingly by the collapse of cottage industries and declining agricultural productivity. This seriously restricted women's access to the skills and capital necessary for small-scale production. Since the turn of this century the State has increased its influence in rural areas through road building, education, agrarian reform, provincial bureaucracies, and not least, conscription. All of these facilitated the transmission and urban middle-class gender ideologies to the peasantry. The higher wages commanded by men, compared with women's subsistence activities, increased their economic status within the communities. Greater familiarity with urban culture, especially with Spanish language, increased their political position as mediators between the communities and the State. Their perception of gender roles in Indian culture now shows remarkable evidence of penetration by the urban domestic ideology (Wilson 1983).

The forms of segregation which appeared in Peru resulted from changes associated with the development of capitalism prior to and during the major period of industrialization. These changes are reflected in both large-and small-scale forms of production. However in both cases, the market forces producing segregation operated with gender assumptions originating from either the Peruvian urban elites or foreign advanced industrial societies. These assumptions were supported by an institutional and cultural framework forged by the ruling class. What is remarkable is that this framework was implanted in the society so early in its history and in an indigenous culture that was somewhat at odds with it. The structures of political and ideological domination which originated in the colonial period and continued after independence, together with the system of class and ethnic relations, were essential to the gradual extension of this framework over time. The domestic ideology has thus gradually penetrated to within the indigenous culture itself. I shall now turn to a society which has shown a greater tendency to withstand and modify the gender assumptions of Western industrialization.

## Egypt

The Egyptian economy is similar to that of Peru as far as the pattern of industrialization and the degree of dualism, dependency and inequality are concerned.[24] Yet there are important differences in the structure of female employment. Women's labour-force participation rates are much lower and there are far fewer women in occupations that are 'normally' thought of as 'female', such as secretaries, shop assistants, textile and clothing workers, and domestic servants.[25] The proportions are low even in small-scale employment.[26] Most curious of all is the fact that the vertical distribution of women workers is weighted toward the top rather than the bottom, especially in wage and salaried employment. Compared with Peru, where low-skilled occupations in production, sales and service work account for 70 per cent of female non-agricultural employment and 55 per cent of female wage and salaried work, the proportions in Egypt are only 32 per cent and 27 per cent respectively. On the other hand, Egypt has a much higher proportion of women in professional and white-collar work than Peru, or even Britain (see table 11.7).

This situation cannot be explained by the structure of demand since the aggregate distribution of employment between occupational classes in Peru and Egypt is broadly similar, even when non-wage labour is included (see table 11.10). Nor can it be explained by women's lack of formal qualifications. Although the general level of female education is much lower in Egypt than in Peru, this would not be a barrier to employment in unskilled jobs such as domestic service. On the other hand, women's access

to higher education is similar and would not explain the greater proportion
of Egyptian women in the professions (see table 11.3).

The pattern of female employment in Egypt is the product of a particular
relationship between the family, religion and the status system. Islam has
played a major role in defining the position of women within the family in
terms of juridical rights and moral prescriptions. It has also placed gender
roles at the centre of Egyptian culture as a major source of personal and
social honour. This is due to the pervasive influence of Islam on all social
institutions and in particular its close relationship with the State. The
Ottoman Empire (sixteenth to nineteenth centuries in Eygpt) was based on
Islamic law and the indigenous State through which the Turks ruled was
strongly associated with Islamic institutions (Eccel 1984). Family law was
administered by religious courts as late as 1956, and higher education was
monopolized by religious elites until the fifties.

Traditionally, family structure was highly patriarchal. Although in
principle women had rights to property and divorce, these rights were
monopolized by men. Women were entitled to only half the inheritance of
men, grounds for divorce were stringent for women while they were
frivolous for men,[27] women had custody rights only over very small children
and they faced serious problems of legal representation in the courts.[28]
Islamic norms stressed domesticity, segregation and seclusion. More
importantly, these norms were the basis for public morality and social
standing in the community.[29] The family was the principal arena for the
demonstration of moral virtue and that virtue was linked to the control of
female sexuality. The social honour of the family and of its male
representatives was tied to the chastity and fidelity of its women (Youssef
1974; Smock and Youssef 1977). This resulted in early marriage, close
surveillance of married women (effected by varying degrees of segregation
and seclusion) and the evolution of sex-segregated institutions such as
schools, hospitals and recreational activities.

The forms and degrees of female subordination and seclusion varied
between social classes, and this differentiated the conditions under which
women in particular classes participated in the labour-market. Amongst
the rural and urban poor, preoccupations with the chastity of young girls
limited their access to education, while early marriage restricted their
participation in the labour-market. This significantly reduced the supply of
labour to domestic service and factory work. Although poverty made it
necessary for married women to work, they were confined to family
labour. Work under free market conditions was considered disgraceful,
and was only permitted for widows (Fakhouri 1972). The strong association
between marital and economic status is one reason for the low female
participation rates in the countryside, not because women do not work, but
because their labour is not perceived as separable from male labour or
from domestic chores. Even when women worked as wage labourers, e.g.

in picking cotton or construction work, they did so as an adjunct of their spouses. Family labour in non-agricultural enterprises was restricted by the strong control of artisanal trades by male guilds, and by the fact that many small-scale activities did not take place within the home and could not guarantee a segregated environment (Fakhouri 1972; Youssef 1974).

Amongst the wealthier classes, women's labour was not so crucial to the household income and their leisure was a symbol of economic status as well as male honour. All work was seen as degrading. Physical seclusion and the use of the veil was most widely practised by this group. Even after the girls from such families had begun to attend schools they were discouraged from employment, thus limiting the supply of women to middle-level occupations such as clerical or sales work. Up until the early 1960s, women employed in such occupations were foreign or non-Muslim (Youssef 1974).

Gender roles have changed substantially in modern Egypt, permitting greater access for women to education and employment. Although economic development and State policies have been important forces for change,[30] they were not sufficient to alter the pattern of female employment. For example, rural families failed to take advantage of the extension of educational provision for girls because of the threat to family honour and the assumption that education did not lead to employment (Youssef 1974). Labour legislation offering maternity benefits for married women introduced in 1959 failed to entice married women into the labour-market. Neither the expansion of demand nor formal emancipation could alter women's labour-market participation until gender roles had been redefined through the value system. This occurred only through changes within Islam and the reconstitution of its link to the status system.

In contrast to Peru, where female subordination and domesticity was stronger amongst the elites than amongst the peasantry, the reverse was the case in Egypt.[31] The secularization process which had produced a separation between the Church and the State in Peru was accompanied in Egypt by a 'modernization' of Islam and was associated with nationalist movements led by the upper classes and the intelligentsia.[32] The State was restructured by these same groups whose enlightened Islam influenced its structure and policies. Although these policies advocated the emancipation of women, they also stressed traditional family values. The early expansion of secular schooling for example, was sex-segregated with a gender-differentiated curriculum. Access to education and employment became acceptable for elite women provided they took place within sex-segregated and high-status institutions.[33] Gender roles were thus modified subtlely in ways that were consistent with religious precepts and social honour. These modified roles then percolated down to the lower classes through the status system.

Since the 1970s, rising living costs have increasingly threatened men's abilities to provide for their families while maintaining a segregated life-style. This, together with increasing male migration to the Gulf States has encouraged women into the labour-market. The anonymity of the city has also made marriages increasingly difficult to arrange, while the massive expansion of the educational system[34] has afforded an alternative arena for mate selection and a source of status for marriageable women (Smock and Youssef 1977; Eccel 1984). Women's increased access to education and employment has thus perpetuated a certain continuity in gender roles within the family (Wikan 1980; Hoodfar 1985). While it has eroded seclusion practices it has been predicated upon continued segregation of the sexes at home, school and work. However, these changes have taken place within a continuing pattern of low female labour-market participation, particularly in low-status occupations. Moreover, the religious underpinning of gender ideology still permeates the culture and reacts periodically against the trend towards female emancipation. For example Muslim Fundamentalism appears to be on the increase in some sectors of Egyptian society, and has resulted in a return to the veil for women and their withdrawal from the labour-market.

In Egypt gender roles and ideology clearly differentiated patterns of male and female employment and affected the structure of some major employing institutions, particularly in the public sector. Gender segregation was not merely the reflection of women's lack of skills or domestic commitments but was the product of cultural constraints over women stipulated by religion and social honour. These constraints were codified originally in religious and civil law, but even after formal emancipation the traditional value system continued to exert normative pressure on women that prevented them from responding to market forces in the early stages of economic development. Secularization, institutional reform and changes in the class and status system were necessary before market forces could 'liberate' women's labour. However, even as gender roles were modified and gradually permitted women to engage in the market as individual agents rather than as appendages of their families, the effects of previous seclusion practices continued to structure the market. The traditional male stereotyping of occupations such as office and bank clerks and textile workers only began to change within foreign companies whose employment practices were sex-typed differently. The rapid influx of such companies following the 'open-door' policy of Sadat in 1974, has had a major effect in breaking down these ideologically based practices from the demand side.

## Ghana

In Britain, Peru and Egypt, women's roles were already oriented somewhat towards dependence and domesticity at the onset of industrialization. Subsequent modifications in gender roles were the result of shifting relationships between the economy, the State and the value system. The influence of politics and ideology was less visible than economics partly because female subordination was already latent in the society and thus appeared 'natural'. The Ghanaian case is different. Prior to colonialism and industrialization, dependence and domesticity amongst women were relatively unknown. Women had considerable autonomy within the family and the economy and had independent sources of prestige and political authority; but today the pattern of female employment in the modern enterprises of urban Ghana replicates that of the West. This situation has come about not only through economic changes but through the imposition of Western values on Ghanaian society by the colonial State, foreign traders, missionaries and through the status system implanted by the colonial elites. This case shows better than any other that the gender roles which underlie gender segregation are cultural products forged by political and ideological processes as well as economic ones.

In southern Ghana[35] traditional indigenous institutions encouraged a high female participation in the economy coupled with considerable autonomy for women in the running of their enterprises. Women had independent access to property and were able to accumulate profits in their own right. They were not accountable to their husbands for the financing or administration of their activities, nor had the latter any rights of intervention or control.[36] Women had considerable skill as producers and entrepreneurs and corresponding status and wealth. Their economic roles were not conditioned by marital status or child-care commitments as in the West, since domestic responsibilities were shared amongst extended female kin.[37] Therefore, even though their activities might involve short or lengthy periods away from home, commitment to production was high and continuous over their lifetime. Their success as entrepreneurs increased rather than decreased over the life cycle (Okali 1983). Although aspects of female subordination were present within this situation, as witnessed by the greater access of men to the more lucrative trades and to political positions, and the existence of notions of male superiority, the extent and forms of subordination were very different from those in the other societies analysed above. Women may have been restricted to less-profitable areas of the economy, but within that sphere, they had autonomy over production and were able to accumulate wealth independently (Westwood 1984).

The reasons for this are complex and can only be mentioned briefly here. They have to do with the relative underdevelopment of institutions of private property, the separation of systems of property transfer between men and women, polygamous kinship systems (primarily though not exclusively matrilineal), the primacy of the lineage over the nuclear family, the existence of corporate institutions which represented women's interests, residential patterns which consisted of multi-household sex-segregated compounds, ease of divorce, and a relative lack of concern with pre-marital chastity. The absence of world religions, the fragmentation of the economy (absence of large estates) and the concentration of men in export agriculture and politico-military activities are also important.[38] This left cash-cropping of food products, cottage industry and trade for women. In sharp contrast with Egypt therefore, Ghanaian women had freedom of movement in public places and became particularly active in both local and long-distance trade.[39]

If the industrialization process was really gender-neutral, we would expect a random distribution of the sexes within the occupational structure, both horizontally and vertically. However, urban capitalism has excluded women from most of its activities and concentrated them into a narrow range of jobs. This has produced a sharp divergence between the pattern of female employment in the modern and traditional sectors of the economy. In 1970, women constituted half the work-force in small-scale urban employment (less than ten workers per establishment) but only 10 per cent of large-scale employment. In the manufacturing sector, they were two thirds of traditional labour force, but only 10 per cent of the factory work-force. The anomaly is most striking in the commercial sector, where despite the heavy concentration of women in indigenous trading systems, they were only a third of modern-sector sales workers (Date-Bah 1984).

Thus the high female participation[40] and the heavy concentration of women in manufacturing and commerce (see tables 11.4 to 11.6) is due to the persistence of petty commodity production in the Ghanaian economy and the importance of women in it. It is the major reason for the low supply of labour to domestic service. Modern-sector employment is heavily biased towards men. Between 1960—70 only 9 per cent of new female non-agricultural jobs were in the modern sector compared with 72 per cent of men's (Steel 1981). Most of these were jobs which are defined as 'female' in advanced industrial economies, i.e. secretarial jobs, nursing and teaching. Almost two thirds of modern-sector women in 1973 were employed in these three occupations. However, because of the male predominance in all modern-sector jobs, even these were not yet extensively feminized.

Within the capitalist sector then, the incorporation of women has been along similar lines to the West, although on a much smaller scale. This cannot be explained in terms of female seclusion as in the Egyptian case, nor in terms of lower labour-force commitment and the burden of child-care responsibilities as in the West. A recent survey of modern-sector firms showed that there were no differences in the patterns of job stability of men and women and that women had an equal commitment to work as men. Of the women in the survey 61 per cent were married and none worked part-time. All were able to resort to the female kinship network for help with child-care and the number who relied on employer's crèches was negligible (Date-Bah 1984).

The study reports that the major reasons given for women's marginalization were discrepancies in the educational levels of men and women and concerns about appropriateness of certain jobs to women's roles and status (Date-Bah 1984). Both these reasons indicate gender ideologies which were inimical to traditional Ghanaian society. Strenuous work and manual labour did not carry the same connotations of status inferiority in the traditional economy as in the capitalist labour-market. Nor were the two factors present which normally restrict women's access to education; their low economic value and the ideology of domesticity. This situation is the outcome of exclusionary mechanisms introduced by a foreign State and based on an alien ideology.

The colonial administration (1874—1957) created a selective process of training and recruitment for administrative jobs which reflected the sex roles of Victorian Britain rather than Ghana.[42] This assumed that only men were suitable for positions of responsibility and that female employment should be tied to marital status. Employment of women was discouraged generally and resignation upon pregnancy was made a condition of employment for those who were hired (Greenstreet 1981). Although legislation was later converted from exclusionary to protectionist, the underlying assumption that women deserved special status in the labour-market persisted throughout.

The educational system replicated that of late Victorian Britain, both structurally and ideologically.[43] It assumed that education should provide moral as well as academic training, and that girls' education should be oriented towards domestic skills and social graces. Schools were sex-segregated, and provision for girls was far inferior to that for boys. The early schools were run by Christian missionaries who disseminated an alien ideology about family structure and sexual morality. The colonial administration and the missions sustained a continual onslaught on indigenous kinship systems. They introduced the pattern of female-dependant, relatively indissoluble, Christian monogamous marriage, together with unequal rights of property inheritance.[44] This type of marriage became associated with the urban middle-class, many of whom had been educated in the mission schools. It deprived women of their autonomy as spouses and cut them off from the traditional support networks which had enabled them to maintain their autonomy.

The increased formalization of colonial political control together with the refusal to recognize women's political offices and associations concentrated power into the hands of male political appointees. Female religious roles were undermined through the influence of the Christian missions. Women were thus deprived of two important sources of social status and political influence in traditional society. Simultaneously economic forces were gradually lowering the value of women's economic activities while increasing those of men. The interference with traditional property rights, increased capitalization of the means of production, the tendency to bypass women in trading negotiations and the concentration of men in export agriculture, all tended to differentiate the wealth and status of men's and women's economic activities. As women's traditional activities were marginalized from the economy, so the benefits of their autonomy began to decline.[45]

Although the post-colonial government removed some of the more blatant forms of sex discrimination, the structural and ideological influences of the colonial period were perpetuated through the incipient class system. Elite families who were themselves a product of the colonial system, who tended to have Christian marriages and nuclear family structures, espoused the ideology of domesticity which had become associated with prestige and wealth. Men's preoccupations with occupational status began to restrict the labour-market behaviour of their wives, a situation that would have been inconceivable in the pre-colonial period.[46] The sex-typing of occupations introduced in colonial times was perpetuated by the post-colonial State which is the largest employer in Accra. Exclusionary practices were also introduced by foreign managements who entered Ghana during the post-independence industrialization process.

The educational system has played a crucial role as an economic and political exclusionary mechanism which worked against women.[47] Although its inegalitarian origins can be traced to imported ideologies, educational inequality is now sustained by the labour-market itself. The restriction of women's opportunities in the modern sector has lowered the return on girls' education compared with boys', and since it represents a considerable drain on the resources of most families, boys are given preferential access to education. Yet even where women have managed to gain access to the necessary qualifications, men are still preferred over women (Greenstreet 1981).

Women's participation in the economy is becoming class-differentiated as are their family structures. Middle-class women are more highly educated and are oriented towards modern-sector employment or a life as full-time housewives. Poor women who still conform to the traditional patterns of autonomy, are increasingly having the worst of both worlds. They have neither the economic security of the monogamous wife nor the benefits of autonomous production in a lucrative trade. Under pressure of poverty and underemployment men are failing to support wives and their families, especially if divorced, and women are being made to shoulder an increased share of the burden of family commitments from declining incomes. Trading occupations which were once a source of wealth and prestige are now associated increasingly with low status and prostitution.

## CONCLUSIONS

My purpose in this chapter has been to challenge the assumed sex-neutrality of economic processes which underlies much of contemporary labour-market and stratification theory. I believe this assumption seriously undermines our understanding of the mechanisms which produce inequality and action in industrial societies. However, this is only a hypothesis since the effect of gender segregation on these questions still requires systematic examination. In this chapter I have concentrated on a prior step in the argument — the notion that the mechanism which *produces* segregation, i.e. the market, is *not* sex-neutral. This argument is important because of the central role attributed to the market in determining stratification processes. If it can be shown to be subject to political and ideological influences, and, through these influences 'gendered', the way will be open for the examination of gender as a mechanism of stratification.

I have attempted to show that different patterns of gender segregation are the product of macrolevel linkages between economic and non-economic institutions and the incorporation into the market of political and ideological pressures deriving from these institutions. This has meant that occupational segregation is not merely the product of individual preferences and endowments but of a more diffuse permeation of the division of labour by gender. We have seen that skills, work commitment and prices have been influenced by gender and although they have constituted important bases for allocating labour to jobs they have not been the only ones. In all the societies analysed, notions that women constituted a special category of labour persisted even where they could no longer be differentiated from men in terms of their supply characteristics. Market forces failed to bring about desegregation when they should have done. This rigidity in the market is an effect of current links between the economy and the wider society and former practices sustained ideologically by the conflation of sex and work roles in the production process itself.

A major aspect of my argument has been that even though gender roles rest on a biological foundation they are cultural products and therefore capable of variation. The ideology of domesticity is also a cultural product, and although it has usually accompanied industrialization, it has appeared in other circumstances. It has been associated particularly with feudal aristocracies and world religions, and therefore appears to be fundamentally a class phenomenon, linked with notions of moral and social order and imposed through politico-religious institutions. The gender ideology which developed in the course of early industrialization may therefore have been as much a product of the incorporation of gender into emerging class relations as of the home-workplace separation.

Another aspect of my argument is the stress on the variability and historical contingency of patterns of gender segregation. Comparisons between societies show significant differences in the degree of segregation and the structure of women's participation in the economy. These differences can be traced clearly to variations in family structure and the role of gender ideology in the institutions which structured the economy. These variations are particularly pronounced within the small-scale sector of an economy prior to and even during industrialization (cf. Collver and Langlois 1962; Boserup 1975).

However, despite these different starting points and differences in the pace of industrial change, there is an unmistakeable convergent trend in patterns of segregation in the four countries. If neither the logic of industrialism nor the separation between productive and reproductive roles are responsible for this, then what is? Two points are relevant here. First, industrialization involves a type of society as well as a type of economy and the market is embedded in the political and cultural institutions of that society. It is a class-stratified society in which State institutions and processes of social mobility are major mechanisms of social integration. Historically, gender played a role in these processes as a mechanism of class reproduction, status consolidation and social control: the ideology of domesticity was important in legitimizing that role. Whether this was historical accident (produced by the fact that European societies were predisposed towards female subordination at the onset of industrialization) or whether it corresponds to a deeper societal function is open to discussion.

Secondly, the spread of industrialization processes to 'late developers' involved not only changes in forms of production, but all the other social and institutional elements asociated with it. However, these processes have been heavily influenced by the First World, directly through colonialism and indirectly through the international market and aid agencies. Also, the incipient class and status order is culturally as well as economically dependent upon the international stratification system. National elites have tended to assimilate and transmit the bourgeois values of the First World through the political institutions they control and through the internal status system. The gender assumptions embodied in early industrialization have therefore spread to other societies through social and political processes as well as economic ones.

Yet these examples have shown that change is not automatic. Political and ideological influences on the market can act as constraints on change as well as forces for it. It has generally been easier to push women out of the economy (for example in Ghana) than to encourage them into it (Peru and Egypt), despite a belief in civil rights and economic individualism. Paradoxically then, an institutional approach to gender segregation can demonstrate variation *and* similarity, change as well as stability.

The 'gender embeddedness' of the division of labour is thus an outcome of the wider structure of gender inequality and of the institutional linkages which shape the division of labour. A weak version of this thesis may see the incorporation of gender into the economy as a coincidental effect of those institutional linkages. A stronger version may seek to explore the wider role of gender in social and class reproduction under industrial capitalism. However, consistent with the premise that gender inequality is a cultural product, must be the theoretical possibility of a future transformation in gender roles which could reduce the influence of gender on the division of labour. However, until that day comes, it must be seen as an inherent feature of the division of labour and its effects on stratification must be examined further.

*– interesting statement of the ideological (or cultural) influence on gender inequality.*

APPENDIX

**Table 11.1   Summary indicators of industrialization for UK, Peru, Egypt and Ghana**

| Indicator | UK | Peru | Egypt | Ghana |
|---|---|---|---|---|
| GNP per capita US$ 1977 | 4,420 | 840 | 320 | 380 |
| Manufacturing as % GDP c.1977 | 37 | 19 | 24 | 9 |
| Value added in manufacturing US$ (millions) 1970 | 34,317 | 982 | 1326 | 253 |
| Non-primary employment* as % total employment | 90.0 | 50.8 | 46.5 | 42.0 |
| Wage and salaried labour** as % non-agricultural employment | 89.9 | 66.8 | 79.0 | 42.3 |
| Adult literacy rate 1975 | 99 | 72 | 44 | 30 |

*Note:*
\*   Excludes agriculture, livestock, fishing, mining, unemployed and unspecified activities.
\*\*   Excludes employers, the self-employed, family workers and unspecified workers, includes miners.
The employment figures refer to the census years: UK (1971); Peru (1972); Egypt (1976); and Ghana (1970).
*Sources*: *World Development Report*, 1979; *ILO Yearbook of Labour Statistics*, 1975; 1980.

**Table 11.2   Achieved level of education of the adult female population\***
**(25 + years): UK, Peru, Egypt, Ghana — (male figures in parenthesies)**

| Level of education | UK (1971) | Peru (1972) | Egypt (1976) | Ghana (1970) |
|---|---|---|---|---|
| Illiterate | — | 47.5 (22.1) | 92.9 (79.4) | 88.0 (66.4) |
| Primary | — | 38.7 (55.9) | 2.6 ( 6.8) | 4.8 ( 6.9) |
| Secondary | 92.0 | 10.9 (16.0) | 3.1 ( 8.3) | 7.1 (26.0) |
| Higher | 8.0 | 3.0 ( 6.0) | 1.3 ( 5.5) | 0.1 ( 0.7) |
| Total | 100.0 (n.a) | 100.0 (100.0) | 100.0 (100.0) | 100.0 (100.0) |

*Note:*
\*   This includes rural population, the urban figures would show much higher levels of education.
*Source: Unesco, Statistical Yearbook, 1983.*

**Table 11.3    Enrolment ratios by sex and level of education: UK, Peru, Egypt, Ghana**

|  | UK (1970) | Peru (1970) | Egypt (1975) | Ghana (1970) |
|---|---|---|---|---|
| **Primary** |  |  |  |  |
| GER* males | 104 | 113 | 89 | 73 |
| GER females | 104 | 97 | 57 | 54 |
| Female enrolments | 49% | 46% | 39% | 43% |
| **Secondary** |  |  |  |  |
| GER males | 74 | 35 | 56 | 21 |
| GER females | 73 | 26 | 30 | 8 |
| female enrolments | 48% | 43% | 35% | 28% |
| **Higher** |  |  |  |  |
| GER males | 18 | 14 | 19 | 1 |
| GER females | 9 | 8 | 8 | 0.2 |
| Female enrolments | 33% | 34% | 30% | 14% |
| Female university enrolments | 29% | 30% | 30% | 13% |
| No. of female students per 100,000 inhabitants | 701 | 644 | 747 | 18 |

*Note:*
* GER = gross enrolment ratio: the total number of male or female children as a percentage of the total number of male or female children in the school age-group. This figure may exceed 100 where children are admitted earlier or later than the school age-limits.

School age-groups for different levels of education vary between countries:
    UK — primary = 5—10; secondary = 11—17; higher = 20—24
    Peru — primary = 6—11; secondary = 12—17; higher = 20—24
    Egypt — primary = 6—11; secondary = 12—17; higher = 20—24
    Ghana — primary = 6—15; secondary = 16—19; higher = 20—24
The Ghanaian figures are not comparable with the other countries in the table at primary and secondary levels.
*Source: Unesco, Statistical Yearbook 1983.*

**Table 11.4  Summary indicators of female employment\* for UK, Peru, Egypt and Ghana**

|  | UK (1971) | Peru (1972) | Egypt (1976) | Ghana (1970) |
|---|---|---|---|---|
| Female labour-force participation rate (base 15 + years)\*\* | 42.5 | 19.9 | 6.4 | 63.6 |
| Female non-primary employment as % total female employment | 92.8 | 71.7 | 51.8 | 39.3\*\*\* |
| Women's share of non-primary employment | 36.7 | 28.5 | 10.0 | 47.9 |
| Female wage and salaried labour as % total female non-agricultural employment | 94.2 | 62.9 | 92.3 | 12.7 |
| Women's share of wage and salaried non-agricultural employment | 38.4 | 26.2 | 11.2 | 14.4 |

*Note:*
\* For definitions see notes to table 11.1
\*\* The labour-force participation rate includes agricultural employment and is underestimated in countries like Egypt which do not have good coverage of family labour in rural areas.
\*\*\* 1960 Census.
*Sources: ILO Yearbook of Labour Statistics, 1973; 1975, 1980.*

**Table 11.5  Distribution of female non-agricultural employment by occupational class**

| Occupational class | UK (1971) | Peru (1972) | Egypt (1976) | Ghana (1970) |
|---|---|---|---|---|
| Professionals and technicians | 12.3 | 16.3 | 37.5 | 4.4 |
| Administrative and managerial | 0.9 | 0.2 | 2.5 | 0.1 |
| Clerical | 31.2 | 13.5 | 28.0 | 2.1 |
| Sales workers | 12.3 | 16.7 | 6.8 | 56.3 |
| Service workers | 23.5 | 32.9 | 13.1 | 3.3 |
| Production workers | 19.7 | 20.5 | 12.0 | 33.7 |
| Total | 99.9 | 100.1 | 99.9 | 99.9 |

*Note:* excludes agricultural and unclassified workers.
*Source: ILO Yearbook of Labour Statistics, 1975; 1980.*

**Table 11.6 Female share of non-agricultural employment within each occupational class**

| Occupational class | UK (1971) | Peru (1972) | Egypt (1976) | Ghana (1970) |
|---|---|---|---|---|
| Professionals and technicians | 38.3 | 33.2 | 25.1 | 23.4 |
| Administrative and managerial | 8.4 | 5.4 | 11.1 | 5.2 |
| Clerical | 60.3 | 35.7 | 19.3 | 15.5 |
| Sales workers | 47.4 | 30.2 | 5.2 | 87.6 |
| Service workers | 69.3 | 57.6 | 7.8 | 23.3 |
| Production workers | 17.1 | 13.7 | 2.8 | 35.1 |
| Total | 36.7 | 28.5 | 9.6 | 47.9 |

*Note:* excludes agricultural and unclassified workers.
*Source: ILO Yearbook of Labour Statistics,* 1975; 1980.

**Table 11.7 Distribution of female wage and salaried\* non-agricultural employment by occupational class**

| Occupational class | UK (1971) | Peru (1972) | Egypt (1976) | Ghana (1970) |
|---|---|---|---|---|
| Professionals and technicians | 12.3 | 24.3 | 40.3 | 29.7 |
| Administrative and managerial | 1.0 | 0.2 | 2.7 | 0.3 |
| Clerical | 32.3 | 20.8 | 30.3 | 16.1 |
| Sales workers | 11.0 | 5.0 | 2.7 | 10.2 |
| Service workers | 23.3 | 40.7 | 13.8 | 16.5 |
| Production workers | 20.0 | 9.0 | 10.2 | 27.1 |
| Total | 99.9 | 100.0 | 100.0 | 99.9 |
| Share of total female employment | 94.2 | 62.9 | 92.3 | 12.7 |

*Note:* excludes agricultural and unclassified workers.
\* Excludes employers, the self-employed, unpaid family labour and unclassified employment status.
*Source: ILO Yearbook of Labour Statistics,* 1975; 1980.

**Table 11.8  Female share of wage and salaried employment\* within each occupational class**

| Occupational class | UK (1971) | Peru (1972) | Egypt (1976) | Ghana (1970) |
|---|---|---|---|---|
| Professionals and technicians | 40.1 | 38.9 | 25.6 | 23.2 |
| Administrative and managerial | 8.5 | 5.4 | 12.0 | 4.6 |
| Clerical | 60.7 | 35.6 | 19.3 | 16.2 |
| Sales workers | 51.9 | 20.5 | 6.9 | 37.7 |
| Service workers | 72.8 | 55.4 | 8.6 | 17.5 |
| Production workers | 18.4 | 5.9 | 2.9 | 8.0 |
| Total | 38.4 | 26.2 | 11.2 | 14.4 |

*Note:* excludes agricultural and unclassified workers.
\* Excludes employers, the self-employed, unpaid family labour, and unclassified employment status.
*Source: ILO Yearbook of Labour Statistics,* 1975; 1980.

**Table 11.9  Principal occupations of the female workforce in Britain and Peru (Lima)**

| | Britain | | | Lima, Peru | |
|---|---|---|---|---|---|
| | 1911 | 1971 | | 1974 | |
| Occupation | % total women | % total women | female % within occupation | % total women | female % within occupation |
|---|---|---|---|---|---|
| Schoolteachers | 3.8 | 4.1 | 63.6 | 6.2 | 62.1 |
| Nurses | 1.7 | 4.3 | 91.4 | 4.1 | 85.4 |
| Clerks, typists | 3.0 | 27.3 | 71.1 | 9.0 | 92.0 |
| Shop workers | 9.3 | 10.8 | 60.0 | 18.0 | 39.5 |
| Textile workers | 13.5 | 1.9 | 53.8 | 2.2 | 27.2 |
| Clothing workers | 14.0 | 3.6 | 80.0 | 8.5 | 68.8 |
| Packers, labellers | — | 2.4 | 72.9 | 1.9 | 45.8 |
| Hairdressers | 0.1 | 1.4 | 78.3 | 1.8 | 90.2 |
| Catering, etc.\* | 3.2 | 7.0 | 82.9 | 5.0 | 51.8 |
| Laundry workers | 3.5 | 0.7 | 77.4 | 3.2 | 94.9 |
| Charwomen, cleaners | 2.6 | 4.5 | 86.0 | — | — |
| Domestic servants | 26.1 | 2.2 | 83.8 | 24.0 | 93.3 |
| Cumulative total | 80.7 | 70.2 | | 83.7 | |

*Note:*
\* Catering includes waitresses, cooks, kitchen hands, chambermaids, and other domestic staff in institutions. The figures for 'Britain' refer to England and Wales.
*Source:* Britain adapted from Joseph (1983; p. 143). Figures for Peru, from *Employment Survey,* (Ministry of Labour, 1984), unpublished.

**Table 11.10 Distribution of total non-agricultural employment and wage and salaried labour in Peru (1972) and Egypt (1976)**

| | Non-agricultural employment | | | | Wage and salaried employment | | | |
|---|---|---|---|---|---|---|---|---|
| | *Total* | | *Women only* | | *Total* | | *Women only* | |
| | *Peru* | *Egypt* | *Peru* | *Egypt* | *Peru* | *Egypt* | *Peru* | *Egypt* |
| Professional | 13.9 | 14.3 | 16.3 | 37.5 | 16.7 | 17.6 | 24.3 | 40.3 |
| Administrative | 0.8 | 2.1 | 0.2 | 2.5 | 1.0 | 2.5 | 0.2 | 2.7 |
| Clerical | 10.8 | 13.9 | 13.5 | 28.0 | 15.6 | 17.6 | 20.8 | 30.3 |
| Sales | 15.7 | 12.5 | 16.7 | 6.8 | 6.5 | 4.4 | 5.0 | 2.7 |
| Services | 16.3 | 16.2 | 32.9 | 13.1 | 19.7 | 18.0 | 40.7 | 13.8 |
| Production | 42.6 | 40.9 | 20.5 | 12.0 | 40.4 | 39.9 | 9.0 | 10.2 |
| Total | 100.1 | 99.9 | 100.1 | 99.9 | 99.9 | 100.0 | 100.0 | 100.0 |

*Source: ILO Yearbook of Labour Statistics,* 1975; 1980

*[Handwritten annotations at top of page:]*

(1) Explaining gender inequality ~~without~~ without conceptual reformat...
  (1) human capital to free market processes / concentrate in gender inequality within occupational...
  (2) discrimination.
  (3) conventional view is
(B) - gender (4) occupational segregation as result of stratification processes. no ~~posing~~ ...
  inequality as result of / secondary to market forces
(2) patriarchy as equal to or primary to capitalism - gender inequality
  is the structure of inequality to be explained - this
  requires major conceptual reformation

# 12

# The Role of Gender in the
# 'First Industrial Nation'
## Agriculture in England 1780–1850

## Leonore Davidoff

*'Keep up appearances: there lies the test*
*The World will give thee credit for the rest'*
    John Trusler, The Way to be Rich and Respectable, *1777.*

By the end of the eighteenth century, a middle class was emerging as a major force in English society.[1] The expansion of capitalist enterprise had transformed forms of property and fostered scientific and practical experimentation, rational acounting and centralized marketing. Commercial, manufacturing, professional and farming families gained in wealth, knowledge and prestige. Their aim was not simply inclusion in the existing system but challenged the legitimate basis of aristocratic domination. Their wealth flowed mainly from liquid property and skill rather than land, hitherto the major source of political and social honour.[2] As employers of wage labour, manufacturers and farmers faced directly that section of the lower strata being transformed into a propertyless working class. Moreover, the middle class was itself riven by internal divisions: between higher- and lower-ranking families, between provinces and metropolis, Anglican and Nonconformist, Tory and Whig.

Within this context, provincial middle-class consciousness was framed by moral and religious values, embodied in the Evangelical movement, both Anglican and Nonconformist.[3] Concern with individual salvation elevated moral probity above the claims of rank through birth. An intensely moral life was to be supported by the rational principles of property management and work organization, both aspects enhancing commercial trustworthiness at a time when formal business institutions were undeveloped. The emphasis on conversion experience meant that inward grace could be demonstrated by outward individual behaviour; restraint in gait and language, soberness, curbing public display of bodily functions or simply wearing clean linen. Such 'seriousness' challenged aristocratic laxity, exemplified in the countryside by the absentee parson and hard-riding, drinking squire. In London the Prince Regent's circle was notorious for drunkenness, licentiousness and gambling at a time when debt to tradesmen was part of the aristocratic code but anathema to the self-respect of the middle classes whose livelihood and social position depended on commercial trust.[4] The challenge of the middle class was, indeed, seen as a crusade against 'Old Corruption'.[5]

Within the middle class, social honour was claimed through *gentility*, a concept undoubtedly derived partly from gentry culture but reinterpreted in crucial ways.[6] *Gentility* and its lesser derivative, *respectability*, were always heavily gendered categories. A *gentleman's* claim to recognition was his independence signified by his ability to protect and support his dependents (primarily wife and children), a definition with chivalric overtones of reconstructed paternalism going hand in hand with market exploitation.[7] The analogous ideal of *lady* placed women in a protected environment away from independent action in market, street or political forum.

Religious and secular status merged in stressing domestic life, the creation and maintenance of the 'Home' in opposition to the public world. This division evolved into a powerful world-view embodied in the doctrine of 'separate spheres', with its gendered resonance which became a unifying characteristic of middle-class identity. Such concepts are never made from whole cloth but had an inheritance from law, theology, custom and classical learning. Men already claimed natural superiority and a place as representatives of household and family in the body politic. They were seen as potential bearers of rationality and controllers of disruptive forces, particularly female sexuality. Since it was the middle classes who had promoted the potentially disruptive and amoral market forces, they were especially concerned with social order and their apprehensions were fuelled by potential political disorder unleashed by the French Revolution. Relations between the sexes often became a metaphor for such threats to the social fabric.

The central place of home and family also rested on the organization of middle-class property and economic resources. Few institutions had yet emerged for transacting business. Early banks, for example, were liable to sudden collapse and family or local community remained the primary source of capital and credit.[8] The main form of enterprise was the single entrepreneur aided by family and household and expandable into the partnership. Wives, often acting as informal partners, would have been the logical choice, but under the legal convention of 'coverture', at marriage a woman 'died a kind of civil death'; she could not make contracts, sue or be sued or declared bankrupt.[9] Single women and widows, while not legally disabled, were conventually regarded in a similar way. Male relatives were favoured partners: brothers, sons, nephews, brothers-in-law and sons-in-law.

One of the most powerful middle-class forms of property, the trust, also marginalized women. Male relatives acted as trustees investing and managing women's property to produce income for their support while capital was freed for investment in the family enterprise.[10] The liquidity of much middle-class property favoured partible inheritance in contrast to primogeniture practised by the landed gentry, although sons tended to inherit business tools, stock and premises while daughters received household goods, cash and government securities.[11] One result was the intensity of sibling relationships since all life-chances were tied to the family enterprise, a pattern reinforced by the late age at marriage.[12] Women's roles were extended beyond mothers and wives to sisters, aunts, cousins or occasionally non-kin in a pattern of male support exchanged for female service.

Since kin were so important to economic survival, marriage was central. Brothers-in-law were brought in as partners or sisters married existing partners. The priority given to such links is indicated by 'sibling exchange' marriage frequently found in town and countryside, across all occupations and religious groups. In this practice, two brothers would marry two sisters or a sister and brother from one family would marry a brother and sister from another. Cousin marriages were also frequent, both patterns reinforcing partnership.[13] Women were central in maintaining relationships upon which business and professional operations rested. They contributed further by bearing and rearing suitabily large numbers of sons as future personnel,[14] and they cared for apprentices, pupils or shopmen, often kin, who lived in their master's home. In addition, women contributed labour and skills to the enterprise although often behind the scenes, since households were largely still located next to, if not within, the enterprise. Bankers' families lived in the Bank House, school masters' in the School House, millers' in the Mill House, while shops were in the front room from which doctors likewise dispensed drugs. Thus women dealt with customers, helped keep the books and undertook other business tasks while running the house.

Women were also instrumental in exhibiting the family's position through consumption. An effort to keep up appearances and display credit-worthiness lay behind much of the expenditure in rising standards of living. Middle-class households bought the furniture, carpets, wallpaper, silver plate, pictures and wheeled vehicles for their renovated or new suburban homes. They read new publications, attended doctors and solicitors, created opportunities for more clergymen, schoolmasters, bankers and architects. This circular process created demand for goods and services which made modest fortunes while fuelling claims to status recognition by the gentry.[15] The necessity to prove probity through life-style increased during the volatile Napoleonic War period. The mingling of family and business finances under unlimited liability made frequent bankruptcies more devastating. High mortality constantly threatened financial support from a husband, father or brother. Thus family and kin, augmented by local and religious community ties, provided a vital source of support. Women, in their active domesticity, were at the heart of these networks.

The contribution of women's property, labour and skill to the enterprise has been outlined. Conversely, men were heavily involved in the household where business and social contacts intermingled, the endless tea-drinking being by no means a purely female affair. Middle-class men, working from the building which housed the home, engaged with their children and the innumerable visiting family and friends. At the same time, these men were active in the expanding public sphere. In addition to their business affairs, men sought political, scientific and cultural recognition through a myriad of voluntary societies, the hallmark of the middle class.[16] Not coincidentally, such organizations were often charitable trusts, their trustees, the same men running the gas companies, insurance societies, and renovated grammar schools, further strengthening the masculine image of the public sphere.

Women were peripheral to such organizations. They might give subscriptions or act as spectators at selected events, but were ineligible as effective members. Forms of property, economic institutions and cultural norms framed middle-class masculinity as action and independence while women received support in return for personal services and dependence.[17] At this time, their role promised positive rewards. It was only as the nineteenth century developed, that the price women paid for exclusion from the expanding public world became manifest.

The provincial middle class has usually been taken as an urban phenomenon. It may be argued however, that similar patterns would emerge wherever conditions for its growth were present. In the last quarter of the eighteenth century farming for profit was well established in the south-eastern and midland areas of England.[18] Here too, Anglicans and Nonconformists were active proponents of domesticity. Therefore, detailed concentration on this local farming community should demonstrate the interaction of class and gender in its historical context. The middle-class challenge might be observed even better in the countryside where gentry and aristocracy were visible than in more middle-class enclaves of provincial manufacturing towns. Farmers were the first to confront wage labourers on a large scale, before the familiar case of manufacture. Thus it is here in the heartland of the upper-class ascendancy, that the men and women of the middle class will be observed as they forged a self-identity in the daily round of business, social and family life.

Despite the growth of manufacturing industry in the late eighteenth century, agriculture remained the basis of English society. Land, in the form of large estates, was owned mainly by the aristocracy. Below them was a larger group of landowning gentry without titles, plus a scattering of owner occupiers. By the mid-eighteenth century, particularly in the grain-growing areas of the midlands and southeast, the uniquely English 'three-tier' system of agriculture was firmly established. Landowners leased out land and farmsteads and were responsible for maintaining buildings, roads, hedges and drainage. The farmers who managed the land were tenants who supplied stock, seed and tools. This division gave a flexibility unlike European peasant farming or even owner occupation of English upland farms of the north and west. Farmers could add or discard acres and move households from farm to farm with changes in labour supply or demand for grain products.

In these areas the system of boarding and lodging farm servants within the farmhouse was giving way to the employment of day-labourers paid in cash. Farm service had been performed primarily by young men and women before marriage whereas day-labour represented a permanently proletarianized work-force.[19] This shift was related to changes in farming practice where arable crops were easing out animal husbandry, an innovation often countered by hostility from the agriculture labouring community.

By the second quarter of the nineteenth century, it was recognized that although landowners provided many of the basic resources, the farmers were 'the active capitalists of English agriculture'.[20] For much of the eastern region, agriculture had become an economic salvation. This area had been the centre of the wool trade through the eighteenth century, its towns and villages prosperous with wool merchants, weavers and spinners. By the 1770s, changes in demand and competition from abroad eroded trade, the blockade of the Napoleonic War providing the final blow. However, the same factors created a protected market for grain, many woollen mills being converted for grinding corn,[21] while capital salvaged by wool merchants was reinvested in growing grain, malting and milling.[22]

The gulf between prosperous farmers and labourers grew. Farmers became disdainful of manual work alongside their men, spending more time in planning, marketing and managerial functions.[23] The gap widened further when the high cost of corn during the Napoleonic wars brought wealth to many farmers but lean years to their labourers, whose lives appeared increasingly narrow and vulgar. Rising expectations among farmers were encouraged by newcomers to the countryside. Families with a little capital were drawn by high profits and the prospect of a rural retreat. Many came to grief in the post-war slump, but their influence as carriers of culture was strong. The ex-naval officer, John Harriott, took over a large farm on marginal lands in coastal Essex, determined to make it pay and enlighten his stolid rural neighbours with innovations such as Sunday schools.[24] At a more opulent level, John Hanson, a wealthy London merchant, bought a small Essex estate as a retreat on which to raise his fourteen children. He was keen to run the Home Farm on commercial lines while his home became a social centre for the area, displaying genteel domesticity in daily life.[25] The war also brought army officers to market towns, some of whom became part of the evangelical community while others sponsored balls, assemblies and theatres. Worldly or religious, these families created demands for goods and services, acting as status leaders to the local population.[26] These towns also attracted retired farmers, and farmers' widows and spinster daughters, swelling the ranks of genteel families living on small investment-incomes, mingling the cultures of town and countryside.[27]

In any case, farming was not yet a fixed full-time occupation during the period under investigation. For the wealthy banking family of Oakes in Bury St. Edmunds (close friends of their neighbour, Arthur Young), the farm was still an important part of their household economy and the banker himself turned out to see the harvest in.[28] Jonas Asplin, an Essex physician, was as concerned about the state of his corn as of his patients.[29] The successful Witham grocer, Thomas Butler, turned the business over to his son and worked the farm whose fields lay behind the shop.[30] Malters and brewers grew their own barley while farming and milling continued in combination.[31] Smaller farms might keep a public house or a shop, work a brick-kiln, blacksmithy or small pottery.[32] These enterprises used family labour, custom dictating activities suitable for boys and girls, men and women.

By the 1820s, the standard of living and status aspirations of farming families had been raised. A Suffolk vicar had noted in 1813 how a generation before farmers had 'lived in the midst of their enlightened neighbours like beings of another order; in their personal labour they were indefatigable; in their fare hard, in their dress homely, in their manners rude. We ne'er shall look upon their like again'.[33] There were modest fortunes in farming but it was risky and capital was necessary. Arthur Young, travelling the eastern counties, noted that houses of small farms 'are frequently wretched hovels, not better, if so good, as decent cottages'.[34] At the other end of the scale farmers lived in converted manor houses, for example families like the Hutleys of Power Hall in Witham, Essex, with extended acres, augmented by judicious marriage, who became a force in the local community. Hutley, farming over 1,500 acres, had the option of becoming part of the local gentry but he chose to remain a farmer whose wealth exceeded that of some of his gentry neighbours.[35]

Hutley dined regularly with the self-made Witham doctor, Henry Dixon, himself the son of a small farmer but who, through marriage, was proprietor of neighbouring Durward Hall and like many of their mutual friends was active in local politics often opposed to gentry interests.[36]

These substantial farmers, whose wealth and contacts made them powerful beyond the bounds of their villages, were becoming a social anomaly if not an actual threat to the status order of the countryside. By the 1820s, peace had brought a sharp drop in grain prices, combining with bad harvests to turn boom into depression and only larger farms backed by strong credit survived. Yet when the Select Committee on Agriculture sat in 1833 to enquire into the distress, it was maintained that farmers and farmers' wives were loath to give up the tastes they had acquired during the prosperous years of the French Wars. 'They may have since been forced to diminish their expenses, but I cannot say that they have returned to their former habits, because they could not have kept their grade in society.'[37]

Local gentry and clergy were threatened by the rising position of farmers while their own fortunes were closely tied to the farming enterprise, a point made painfully clear in the 1820s and 1830s when, as landlords, many were forced to grant rent abatements on farms no longer profitable.[38] Jane Austen encapsulated the social bewilderment expressed by local gentry. In her novel of 1816, *Emma,* the heroine of the title had befriended a young woman of gentry origins who had been at boarding-school with the sisters of an up-and-coming young farmer neighbour. This young man read a great deal but not 'what you would think anything of. He reads the Agricultural Reports'. When Emma is asked if she has seen him, she replies that she may have seen him fifty times but has no idea of his name:

> The yeomanry are precisely the order of people with whom I feel I can have nothing to do. A degree or two lower, and a creditable appearance might interest me; I might hope to be useful to their families in some way or other. But a farmer can need none of my help, and is therefore in one sense as much above my notice as in every other he is below it.[39]

Austen recognizes here the role of women in giving or withholding social recognition while satirizing the gentry for false pretensions over their farming neighbours. At the same time, radicals such as Cobbett fulminated against upstart farmers who disdained the plain ways and honest oak furniture of his youthful days.[40]

Status problems among farmers were furthered by the wide range of incomes and life-styles. The ambiguous division between managerial and manual tasks for both the farmer and his wife allowed no breaking point in the scale of status demarcation as between, for example, wholesale and retail trade. Furthermore, in the earlier part of the period under discussion in this chapter, young people from small farming families had entered higher echelons of domestic service. Ladies' maids, children's nurses, cooks, grooms and footmen were often recruited from farms and when married settled back in the countryside carrying with them urban standards yet remaining socially tainted in the eyes of the gentry by their service experience.[41]

The ambiguity of farmers' status seemed most disturbing to the clergy, traditional cultural leaders in the countryside, particularly Anglicans with close ties to the gentry but whose incomes might be closer to those of their farming parishioners.[42] Unease about the degree of social intimacy between farmers and clergy surfaces in local sources. An Evangelical curate in rural Suffolk wrote a tale in which the clergyman hero is shocked when his sister is courted by the son of a local farmer, a young man given a gentleman's education which raised him above his station.[43] Clergy-farming relations were acerbated further by the tithe question particularly where farmers were Nonconformist and clergymen doubled as landowners. But even Anglican farming families might seek to preserve independence by refusing to remove a cap or curtsy to clergy.[44] Nevertheless, Evangelical religion permeated the farming community as much as the urban middle class. Nonconformists and Anglicans recruited farmers as the backbone of revitalized rural congregations.[45] Prosperous farming families drove their gigs to more distant town churches and chapels often staying on for afternoon Sunday services.[46] Here they mixed with trade and professional people, raising aspirations for a more refined life-style.

Religious impetus combined with changing farming practices to emphasize the need for an enlarged education for farmers' children. In 1807, Arthur Young noted that the 'greater opulence of farmers led to improved education of their children and a greater taste for reading.' No longer did incessant drudgery shut him (sic) out from 'intercourse with the world which enlarges the mind and increases knowledge'.[47] More prosperous male farmers mixed socially at markets and other functions, their mobility increasing with ownership of riding-horses and wheeled vehicles. Modern farming also required increased literacy and numeracy for the keeping of accounts and records, writing business letters and keeping up with new literature on farming methods. School curricula were expanded with surveying, geometry and bookkeeping alongside Latin and Greek for sons of farmers and tradesmen in the renovated grammar schools and numerous private academies of the market towns.[48] Gentry, clergy and professionals may have felt threatened by the educated, more 'gentlemanly' farmer, but farmers saw education as a means of raising their social status *vis-à-vis* labourers. In a survey of Suffolk it was stated that the smaller farmers could not afford the annual fees of £40 or £50 for the grammar schools and 'owing to the advantages of the free and parochial schools now spread throughout the county, our labourers' children will be better taught than our own.'[49] Since the clergy were mainly responsible for the drive to educate labourers' children, this further aggravated tensions.

While the sons of farmers were beginning to receive a general education augmented by practical subjects, girls' brief formal schooling and home training alike emphasized the expectation of a domestic future. In Lincolnshire a farmer sent his sons to school but not his daughters as they needed only to milk, sew, cook and bear children.[50] Girls had long been excluded from the grammar schools, many of whose original founding charters had specified that both sexes should attend. The girls' private schools which existed at this time stressed deportment, music, drawing and a smattering of foreign languages in addition to the all-pervasive religious and moral training. Since the content of the education offered to girls from farming families was not directly useful or seen to be relevant to their lives, they were more open to censure for pretentiousness than young men whose schooling might at least turn them into better farmers.

In fact, the standard of living of the family was partially determined by the level of literacy, skill and outlook of its female members. Wives and daughters who had received a better education might manage to keep some literary pursuits and mix more freely with other middle-class women. Jane Saffrey, who had run a boarding-school before marrying a Baptist farmer, organized a small magazine and literary society,[51] while Jane Ransome Biddell, daughter of an Ipswich Quaker manufacturer but married to a wealthy Anglican farmer wrote poetry and mixed with the upper echelons of the town.[52] Yet the literary output of both women is a celebration of domesticity. 'Commonplace books' of young men and women illustrate their differing preoccupations. While all were concerned with moral questions and individual salvation, masculine entries include exercises in measurement, comments on politics, scientific facts, or the weather. The cultural milieu of young women, gleaned from books, newspapers, school stories, local sermons and their diary entries favoured family relationships, friendship and domestic happenings. Jane Seabrook was a farmer's daughter and future farmer's wife when she kept such a book in her late teens. Her brother-in-law copied for her the well-known homily, 'The One Thing Needful': religious duties, which 'particularly belong to woman to gain for her family'. She is to daily read and explain the Scriptures, to lead all family members 'to the alter of God'. If her husband stands aloof from these important duties and 'suffers the cares and troubles of the world more to possess his mind' there is nothing she can do but 'humbly hope and pray'.[53]

Local evidence suggests that farmers' wives, sisters and daughters took seriously their role in creating a domestic atmosphere and training their children. They saw the home as a means of overcoming divisions between master and man, as strong in the countryside as in the town. Earthly homes were a foretaste of the immortality open to all in the heavenly home. In an unpublished poem entitled simply, 'Home', Jane Ransome Biddell (farmer's wife) states many of these themes explicitly:

> *Alike in day-built shed, or marble hall*
> *Thy magic name has power o'er every heart*
> *The quiet nest, through life so dear to all*
> *The goal from which the spirit may depart.*

But home had a different meaning for men and women:

> *How sweet the atmosphere around thee thrown*
> *Where youthful daughters grace thy social hearth*
> *Nor less, though sadder, is thy influence known*
> *By son's self-exiled wandering o'er the earth*[54]

For both men and women, the material basis of that home was an equally important preoccupation, for both spiritual and worldly reasons. Changes in farming practice and higher levels of income combined at the end of the eighteenth century to institute changes in the layout of farmsteads as well as internal alterations to the farmhouse in keeping with middle-class concerns for privacy, comfort and family life. By the early nineteenth century there had been extensive alterations to existing farms as well as the planning of new farmsteads. New farming methods tidied away many functions into barns and sheds. The use of manure as fertilizer meant providing for its storage which cleared farmyards, while more expensive machinery was kept under cover. The older pattern had been a square of utilitarian buildings with the farmhouse making up the fourth side, no garden to speak of and an entrance through a mucky yard.[55] This was changing as the 'casual chaos' became a 'more planned and purposeful lay-out of the new order'.[56] Many farmhouses were given brick fronts with sash windows and door lintels covering their old-fashioned muddle of elevations, hiding mud and wattle exteriors. By siting the kitchen and working places firmly at the back and presenting such a front to the road, 'farmhouses could approximate to mere . . . residences that could just as well have appeared in town.'[57] By the 1840s, 'Essex farmhouses and buildings are for the most part substantial and ornamental with neat gardens and choice evergreens.'[58]

The interior layout of the farmhouse also changed. The size of the work-force on larger farms would have prevented traditional boarding of all labourers even without social conventions of family privacy.[59] Initially, labourers were segregated at a separate table in the living kitchen, which later gave way to feeding the men in the 'back-house' (bak'hus) for a midday meal only, while the family ate in a separate kitchen and sat in a parlour. A door to this room avoided entrance through the kitchen, keeping family and hired hands apart. Segregation was not simply a social pretension but part of a desire by farmers' female relatives' for freedom from heavy manual tasks. A farmer's daughter who remembered the work involved in the hot dinners and, at harvest, special cakes and home-brewed beer, could understand that farmers' wives welcomed paying men in cash to board themselves although it 'snapped some of the ties which bound the servant and master as fellow creatures'.[60] From the eighteenth to the nineteenth century, the tradition of the harvest supper (in Suffolk, the 'Horkey') with its special ales, songs and rituals, was transformed from the lavish spread in the common 'house place', with tables laden with roast and boiled meat, plum pudding and Horkey ale, master and mistress at the head of the table taking part, to a separate meal provided in the kitchen where the farmer and his wife put in an appearance for the final toasts. Later still the publican was paid to provide the whole affair at the local inn where much heavy drinking took place and women were seldom present.[61]

Furnishings of farmhouses also altered. There were signs of a more rational life-style in wall clocks and barometers. Stone-flagged floors gave way to carpets, open fireplaces with chimney-breasts hung with cooking and farming implements were replaced by closed grates and overmantels. Curtains and padded chairs or a sofa were introduced. There might be books in cases and possibly a piano.[62] The diary of a farmer's wife covers 1823 when extensive alterations were made to their farmhouse, including new grates and chimney adjustment, a parlour with carpets and curtains, the purchase of pictures and, significantly, bell-pulls to summon the servants from the kitchen. The alterations took over five months and by July, she recorded: 'I feel much pleased that I can prevail on Mr Green (*the new vicar*) to take a glass of wine for the first time at our house.'[63]

Men in farming families too, shopped for the new furnishings, helped hang the wallpaper and appreciated the various refinements of their daily lives. However, many, in addition to running the farm, were becoming involved in the voluntary societies which were beginning to redefine the public sphere. For example, the Thaxted Book Society, a group of farmers in Essex led by the Nonconformist minister, met monthly to discuss books brought from London. Despite the fact that they met at each other's houses with only the annual dinner held at the Sun Inn, there seems to have been only one woman member.[64] Some organizations built the concept of men's responsibility for dependants into their activities, setting up funds for widows and children while also emphasizing their masculine ambience through ritual dining and drinking. Their meetings were almost always held in public houses and ranged from purely social affairs such as the Chelmsford Beefsteak Club, to more political Whig and Tory strongholds. Freemasonry, too, flourished in the eastern counties and was almost entirely middle class despite its aristocratic patronage at the national level.

While innkeepers, tradesmen and professional men tended to dominate in lodges in Colchester and Ipswich, farmers made up 6 per cent of the total.[65]

The contacts gained through an organization like the Freemasons were used by farmers to promote business, but Agricultural Societies and Farmers Clubs were their special milieu. The latter were less prestigious and had fewer aristocratic titles but they had more working members who exchanged practical information.[66] In Suffolk in 1804 there had been one Agricultural Society, but by 1846 there were five as well as ten Farmers Clubs.[67] Women might go as spectators to Agricultural Society shows and social affairs but they were totally excluded from the Farmers Clubs which met in local public houses. Farmers also joined forces to protect their property as rural police were unknown before the 1830s. The Napoleonic wars and their aftermath of depression meant much unrest among the hard-pressed rural labouring community, with rick-burning and cattle-maiming as well as stealing horses, fodder and food. Attacks were directed at the larger farmers as well as clergy and gentry.[68] Farmers formed the core of rural Protective Associations to track down culprits, raise rewards and follow up prosecutions. These Associations also met in public houses where dining and convivial drinking were combined with business. Only a handful of property-owning widows was scattered among the male membership.[69]

Changes in local administration transferring church functions to the state, favoured farmers' involvement at village level. The appointment of permanent officials left local people with vestry duties, larger farmers demonstrating their new levels of administrative competence as Poor Law overseers. Traditional offices were attached to the property rather than the person and technically open to widows and single women who worked farms.[70] Up to the 1830s some women exercised this right, helping to take the collection at church services, levying rates and administering relief, for example the notable Mrs Whitehead who dealt with 165 applicants at a single meeting.[71] However women so acting were potentially anomalous. While the verger, sexton and parish clerk were posts occasionally filled by women, the latter office derived from clerical assistant to the priest, 'a man who is able to make a will or write a letter for anyone in the parish . . . the universal father to give away brides, and the standing god-father to all newborn bantlings'.[72] In parishes with a dearth of literate men, a woman might take on some of these functions. Attitudes of Evangelical clergy to this situation are illustrated by the shocked reaction of Revd John Charlesworth, on first taking his appointment in the remote parish of Flowton in Suffolk where he 'found a *woman* acted as the clerk giving out the responses' (his italics). He immediately substituted a male farmer although this man's reading was 'inferior to hers'.[73]

The use of the public house for transacting all types of business was a major obstacle to respectable womens' activity in local affairs. The heart of the farmers' world was the market where buying and selling of produce, exchange of information on prices, land availability and farming practice changed hands and bargains were sealed over a drink. On market days the innkeeper and one or two leading farmers organized the weekly 'ordinary' — a meal at a fixed price high enough to exclude labourers.[74] Farmers' wives might accompany their husbands to inns when on a visit to a town, but women seen in public houses were increasingly jeopardizing their reputations. Evangelical opinion equated public houses with sin. While men might have to go to such places in pursuit of legitimate business, women should never be seen crossing their thresholds. In the 1830s, a Suffolk man commented on the notoriety of a female cattle dealer — by that date considered an eccentric — who used to sit with other dealers at the Swan, drinking and smoking a pipe and known locally as 'The Duchess'.[75]

Changes in marketing also hampered women's business activities. The informal open market was superseded by Market Halls and Corn Exchanges. The building of these impressive structures with neo-classical facades was organized by men as committees of trustees or directors. Women might have bought shares as an investment but they never became active committee members.[76] These purpose-built structures were partly promoted to replace fairs. The control of fairs was part of the Evangelical moral crusade against public displays of dancing, singing, drinking and games with an undercurrent of sexuality. The new morality was exemplified by the Essex magistrates' support for Wilberforce's Society Against Vice and Immorality to stop the licensing of local fairs, while an Essex vicar maintained that Chelmsford Fair was, indeed, an 'abode of Moral Darkness'.[77] Such strictures were becoming easier to enforce as fairs were being partially replaced by shops or tinkers and packmen travelling to farm doors.

Hunting, too, was becoming a more questionable activity for women. The hunt had traditionally been the place where the three tiers of the English countryside could meet, for even labourers followed the hunt on foot. By the late eighteenth century, more formal subscription packs replaced private arrangements which had allowed women to take part occasionally (Lady Salisbury had once been Master of the Hunt by inheritance). The wildness of the chase, the 'blooding' with the fox's tail — exactly those elements which made it a 'manly exercise' — were inimical to feminine decorum. The costume of pink coat and breeches (evolved from wartime uniforms) was not for ladies whose long skirts when perched on a side-saddle were a further disincentive to hard riding. Emphasis on masculine chivalry, the need to protect women through any supposed difficulty and maintain ceremonious intercourse between the sexes made men feel constrained with women in the chase. 'Surtees', the great hunting journalist, maintained that: 'women are as much in their place at the meet watching and cheering the men on as they are out of it tearing across the country.'[78] Hunting provided an ideal 'male bonding' for all classes, the 'strongest preservation of that natural spirit . . . for a life of active energy, independence and freedom . . . and corrective to effeminacy' in the words of a fox-hunting MP.[79] Meanwhile, the women, whose men had organized the Suffolk Hunt, 'played the harpsichord and the new forte-piano, paid visits to each other, organised balls and made up theatre parties'.[80] Male farmers were thus able to mix with both social inferiors and superiors in market, hunting field, agricultural show, horse-race or club, but such masculine camaraderie had no equivalent for their female relatives. Women's activities were encapsulated by family and friends, the marking of social boundaries through informal shopping and visiting.

Women had traditionally been excluded from the public sphere of politics so that masculine monopoly of voluntary societies, civic activities and leisure pursuits is not unexpected. The role of women in the economy was more problematic in both farming and the new occupations which were evolving in the countryside. Auctioneers, estate agents and bailiffs were dealing in land and specializing their nascent professions while others became solicitors. The demand for enclosure surveys, the estimation of tithes for commutation into cash, and later the railways, created a lively demand for surveying. Many men practising these skills had risen from the ranks of working farmers while other farmers combined activities.[81] These occupations stressed training on the job and experience. Their professional standards were promoted by newly formed organizations such as the Land Surveyor's Club, forerunner to the Institute of Chartered Surveyors.[82] Women were in no position to grasp such opportunities for they had neither the education, training nor legitimate acceptance in professional circles. A farmer's daughter with a talent for drawing might give a few art lessons to the neighbour's children or use her talents in cookery and needlework for the family.

Even in those areas where farm women had contributed directly to household production, a combination of factors was making them marginal to the economy. Specialization in arable farming and the accompanying use of male waged day-labour affected women's position at all levels of agriculture. The traditional association of men with ploughing and reaping furthered a gradual displacement of female labour from the fields, except for casual seasonal tasks.[83] There is a debate about the origins and timing of the decline in women's field labour, but it is agreed that by the early nineteenth century there was concern about the suitability of field work for women.[84] Whatever the underlying economic reasons, the discussion of women's field work was couched almost entirely in moral terms.[85] Exclusion affected women in farming families, creating difficulties in their enforcement of authority over the now predominantly male labour force, particularly as they no longer overlooked the men's domestic lives as house-mistresses. Supervision of field labour on far-flung acreages meant riding horseback, often alone. While this may have given added status and authority to male farmers, thus 'elevated above their work-force',[86] it ran contrary to notions of feminine decorum. Male farmers could slip into colloquial speech when dealing with labourers but respectable women were in a dilemma since rural lower-class culture was increasingly regarded as crude.

A more serious loss was dairying, traditionally women's work, which was a casualty of the shift to arable agriculture. Cheese and butter rapidly declined from being export products in the eastern counties as 'factors' made the rounds collecting more standardized products,[87] concentrating production in certain areas such as Gloucestershire where men were taking over enlarged operations.[88] Women's dairying which had taken place on almost every farm was slowly phased out while growing corn and fattening cattle, 'give but little trouble to the housewives of the present generation' according to an Essex commentator.[89] By 1843, the Royal Commission on Women and Children in Agriculture announced that the patience, skill and strength needed to produce cheese made this work unsuitable for women.[90] Specialized organization accompanied a move towards more scientific methods of cheese making. The shift from craft skills to more experimental methods is exemplified in a manual dated 1784 where the male author based his rules on information 'collected from the most experienced Dairywomen of several counties' but then proceeded to upbraid them for their empiricist approach:

> The general way that the art of Dairying has been carried on for Ages has been progressive or traditional, being taught by Mother to Daughter, from common or continual experience, naturally adopting from time to time, the methods that appeared best, from such as have happened to come within their knowledge; without ever calling in the assistance of either materials they use, or knowledge of how to apply them in a Physical or Practical manner.[91]

At this early date the handbook is still designed for women, 'an attempt to instruct or inform Dairy women' despite the 'unthankful office' as the author anticipated the question: 'how should a Man know anything of Cheesemaking.'[92] As long as the process was in transition it was possible for women to contribute. The only entry by a woman in the *Farmer's Magazine* which began in 1800, was an article setting out a gravity test to measure the richness of milk, including the concept of a weighted index.[93] In the 1800s, a Suffolk farmer's wife was commended in the survey undertaken by the newly formed Board of Agriculture for her method of comparing milk from cows of different breeds and feeding habits. William Marshall combined gallantry with approval in his comment: 'This is a charming thought — which conveys to my mind, new and interesting ideas. And I value it the more as it aptly emanates from that of a sensible enlightened mistress of a dairy, whose experiments and observations on the subject in view, are truely scientific.'[94]

By the second quarter of the nineteenth century, only a few avocations were left to farmers' female relatives, activities which hovered between money-making, production for family use and hobbies of interest mainly to the women themselves. Poultry keeping remained uncommercialized and farms continued to keep a few cows since large-scale sales of liquid milk were not possible until mid-century railroad development. The wife of Robert Bretnall of Witham, (prosperous enough to sign himself 'gent' but from his diary more a farmer) kept two cows. In the first week of November, her husband recorded: 'My wife opened her Cow Box found in it saved cash £37=9=6 allowed for butter and milk for the use of our own house at 1 shilling per week is £2=12 shillings or £40=1=6.' Considering that this would have been a good income for a schoolteacher or curate, Mrs Bretnall had done well with her minuscule herd although how much she benefitted personally is doubtful for the next year's entry reads: 'Total amount for the two Alderney's made in the Year £50=6=6. My wife took for her hard labour in managing the two cows £5=0=0 and I received £45=6=6 like all other lazy persons for doing nothing.' Bretnall paid his daughter-in-law small sums for raising puppies for him and his married sister one penny each for ducks she had raised on her farm.[95]

Developments in farming and status considerations had combined to make profitable farming more difficult for women. In the eighteenth century it was still not considered unusual for a farmer's wife, even of fairly high rank, to be seen taking an active role in running the farm. In the 1780s Mary Hardy dealt with her solicitor, directed workmen and recorded in her diary 'the sale of my turnips' and that she 'ground malt for brewing'. She often rode horseback from her home at Letheringsett Hall the 22 miles to Norwich to transact business including the purchase of land.[96] On smaller farms where mainly family labour was employed, wives and daughters would contribute directly, particularly at harvest, if not actually raking hay or stacking corn, then brewing and baking to feed casual workers. Even the rather flighty 17 year-old Mary Parker, daughter of a farmer, whose mid-nineteenth century diary is filled with genteel visiting and hints at attachments with young men at chapel, breaks off in June to record that she and her two sisters 'have been working at hay making in the Mill Field' which prevents her visiting but, 'I don't dislike it half as much as I thought.'[97]

Nevertheless, women who wished, or had, to farm on their own were at a disadvantage in the larger scale of operations, in the need for heavier capital investment for tools, fertilizer, seed and better storage facilities, as well as credit to carry over from planting to harvest. Formerly when cash needs had been intermittent and informal borrowing the norm, it had often been the woman's butter, cheese or egg money which provided rent or small sums for stock, a practice recalled disdainfully by the son of a small farmer: 'The farmer's wife was an especial hoarder in making a purse of her own from chickens and poultry of all kinds.' He noted that such a woman had saved £150 in notes over the years, hiding them in the thatch where they were eaten by mice.[98] Under the new conditions, women controlled the necessary large capital sums less often and were not seen as legitimate borrowers for investment. In the burst of prosperity during the Napoleonic War, farmers began to use country banks to raise capital on a larger scale.[99] The ensuing use of cheques created problems for women without credit. Bankers often asked for references and referees were likely to stress 'diligence in business, experience and capital', all elements difficult for a woman to demonstrate.[100]

Farmers' female relatives continued to bring capital and skill to the enterprise but rather in their capacity as family members and kin. At marriage a wife might contribute her savings or inheritance to stock the farm. William Fairhead, whose family had once farmed independently, was reduced to labour as a team man but his fiancée had skills in dressmaking gained when employed by a Norwich family and after marriage 'this remarkable woman' brought the family back into farming.[101] Older women made loans at low interest to family members while women's property in trust or trust-like arrangements could be used as investment on an existing farm or to take on additional land. The trust device seemed to have particular appeal in the farming community, possibly because farmers seldom went into formal partnership to raise capital and were slow to take up other forms of credit. Among the 158 wills examined between 1780—1850 for the Essex town of Witham, virtually all of the higher strata of the middle class left their property under some form of trust arrangement, while 43 per cent of the lower strata left theirs directly under the control of their wives. Yet among yeoman and farmers, even among the lesser type, only 19 per cent gave complete control to their wives and 81 per cent left property either in trusts or other regulated forms.[102]

Farm women were pivotal in marriage alliance as a resource. The special relationship between town enterprises such as grocers' shops and farms was often maintained through family ties. For example, three daughters out of the ten children of a Suffolk farming family married Ipswich shopkeepers. In this way, farm produce became fresh supplies for town shops travelling along kinship networks.[103] Some farm families had relatives in larger cities, particularly London, so that products would be exchanged for urban contacts and country holidays were traded for placing farm youngsters in town employment. Marriage also linked farming families with nascent manufacture in the countryside or market town. The farmer/surveyor Arthur Biddell enhanced his operations by his marriage into the iron-manufacturing family of Ransome. Biddell sons' professional careers benefitted while the Ransomes were rewarded by close association with their farming customers and by Biddell's knowledge for they specialized in manufacturing agricultural machinery.[104]

Farm women were instrumental in training young people in farming skills, particularly girls. The Wright family took in the 15-year-old daughter of a distant cousin, also a farmer, whose wife had died leaving a houseful of young children. Mrs Wright taught her to bake and the basic skills in running a farmhouse so that she could manage the household for her father.[105] Farmer's wives needed extra hands even if they were not working directly on the land for during the daily round they were kept busy smoking, pickling and preserving food, baking bread, puddings and cakes as well as the daily cooking for large families and, perhaps, the midday meal of labourers. Part of the farming family's claim to local status lay in the ability to 'keep a good table' at a time when three-quarters of the population could drop into destitution if not starvation. Food and farm produce were favourite gifts for maintaining kinship networks and expressing thanks for favours. It was usually the farmer's wife who controlled the distribution of items such as the Christmas goose. The raising of the seven or more children of the average family carried on whether farm work was undertaken or not. Higher standards of child-care had to be fitted into farm life. It was these demands, as much as the often criticized refinements, which occupied farmers' female relatives by the early nineteenth century.

The efforts of farm women to live a respectable, domesticated life could play a central role in demonstrating the farm as a going concern. Oxley Parker, the Essex agent, noted that the church-going habits of farmers' wives acted in their favour as tenants. The sobriety, sense and experience of a wife could ensure the granting of leases, their terms and possible renewal.[106] Farm women had to balance spiritual and material rewards of domesticity against a direct contribution to productive farm work. The contradiction of these demands was most evident when women attempted to run farms in their own right as widows and spinsters. It was, in fact, usually expected that such women would take on a bailiff or agent to act for them but only those above a certain level of income had this option. In an 1851 sample from Essex and Suffolk, 9.3 per cent of farm households were headed by women, almost all widows.[107] The occasional spinster might farm property she had inherited but single women farming on their own found their scope limited. Louisa Fairhead of Wickham's Bishop in Essex inherited the family farm and ran it 'with equal skill to that of male members of the family' throughout her long life. It is instructive to compare her career with that of her brother who farmed at nearby Birch Holt. Golden Fairhead became a well-known local agriculturalist, a 'familiar figure at different markets', active in the Braxted Agricultural Society and in his local church. His wife, from a successful farming family, played the organ at their parish church and was presumably more refined than her farming sister-in-law.[108]

Age, experience and the mantle of her former husband gave the widow advantages over young and/or unmarried women, but it was still difficult for her to run a farm actively. Records indicate that widows often farmed as a 'holding operation' until a son was old enough to take over.[109] While the combination of widow and young adult son might make it possible to pass the lease from one generation to another, the tenancy system could make a widow's position vulnerable. The landlord or his agent had to be convinced that the widow would be able to carry on a profitable venture. Those landlords who had invested heavily in improvements sought tenants who were 'intelligent and enterprising'.[110] However the landlords and agents were themselves often imbued with preconceptions about female respectability which was characterized by dependency.

By mid-century, these expectations were less compatible than ever with a woman remaining active in running a farm. George Eliot, a farm steward's daughter, put forward the fictional case of the farmer's widow whose husband's dying wish had been for her to carry on the farm. When she goes to plead her case with the landlord she is dismissed in just these terms, of an appeal to both the supposed capacities and right conduct of femininity. 'You are about as able to carry on a farm as your best milch cow. You'll be obliged to have some managing man, who will either cheat you out of your money, or wheedle you into marrying him.' The landlord goes on to predict that the farm will run down and she will get in arrears with the rent. She argues back that she knows 'a deal o' farming an' was brought up i' the thick on it' and that her husband's great-aunt managed a farm for 20 years and left legacies to her 'nephys an' nieces'. 'Phsa! a woman six feet high with a squint and sharp elbows, I daresay — a man in petticoats; not a rosy cheeked widow like you.' This widow knows that once all the stock has been sold and debts paid she will have hardly anything to live on. Since this is fiction, the secretly benevolent landlord arranges to have a cottage let to her at low rent with a plot for a cow and some pigs where she will be able to live in suitable retirement.[111]

However, landlords in the real world, while subscribing to a similar view of women's place, were not as helpful or often unable to be as liberal. John Oxley-Parker, the agent for a large number of landowners in mid-Essex in the 1830s, was called in to negotiate the lease of a widow who had kept on a farm after her husband's death. He, along with her neighbouring farmers and her brother-in-law, urged her to give up the attempt. He noted in his diary in connection with this case how important it was for tenants to have both character and capital. The questions he asked himself about a prospective tenant were: 'Was he an energetic farmer? Did he know his job and use his initiative in doing it?' Oxley-Parker finally urged the widow to throw herself on the mercy of the landlord, but to no avail and she had to leave the farm with no compensation.[112]

If maintaining a farm was problematic for women, acting in the market-place, the core function within capitalist farming, was even more of a challenge for it exposed them to public evaluation. In *Far From the Madding Crowd*, Thomas Hardy's heroine, Bethsheba Everdene, tried to farm an inherited property. Hardy uses her situation to portray the deviant nature of such ambition including the sexual provocation of a woman acting independently. In her first appearance at the Corn Market, Bathsheba's co-farmers carried sticks with which they poked at pigs, sheep or 'their neighbours', hardly an option for a respectable young woman. In the Corn Market itself:

> Among these heavy yeomen, a feminine figure glided, the single one of her sex that the room contained. She was prettily and even daintily dressed. She moved between them as a chaise between carts, was heard after them as a romance after sermons, was felt among them like a breeze among furnaces. It had required a little determination — far more than she at first imagined — to take up a position here, for at her first entry, the lumbering dialogues had ceased, nearly every face had been turned towards her and those that were already turned rigidly fixed there.[113]

In this fantasy, Hardy highlights the damaging fact that Bathsheba had to deal with men to whom she had not been introduced by reliable intermediaries.

The model of feminine gentility, unlike its male counterpart, had no place for even managerial involvement in a productive enterprise. Many women went so far as to have nothing to do with the sordid world of business no matter what the cost. Helen Uvedale, a clergyman's widow living in an Essex village on the modest rents from two farms gave the complete management of her property to a local attorney. She had little interest in it except to get maximum rent paid promptly and grumbled at the need for rent abatements in the 1820s. Unlike the model ladies of the religious tracts, she cared little that her tenant had a large family or lacked sufficient capital to farm efficiently. A male farmer/clergyman might have taken charge himself but Helen Uvedale confessed to being too ignorant in such matters for her opinion to count. She had neither education nor experience to expand her operations even had she been taken seriously in the farming fraternity and, most significantly, as a widow she had only a life-interest in the farms. As a result she was unable even to stem the decline of her small property, having placed herself completely in the hands of her powerful if somewhat shady Colchester attorney.[114]

The only completely respectable public presence for women was at church or chapel. They were an important, if usually silent, part of rural congregations where they listened to sermons on, among other subjects, the importance of family life and women's place. However they could express informal influence in the local congregation as the Independent minister of Kelvedon in Essex found to his cost when he fell out with his deacons and had to solicit farm women's support.[115] In remote villages farming families could be the main representatives of a more refined and religious culture. The farmer's wife who had invited the new vicar to sup wine in her renovated parlour was anxious for his approbation, but she had reserved judgement on his sermons and demeanour when he first came to the parish. Her invitation could be seen as putting the community seal on his tenure of office.[116]

Women took part in the philanthropic activities organized by zealous clerical families, for example the ubiquitous Bible and Missionary Societies. However fancy-work bazaars, garden parties and organized sick visiting were less well developed in the countryside. Much informal aid to labourers was organized by farm women but Sunday School teaching remained their staple contribution to the religious effort. In even more remote villages where no clergy resided and no doctor practised, farmers' families might be the only carriers of the more enlightened culture. Some farm women saw themselves playing a leading role against superstition, folk belief and rural ignorance and apathy. Against this they pitted their intense conversionist religious belief and a commitment to rational modes of thought, although many farmers' wives continued to use herbal medicine to perform the role of village midwife, nurse and doctor. But farm women's expertise even in this role was slowly being undermined. In addition to their own commitment to new ideas, enclosure of common lands was cutting supplies of plants for both medicines and cosmetics. The rise of professional medical men, apothecaries and chemists denigrated many of the women's skills and beliefs to the status of 'old wives tales'.[117]

Yet there is no doubt that educated and religious women were proud of their role. In early nineteenth-century Suffolk, a Quaker farmer's wife, as the sole 'lady' in an isolated village, deliberately exposed her children to smallpox after having them vaccinated to demonstrate to the villagers the efficacy of the new, frightening procedure.[118]

In areas with resident clergy, tension over leadership and status recognition could be played out between women. The Revd John Charlesworth formed part of a network of Evangelical Anglican clergy in early nineteenth-century Suffolk. His eldest daughter Maria later became author of the best-selling treatises, *Ministering Children* and *The Female Visitor to the Poor.* Her text reveals these anxieties in describing an imaginary school fête, to be the high point of the village year, where farmers' wives and daughters are enlisted to provide food, small farmers or cottagers' wives to wait at table while the vicar's daughter, presiding from a throne decked with greenery, dispense prizes as rewards for good and bad behaviour to the village children.[119] In the fantasy, farming families with their new wealth and enhanced education are held firmly in place.

The status ambiguity in the position of farmers which lay behind such fears has been investigated. The symbolic role of farming in English consciousness also played a part. Unlike factory production, farming had a long history, still seen more as a 'way of life' than as a means of earning a living within the cash nexus, a view which lingers to the present.[120] Unlike other sections of the middle class, farmers' families continued to live where they worked. Farmsteads were reorganized instead to separate domestic life spatially and socially from farming operations, but outsiders continued to expect a more unified existence, part of an image of a traditional way of life. As English society became ever more embedded in market relations, as production moved into factories and the population crowded into towns, the yeoman of Olde England with his roast beef and real ale came to embody attributes of independence and patriotism. To this day, John Bull wears the dress of an eighteenth-century farmer.

Within the symbolic imagery of farming, women held a special place and, as so often, they carried the negative qualities of the group as a whole. Claims to spurious gentility and the greed of wives and daughters were seen as prodding the farmers' search for profits, often at the expense of labourers. It was the expensive habits of the women which upsurped the 'honest and manly simplicity of manners which has so long dignified the British character . . . the very farmer's daughter has laid aside her stuffs for muslins, her handkerchief for the metretricious display of naked charms, her diffidence for coquetry and the bloom of virtuous industry for the harlotry of paint'.[121] The use of such gendered messages confuses the historian's investigation, already hampered by limited sources from the women themselves. As an eminent historian of rural England has said: 'The farmers' wife and daughters do not emerge very clearly from the contemporary records.'[122]

Neverthless, it is clear from sources we have, the general ideas about gender permeated the countryside as a consequence of increased literacy and general education, through travel, the circulation of newspapers, journals and books, through sermons and lectures and, above all, through lived example. Farmers and farm women alike experienced the contradictions inherent in the middle-class model. Cornelius Stovin, a devout Nonconformist farmer, had a wife manifestly suffering from isolation and chronic ill-health associated with multiple pregnancies. He tried in his bumbling fashion to make up to her for being cut off from genteel refinements in the draughty old-fashioned farmhouse:

> If God permit us to enjoy the great gift of a new or restored, enlarged and more commodious dwelling, my Lizzie will find more scope for her tasteful devices. She is fond of a vase and understands the adornment of a home . . . I

notice a great change towards a loftier and more refined civilization hallowing
our dwellings which had not taken place during my childhood.[123]

The exclusion of women with ambitions for gentility from active
participation in the running of the farm was complete by the mid-century
'golden age' of high agriculture. Such ideas were only reaching the
Lincolnshire countryside in the 1860s and 1870s when Cornelius and
Elizabeth Stovin started their farming life. Many of the couple's aspirations
stemmed from visits to and from their respective families, particularly
Cornelius' first cousin, who was married to his sister and a doctor in
Oxford. Cornelius Stovin's bewilderment about his wife's unhappiness is
understandable. The couple were part of a culture which had built an
edifice of gender differentiation whose contradictions bore particularly
heavily on women. As a working farmer pressed with debt, Stovin could
scarcely afford to keep a wife in non-productive refinement (Elizabeth
even refused to bake the household bread although she knew how). To
Cornelius, Elizabeth's 'inability for accomplishing life's duties' was a
'mystery' and far from being angry, he regarded her weakness as part of her
gentility, her devout, meek, Christian character. The stress on pious
domesticity and the expected pattern of family enterprise meant no
reduction in constant debilitating child-bearing which undermined Elizabeth
Stovin's health and strength. Her craving for respite and company was
partly the product of beliefs which made active farming appear vulgar and
degrading, especially in comparison with her town kinsfolk. The wish of
such women to move beyond the drudgery of farm work should not,
however, be dismissed as mere snobbery. The grinding physical labour and
social isolation of the farmer's wife must be remembered and may be a
factor in the dearth of their surviving diaries, memoirs and letters.[124]

By the 1870s English agriculture was once again in a period of depression.
It was the grain-growing midland and eastern regions which were hit
hardest. Many farms were deserted while arable land was converted back
to pasture. Towards the end of the century some farms were taken at
extremely low rents by Scots coming south to seek new opportunities. As
farmers willing to take a lower standard of living while using mainly family
labour, they prospered. Their wives willingly undertook tasks such as
mucking-out sheds and sties which no English housewife would contemplate
but, as a contemporary observed, 'they came as stranger; they have no
position to lose.'[125] Such a comment demonstrates how deeply the concept
of 'separate spheres' and its association with both gender and class had
entered into the heart of Victorian identity, even to the depths of the
English countryside.

The power of this model has been profound. The impersonal market
economy, constructed as part of the public sphere, became even more
identified with men, the private sphere of individual morality and the home

with women. Men began to be identified by their means of earning a living for themselves and their dependants, giving the concept of 'occupation' heavy masculine overtones. Women's status however, remained overwhelmingly familial during this period.[126] The identification of manhood with the ability to support a domestic establishment became part of the conditions for the franchise. Women's passive relationship to property was maintained through successive legal reforms and feminine dependence became a serious obstacle to women's wider citizenship claims as well as the narrower issue of suffrage. As the middle class moved into leadership in the late nineteenth-century, the model was used to evaluate working-class behaviour and attitudes. It became a standard in administering state policy and dispensing charity, in education and in recognizing working-class claims for social and political incorporation. It was an important part of the culture which the English carried with them to administer the Empire. Contemporary English society continues as the inheritor of this gendered model of the social world.

# 13

## Gender and Stratification
### One Central Issue or Two?

### Margaret Stacey

What are the core characteristics of the social order in our society in the late twentieth century? Do these relate crucially to the market place, to the ownership and control of the means of production? If so, are they gendered? Is gender of any consequence? Is the familial and kinship system marginal nowadays or does it remain of central importance to structural social inequalities? How can one (or does one need to?) relate social inequalities associated with paid work and the mode of production to the differential position of women and men in the familial and kinship system? This last problematic is one which has been with me for more than three decades, right from the days when I was trying to make sense of the social order in Banbury shortly after the Second World War.

The many hours of debate that went into how we should measure social class and what to do about women is reflected inadequately in the pages of *Tradition and Change: A Study of Banbury* (1960). The gendered nature of occupations both by status-grade and industry was displayed but not discussed, although the absence of women in managerial and professional occupations was commented on. The domination of women's expectations and the actual lives of most of them by the unwaged wife-mother role was clear and was discussed extensively. The essential problematic was stated thus:

> A wife cannot resign from her work without breaking from her husband and children, nor can she leave her husband without losing her job. Her occupation is rightly returned as 'married woman'. This is a unique status in a society otherwise based on individual contract, specialization and separation of function. (Stacey 1960: p. 136).

The centrality of the status of married women, especially wife-mothers, to the problematic of gender and stratification has emerged again in this Symposium, albeit in a variety of guises — see, for example, the chapters in this volume by Crompton (chapter 9), Davidoff (chapter 12), Harris and Morris (chapter 7), Leonard and Delphy (chapter 5), Siltanen (chapter 8), Walby (chapter 3). It was this centrality which led to the remarkably short life in paid employment of the majority of women in Banbury around 1950. For them the end results of the domestication of women in the nineteenth century, so ably discussed by Davidoff in this volume, still applied strongly. By the mid 1960s, when Banbury was studied again (Stacey *et al.,* 1975) the bimodal employment pattern of married women (Hakim 1979) was well established in association with Banbury's second twentieth-century phase of industrialization.

While the problem was recognized and displayed in the early study, it was discussed inadequately because of an absence of terms appropriate to its conceptualization. One consequence of this was that while care was taken to refer to 'gainful employment', women's domestic work was discussed in a chapter on the family rather than in one which took an earlier place in the book, namely that on 'earning a living'. The central importance of the economy to an analysis of the social order was clearly understood, the crucial importance of domestic labour to that economy was not spelled out. The dependent and subservient position of women within both their families of origin and their families of marriage was recognized. The part played by domestic arrangements in the social-status allocation and life-chances of all the members was understood by those of us working in Banbury around 1950s. This theme was developed further by Littlejohn (1963) for his study of Westrigg. No proposal, such as that developed by Delphy and Leonard (1982), part of which argument is developed in chapter 5, had been made at the time. Since the latest phase of the feminist movement — the Women's Liberation movement of the late sixties and early seventies — a good deal of work has gone on which has helped to provide the concepts for the analysis of the anomalies noted so long ago. It is the fruits of this work, the great majority of it women's work, which made the Symposium and this volume possible.

The most striking feature of the Symposium to me, and it is a feature which derives from the history to which I have just alluded briefly, is that the Symposium divided into two groups. One was composed mostly, but not quite exclusively, of women who were familiar with the conventional, 'male-stream', literature on stratification, as well as with all the new work which has collected data relating to women and stratification and which has also been involved in the reconceptualization process. The second group, composed of men, were well versed in the conventional stratification literature, had contributed to and developed it in a variety of ways, but for the most part were less well acquainted with the new knowledge, albeit obviously prepared to take it seriously. This unevenness in shared knowledge had the consequence from time to time of interrupting the dialogue when the second group was unable to respond in the terms postulated by the first.

This division derives from circumstances which I have discussed in 'The division of labour revisited or overcoming the two Adams' (Stacey 1981). There I argue that the historical origins of sociology in the nineteenth century — when the public domain, and specifically institutions of higher education, were not only male-dominated but also exclusively male — led sociological theory to concentrate upon the social order of the public domain. 'In so far as they considered changes in the private domain, it was from their stance as mediators of the private to the public domain.' (Stacey 1981: p. 175; Smith 1974).

The 'naturalness' of the division of labour in the domestic domain long went unchallenged and has, as Leonard and Delphy argue in chapter 5, seriously impeded our understanding of the social order. This stance and the assumptions on which it is based, they argue, stress one form of inequality (that deriving from the labour process or the occupational structure) over against those inequalities which derive from the system of family and kinship and which lead to inequalities associated with gender order. The consequences are to misrepresent life-chances, life-styles, patterns of association and socio-political orientations in class analyses. Because of a failure adequately to analyze inheritance of property, skills and other resources through the familial system, the mechanisms 'which account for the perpetuation of and change within classes and between classes over time' are also misrepresented (p. 73).

This last point is also overlooked by Michael Mann in this volume in his otherwise most insightful chapter. Notwithstanding many changes in the domestic domain, the inheritance of capital remains crucial to class formation and also to male domination.

In addition to the major division as to whether members of the Symposium were thoroughly familiar with work which has sought to relate the gender order and the class order to each other, there were two subsidiary divisions, although these were less sharply defined. These subsidiary divisions were between, on the one hand, those who were concerned about how and why class is measured and, on the other, those whose major focus was with the issue of whether we have one major source of stratification in our society or two. A focus on how and why class is measured links with issues of social policy and social administration and also with a wider social and political understanding of our society. Both women and men were engaged with the second issue of whether the crucial characteristics of the social order derive from the economic structure or whether they derive also, or even primarily, from the familial and kinship system. However, those seeking for a radical revision were all women, with the exception of Michael Mann. For him problems with gender are only one of the reasons for his belief that stratification theories are wanting as sufficient analyses of the crucial issues in contemporary social order.

Among those who focused on the second issue, three main positions emerged. The conservative position of the dominance of market-related class positions is represented at its strongest by David Lockwood in chapter 2; a strongly radical position from the feminist standpoint is expressed by Sylvia Walby in chapter 3, Cynthia Cockburn in chapter 6, and by Diana Leonard and Christine Delphy in chapter 5. Others, such as Christopher Harris and Lydia Morris (chapter 7), Janet Siltanen (chapter 8) and Rosemary Crompton (chapter 9) could be said to occupy a revisionist position, which is probably also true of Michael Mann (chapter 4), although his conclusions stand in direct opposition to those of David Lockwood.

I am acutely aware of the importance of developing a proper method of social accounting so that data collected shall properly reflect the inequalities which derive from gender as well as those which derive from occupational status. I applaud the efforts of those like Linda Murgatroyd who strive to achieve this. However, in these remarks I would like to focus on the proposition that inequalities in contemporary society derive from two sources, the familial and kinship system on the one hand, and the occupational hierarchy and its relationship to the means of production on the other. In particular I would like to draw out some of the changing relationships between these two systems of social organization which have been raised in the preceeding chapters.

No one denies the existence of the familial and kinship system or of a domestic arena where crucial tasks are performed and relationships forged. The domestic arena and the familial and kinship system are often, but not necessarily closely, associated. The question is whether the analysis of this domestic arena is of central importance to the understanding of the social order or whether it has only marginal significance, such that sociologists of the family are themselves necessarily marginalized, as Harris has suggested.

Neither does anyone deny that roles in the family and kin are differentiated between women and men, and furthermore that waged work, managerial roles, administrative and political leadership exhibit systematic gender biases. The question is how important is this for the social order? Is it so important that studies of stratification must be articulated to it?

Lockwood completely denies the importance of gender to a proper understanding of the social order. He argues in chapter 2 that patriarchy has not proved to be a concept that entails any radical revision of conventional stratification theory whose purpose is to explain variations in the degree of class and status formation. Thus he does not accept the validity of the feminist thesis which argues that the structure of social inequality has at least as much to do with gender as with class or status relations. In asking whether women and men constitute anything analogous to 'classes' or 'status groups', Lockwood concludes that they do not because the war between the sexes does not eventuate in a society-wide 'class struggle', or that such conflicts as have taken place have not had enduring or systematic consequences. This case is somewhat difficult to sustain in the face of the empirical evidence 'There's always been a women's movement this century' as Mary Stott said to Dale Spender (Spender 1983b). To ignore the existence of disconcerting behaviour is a well-known method of social exclusion, used effectively in the formation and maintenance of status groups (cf. Stacey 1960; p. 148). It is also a mode whereby ruling groups seek to control those they rule.

Drawing on the European tradition of class analysis as opposed to the hierarchical ranking more typical of the American tradition, Walby argues in chapter 3, in agreement with Lockwood, for the inclusion of gender politics in any attempted assessment of women's class position. She moves however in an opposite direction. Starting from the position that housework is work, and work which is undertaken under distinctive relations of production, she argues that housewives constitute a class. They are engaged in a patriarchal mode of production as members of a direct producer-class where their husbands are non-producers and members of an exploiting class. She accepts that there are reasons for distinguishing between housewives according to the class positions of their husbands, but at the same time they share a common class situation, as do their husbands. She does not however think that all women constitute a class. The class-like nature of the occupation of housewife derives from the patriarchal relations in which housewives find themselves. I agree with Walby that married women who work as housewives, whether part time or full time, have a distinctive place in the stratification system. I would also accept the view that the situation of all women has been affected and depressed by the general normative expectation that all women will marry and have children and that those who do not have somehow failed. It is only relatively recently that single women have proudly proclaimed their spinsterhood. Perhaps also very recently this proposition has begun to be modified by the combined effect of fertility control and a greater range of job opportunities for women.

Notwithstanding their radically different analyses of the importance of the gender order to the social order, Walby and Lockwood agree on the importance of political action as an indicator. We should recognize that the very existence of the Symposium is evidence of such political action. It is ten years since the combined efforts of women sociologists at the 1974 annual conference of the British Sociological Association turned the attention of that body seriously to consider the extent to which policy and practice among sociologists discriminated systematically against women.

Many women present would accept that the calling and funding of the 1984 Symposium represents one positive outcome of the continuing struggle. Serious consideration is now being given to the work of women sociologists and to their charge that stratification studies, along with the great bulk of sociology, has in the past helped to fuel the ideologies which support the male-dominated society in which we live. Women continue other struggles, around issues of welfare rights, of equal opportunties and equal pay. The struggle is not spearheaded by the most depressed or the most deprived, for as Lockwood has reminded us it is not they who combine in the forefront of any struggle for radical change.

Less radical than the position adopted by either Lockwood or Walby were those of Harris and Morris and Siltanen. The Harris-Morris data in chapter 7 explores relationships between the domestic and public domains, in this case in relation to job opportunties and the way in which the local social structure operates to mediate these. My theoretical difficulty with this analysis is that the market is made central to the argument. The question of the conventional position of women in the domestic domain is taken for granted, it being recognized that this is disadvantageous to women in market terms. The chapter argues also, and correctly, that men may sometimes find themselves in a similar situation. Harris and Morris seek to make women visible to stratification theory but they do so in a way which avoids analysis of the gender order. Indeed it was their intention to do just that. While the chapter therefore points to an important aspect of the process whereby gender and stratification come to influence each other, as it stands it constitutes only a beginning.

The careful disentangling of gender in relation to domestic responsibilities which Siltanen undertook in chapter 8 and her notion of a component wage and a full wage is an interesting approach to relating domestic and public economies. 'Component-wage' jobs are done mostly by women and 'full-wage' jobs by men. But as she tells us this is not the whole story. Both women and men in component-wage jobs have limited financial obligations with regard to household maintenance (wives of employed men or single sons living in their family of origin); in full-wage jobs both women and men are solely responsible for the maintenance of a household. As Siltanen argues, her data show that '"occupational segregation by sex", and a distinction between "women's work" and "men's work" are inadequate understandings of the nature of the skewed sex composition of jobs.' This is obviously right, but the notion that in households where there is a male wage-earner a wife need earn only a component wage (and that a young adult male is in a similar situation) can only be understood in the light of the ideology of the 'male breadwinner' and the 'family wage' of the nineteenth century. What is useful about Siltanen's account is that it teases out ways in which this ideology has been modified in the late twentieth century. Change there may be, but Cynthia Cockburn's trenchant analysis of the exclusion of women from skilled tasks in developing high technology industry (chapter 6) can leave us in no doubt of the continuation of the male-dominated society and the intrusion of the gender order into the system of occupational stratification.

A number of points have emerged which help to elucidate why the ample evidence of the inequalities surrounding sex and gender should be open to such a wide range of recognition and interpretation. One of the most important relates to the division between the public and private domains and to the meaning of 'patriarchy', and a second to the way in which those domains have altered over time, as has the relationship between them.

Empirically we have two systems of occupations, the waged or salaried and the unwaged. The system of rewards and sanctions is quite different in the domestic domain from that in the public domain; working for one's keep, for 'love' or out of duty is an altogether different kettle of fish from working for a wage or a salary under contract, unequal though we know such a contract may be. The use of the gift in the system of rewards and sanctions in the domestic domain underlines the differences in the two systems (Bell and Newby 1976). The social order has rested upon these two systems associated with the public and the domestic domains. The gender order, defined in the domestic domain, is also expressed in the public domain; the gender order permeates the whole society, affecting most unequally the life-chances of women and men in the public domain, but also their power in both domains. The Symposium revealed wide agreement that the stratification system of the public domain can no longer be understood without reference to the gender order. It is doubtful whether there was ever a time when it was intelligible simply as a public domain phenomenon. As Leonard and Delphy show in chapter 5, the gender order embodied in the kinship system has and always has had important consequences for the inheritance of property, resources and skills and therefore for the formation of class and status groups. As Davidoff shows in chapter 12, the very form which nineteenth-century capitalism took was associated with the family form. The development of capitalism itself also transformed the family. The domestic and the public domains changed and  still change together.

Part of our problem is how to conceptualize the relationships between these two domains, which are themselves both ideology and empirical reality. There is a problem with the use of 'patriarchy' — see Mann, chapter 4 and Beechey (1979), among others. Patriarchy, strictly speaking, refers to a particular form of the family, kin, household, lineage. It was this form which was found extensively in Europe before the modern period. As Mann has reminded us, at that time the patriarchs constituted the society and what there was of the state (see also Stacey and Price 1981: pp. 27—8, 29—33). Such a society could reasonably be called 'patriarchal'. What we now have is what I prefer to call a 'male-dominated gender order', what Cockburn refers to in this volume as the 'sex-gender system' extending beyond the relations of reproduction. Mann uses the term 'neo-patriarchy'.

What happened so far as I understand it (and this analysis has much in common with Mann's) was that because the family and kinship system had a patriarchal form before a distinct public domain developed, when that domain developed it was occupied and controlled by the men. When production also left the domestic domain in the industrial revolution, the men were again in a position to direct its development (Stacey and Price 1981; ch.3).

It was an empirical reality that the public domain was male dominated before the industrial revolution, although there were women in many of the medieval guilds and women were traders as well as producers. Beyond the domestic domain and the local market any such women were mostly either feme sole or widows, that is to say they lacked a husband or father to act for them and were in some sense acting in place of men.

During the eighteenth and nineteenth centuries the nature of the public domain changed profoundly, but so did the nature of the family. Judy Lown (1983; 1984) has shown how the Courtaulds domesticated their own women, withdrawing them from their factory and office, thus supporting the ideology that 'a woman's place is in the home'. At the same time they employed women workers at rates below those of men and salved their consciences by developing a paternalistic form of capitalism. In chapter 12 Davidoff has shown how in agriculture as well as in industry the notion of the 'separate spheres' of women and men emerged in association with the emerging class and status system. She also shows that women were themselves involved in both those creations. 'The impersonal market economy, constructed as part of the public sphere, became ever more identified with men, the private sphere of individual morality and the home with the women.'

Women of the middle classes thus helped to create and purvey the ideology which justified and sustained these two spheres. They were important agents in forging the alliance between the new medical men and the bourgeoisie, an alliance which led medicine to a position of high status among occupations (Johnson 1972; Parry and Parry 1976). Women, specifically middle-class wives, were persuaded to believe their age-old healing lore was unreliable and also that they were utterly unfitted by nature to become doctors. But here was an internal contradiction in the newly emerging ideology: because of the separateness of women from men, because of the essential moral need for women to remain pure, some were unhappy to be examined and treated by men. Such women of the middle classes supported the struggle of those women, like Elizabeth Blackwell, Elizabeth Garret Anderson and their successors in their attempts to study and practice medicine. We now know that there is nothing in

women's 'nature' which makes them unfit for medicine or indeed any
professional occupation. These and similar allegations about the 'nature' of
women were part of the ideology which created and sustained the notion of
public and private spheres. Men used the ideology (and were actively
involved in its creation) to restrict the access of women to the public
domain.

The empirical reality was that that domain was a male domain. As
Davidoff says in chapter 12 'Contemporary English society is the inheritor
of this gendered model of the social world.' From the outset the men could
not do without women in some of their factories, as in the case of
Courtauld's. But from the outset when women were employed in the public
domain it was on the basis of this gendered model.

Many of the strains in the gendered occupational structure arise in the
area of the caring professions. I have drawn attention elsewhere (Stacey
1984) to the contradictions within nursing which result from workers in a
paid occupation being expected to exhibit the caring responses which
generally go along with domestic domain relationship. The increase in the
activities of the state and its intrusion upon the domestic domain is
identified correctly as crucial by Mann (see also Stacey and Price,
1981: pp. 83—4). Many aspects of the struggle to establish a new gender
order take place in what I have described as an 'intermediate zone' (Stacey
1984), heuristically conceptualized as between the public and domestic
domains, where tasks are performed which are done both for salary or
wage in the public domain and for 'love' in the domestic (see also Finch
and Groves 1983). The labour ward constitutes an interesting microcosm
where, in a protected environment, (protected usually by male
obstetricians), what it is to be a man can be redefined (Richman 1982).
Mann refers correctly to similar changes in the relationship between
private and public domains associated with the citizenship of women and
the operation of welfare legislation. As he says it is quite clear that
'stratification is now gendered, and gender is stratified' (chapter 4),
notwithstanding the great complexity of modern capitalist nation-states.

The Symposium made a most promising beginning in showing how we
must proceed to untangle that complexity and to understand the nature of
contemporary social order. It is critically important to examine the
relationship between the domestic economy and the market economy and
how these influence each other and how each is changing in relation to the
other. This examination has in the first place to be undertaken in terms
which are domestic-domain terms. Public-domain terms are inadequate.
One of the reasons why Lockwood rightly finds the domestic labour debate
unsatisfactory (although it produced important analyses and ideas along
the way) is because the participants were attempting to understand the
domestic economy in terms derived from concepts developed to understand
and analyze the public domain. Ultimately we have to develop terms for

## Gender and Stratification: One Central Issue or Two? 223

concepts which transcend both domains and refer to the social order, *tout entier*. I have already referred to the need to rethink what we mean by work and what the relationship between paid and unpaid work is, where the whole issue of human service work and welfare payments are undoubtedly crucial.

A number of chapters here make an important contribution to this understanding. Collectively they have shown that there is a stratification system associated with the gender order. Proportionately more of them have been about women than men. As we know from studies of occupational stratification and other hierarchies, the processes of dominance and oppression cannot be understood from the underclass alone. In studying the relationship between the domestic domain and domestic economy and the public domain and public economy it will be important to focus on the part played in both domains by the men. There is evidence that they do act as a group (albeit without always being very conscious that that is what they are doing) to sustain their privileged position. All women who have been involved in attempts to effect change become aware of that concerted exercise of power. Like the women, men win some and lose some. We need to know more about what they are up to and how they do it. Only so shall we understand crucial facets of the contemporary structure and processes associated with our changing social order.

It is undoubtedly most important that, this dialogue about gender and stratification having begun so fruitfully, it should continue.

- conceptualize a private/public split and then ask what is relationship between them.
- debate there is about how relations in private sphere are influence (or, on conservative view, are marginal to) the inequality evident in public sphere
- but, these spheres are themselves constructed by actors to enforce inequality – they are part of the structure of inequality –
either by
(1) ... excluded from ... public
(2) rewards in public ...
- the distinction itself is a social reality that requires explanation
- the current public/private organisation is contingent – is it right to conceptualize patriarchy ... predates it – is it right to conceptualize the problem in terms of dealing that are so recent?

# 14

## Gender and Stratification
### Some General Remarks

### Frank Bechhofer

The state of the art in studies of gender and stratification is somewhat confused and does not lend itself to a small number of sharply focused and neatly argued conclusions, and my intention is rather to draw attention to what seem to me to be some important general issues.

Although it is not included here, a paper by Goldthorpe is the backdrop to a good deal of what follows. That paper (Goldthorpe 1983) gave rise to considerable controversy (Stanworth 1984; Goldthorpe 1984) which in turn, though valuable, has sometimes defined the agenda in a misleading way by opposing 'stratification theorists' to 'feminist theorists' — which clearly fails to capture some important distinctions. In terms of this dichotomy Lockwood and Goldthorpe are both 'stratification theorists', yet closer examination shows their position to be different; not all approaches can be equated simply with a 'stratification' perspective or a 'feminist' perspective. Much of Goldthorpe's (1983) paper defends the practice of taking the family as the unit of stratification and the occupation of the chief breadwinner as the defining characteristics for allocation to a class position. One of Goldthorpe's main targets is the debate over the allocation of couples where both are employed and he contends that stratification theorists have to take the gender inequalities in society as a 'given', recognize them as an empirical regularity, and thus in most cases focus on the occupation of the (usually male) head of household. At least some of the opposition to this view, for instance that of Heath and Britten (1984), engages Goldthorpe's argument in its own terms to a considerable degree.

Lockwood's contribution to this volume (chapter 2) seems to me to operate at a different level. It starts from a clearly stated premiss that the purpose of conventional stratification theory is to explore and explain variations in the degree of class and status formation. This task involves above all two kinds of enquiry: into the extent to which class or status systems are the predominant modes of social action at the societal level, and into generalization about the determinants of class and status formation. To a lesser degree for Lockwood, it involves documenting and explaining the inequalities of opportunities and outcomes arising from the factors accounting for the degree of class and status formation. This last task is then a 'by-product of stratification analysis'. It is apparent that from this perspective the study of inequality in society, which clearly must include gender inequality, is to be distinguished from the study of stratification. The 'conventional stratification theory' with which Lockwood is concerned is perhaps similar to that of Goldthorpe in the last analysis, but the chapter makes a far more general argument, which we might characterize somewhat unfairly as 'conceptual' while Goldthorpe's is 'empirical'. If the initial starting point is accepted, then Lockwood puts up a closely argued and spirited defence, allowing only the theory of 'patriarchy' as a serious contender, but rejecting it on grounds which have also been argued by some feminists (e.g. Beechey 1979). Lockwood's chapter leads me to believe that 'conventional theories' will be with us for a long time yet for they do provide powerful explanations of certain kinds of class and political action. It became quite clear however during the Symposium on Gender and Stratification that many participants did not accept the premises on which his chapter is based.

As we turn to the opponents of the 'conventional view(s)', we see however, a far from simple picture. One might start from the position that stratification is about the distribution of power and that power relations between men and women undoubtedly exist and are of great antiquity. Some people argued for the existence of *two* systems of power at least, generally characterizing one as economic power and the other as patriarchy, possibly with the addition of a 'social' system. To put it in this stark way suggests that not only the 'conventional view' may need some rethinking. Patriarchy is a useful idea, but, as Mann and others remind us, has existed for a long time and predates capitalism. The problem is that it is an all-embracing concept. It can readily be *understood* that women have long been and are oppressed by men and patriarchy *expresses* this well but does not *explain* it. One problem is that capitalism is to be understood in relation to feudalism and socialism; what is patriarchy to be understood in relation to? If comparative analysis enabled us to refine the concept and possibly give it a variable form, then we might get more leverage.

There is perhaps a theoretical Holy Grail envisaged by some whereby one could definitively see capital/labour relations or gender relations as having theoretical priority. This would only be possible if, comparatively and over time, class systems shaped gender systems or vice versa.

Many problems were located in the separation of the 'economic' from the 'social' which is to be found in both the competing 'schools' but which no longer seems viable in the face of the empirical evidence. This issue however, illustrates nicely the way in which this area of sociology is deeply entwined with political and ideological beliefs, not as analytic tools but as part of the stance of the sociologists themselves. One should not underrate the difficulties faced by attempts to integrate analytically the various 'systems of power' in view of the felt political need to keep gender inequality and patriarchy in the forefront of action. This concern was expressed frequently during the Symposium. For example Leonard pointed out that patriarchy addressed issues other than stratification such as sexuality and violence. She thus saw the merger as premature, convinced as she was that the issues brought on to the agenda with immense effort by feminists over the years would once again be submerged and the debate turned back to class. One can appreciate this alarm, justified perhaps in the length of time it took for these issues to be placed in the forefront of the agenda of the Stratification Research Seminar itself, while questioning its academic validity. For some however, academic matters cannot be separated from the political issues, which formed something of a hidden agenda for the Symposium.

The need to face these ideological and political questions suggests that the road forward involves a learning process. It is crucial that *male* sociologists have to learn to be more *sociological* which involves a far greater willingness to try and take the 'view of the other'. It is worth commenting in passing that there appears to be no solution to the impasse which is created by those who would argue that this is impossible. To a lesser extent, I suggest with trepidation, if feminists are to contribute to this debate, they will have to become more sociological also. Parenthetically it is interesting to note how the tendency of feminists to study *women* to the neglect of women *and* men bears an uncanny resemblance to the tendency of many sociologists in the 'conventional' mode to study the working class to the exclusion of the middle class, something which I have opposed with varying success for the last fifteen years or so.

It is not surprising that these political undercurrents surface partly, though not exclusively, in the chapters by Prandy (chapter 10) and Siltanen (chapter 8), both from what might be described as the 'Cambridge' school of stratification research. The distinctiveness of their contributions tend to be somewhat lost in the 'conventional'/'feminist' debate and this is unfortunate. Although to my mind they have not so far provided a fully worked-out adequate alternative, the researchers at Cambridge have made cogent points which weaken the 'conventional' approach(es) (Stewart *et al.* 1980). Prandy's chapter does considerable damage to the attempts to solve the problems by allocating a male and a female in a couple relationship each to their own class. There is considerable force in the view put forward in this chapter that a man and a woman in a close and reasonably permanent relationship cannot sensibly be seen as being in different classes. It is perhaps here that the nub of the problem lies. For at least some of the participants at the Symposium (myself included) gender relations could not be reduced simply to a relationship between exploiter and exploited (cf. Walby, chapter 3). The analytic tool falls so far short in subtlety of the reality which is part and parcel of sociologists' own social experience that it seems inadequate. Here again we encounter a growing awareness that the 'economic' cannot be separated from the 'social'. Prandy makes it clear that his chapter is to be seen as part of a larger enterprise in which the whole basis of the study of inequality is challenged.

Siltanen's chapter 8 deserves to be emphasized because as I have already suggested, it has a more radical thrust than was perceived initially. At the heart of her argument is the view that gender cannot be seen as a *theoretical* category which has meaning across all areas of social experience. This is not to deny the reality of gender inequality and of gender outcomes, nor to question that gender may be the basis for some kinds of political action. The essence of the argument is that inequality in the labour-market and in employment is not to be explained by gender itself. Rather, structural forces and social factors determine, in her example, whether people seek what are described as full- or component-wage jobs, which in turn leads to a pattern of outcomes which, if examined by gender, shows inequalities. Gender is not in itself the explanatory variable. The arguments in this chapter, which are more complex than can be summarized in this brief contribution, have, if accepted, profound implications not only for the various conventional views of stratification, but also for a good deal of feminist theory.

Yet another strand ran through the Symposium, raising questions for most of the existing theories, but also incompatible with the arguments discussed in the previous paragraph. This is best illustrated by another chapter.

Scott's argument in chapter 11 is that 'the allocation of men and women to different occupations has been produced by an interaction between economic, political and ideological forces rather than by economic ones alone.' This chapter was exemplary in that it examined variation both across cultures and over time. The Symposium further convinced me that cross-cultural and transhistorical work is essential for further progress. At the heart of Scott's chapter lies the notion that 'domesticity' is a culturally relative ideology whose origins predate industrialization, which sometimes developed in societies 'against the odds' as it were, not because it encouraged low prices and efficiency but despite the fact that it did not. In all the societies examined, women were seen as a special category of labour although their supply characteristics in the labour-market did not justify this distinction. This chapter raises familiar but none the less central questions about the relationship between the structure of stratification, ideology and action.

Davidoff's contribution (chapter 12,) while somewhat different in emphasis, focus and thrust, nevertheless has some interesting similarities. It demonstrates in a superbly detailed and thorough historical analysis, the way in which domestic life in England came to be opposed to the public world. Here we have something more than an ideology, an entire world-view which Davidoff argues was 'embodied in the doctrine of "separate spheres", with its gendered resonance which became a unifying characteristic of middle-class identity'. These two chapters together represent an emphasis on culture, ideology, and patterns of thought which contrasts sharply with some of the other themes developed during the Symposium. There is here an emphasis on the normative which was well captured by a remark by Harris to the effect that women were 'working on normatively approved terms' which needed to be explained historically.

There was then in the Symposium no shortage of reasons for taking seriously the weaknesses and limitations of conventional stratification theory. This theory has however, gone through two important transformations over the years which may be worth reflecting on in the light of some contemporary feminist theory. My first point is undoubtedly controversial. The wave of Marxist theory which swept British sociology in the late sixties and early seventies was, as I have remarked elsewhere (Bechhofer 1981), notable for taking a highly theoretical and arid form. The experience of stratification theorists at the time would lead me at least to be doubtful of the wisdom of swallowing holus-bolus the entire Marxist apparatus in an unreconstructed form. Lockwood (chapter 2) also offers a powerful criticism of the 'attempt to accommodate gender relations to Marxist theory'. It was clear at the Symposium both that this caution would (not surprisingly) be taken badly by some Marxist-feminists and also that it enjoys a degree of general support. Secondly, and perhaps less polemically, the vast forests of trees sacrificed over the years on the altar of false consciousness should give sociologists pause when they examine the position and experiences of many women and may wish to deny, denigrate or devalue what the women themselves have to say about their situation because their views do not accord with theory or cherished sociological belief. The whole area of the perceptions held by men and women of their situation and the relations between them, and the processes of decision-making between couples, deserve far more examination.

This mention of couples brings up another matter which surprised me somewhat at the Symposium. Quite frequently but by no means universally, the concepts of family and household were confused or differentiated inadequately, and further the focus seemed frequently to be not only on marriage as a relationship, but indeed on the household of married couple and children. This is already not the 'norm' in Britain and American research suggests it will be statistically very much a minority in that society by the 1990s (Masnick and Bane 1980) even if many pass through it in the course of the life cycle. We need to bear in mind both the variability of households and the existence of the life cycle. As part of the general programme of examining *process*, we must incorporate the life cycle into research in this area. For instance, the first and subsequent return of women to the labour-market is an issue which runs through several of the debates touched on during the Symposium. This important stage in the life cycle of many women (and couples) should be seen in the light of other 'milestones' such as birth of first and last child, children reaching school age, departure of last child from the home and so on. Since the Symposium, an interesting paper (Anderson 1985) has thrown light on the historical development of the life cycle in a way which can be seen to have considerable implications for the study of gender and stratification.

There remain for comment a couple of issues of considerable generality. I have come to believe increasingly that we have a great deal to learn from the historians. One should not take too seriously the claim by an historian, at any rate a good one, to 'tell it how it is', although they do, I agree, 'tell a story' as someone remarked at the Symposium. It is I think, interesting to note that those doyens of the British profession, the Marxist historians, wrote history with the women largely left out; it was almost the making of the male English working class. Feminist historians are now busy redressing this balance, just as feminist sociologists are redrawing the map of a good deal of sociology. But interestingly the historians seem able to achieve this with rather less trauma than we sociologists can manage, at least partly through the kind of detailed and careful empirical enquiry exemplified by Davidoff (chapter 12).

This kind of historical enquiry contrasts interestingly with some of what is going on in sociology. First there is a great deal more theoretical debate of a rather arid and unproductive kind. More crucial however, is the nature of empirical work. Partly by inclination, partly following the notion of a distinctive 'feminist methodology' and partly owing to the power and funding structure of the profession, much work in this area is small-scale, ethnographic and qualitative. I have no quarrel with either a professed preference for this kind of research or with qualitative methods. I do have reservations about the validity of the concept of a feminist methodology (or its converse) and I believe that the lack of larger-scale and also quantitative research by feminists is a barrier to progress. There is a strange tendency for British sociology to repeat its tragedies as farce. The ethnomethodologists succeeded in putting vast numbers of people off most forms of empirical enquiry, especially the quantitative; the Marxist revival in Britain, though noticeably not elsewhere, had much the same effect in its earlier stages. It would be a pity if research on gender followed the same path. We need a great deal more empirical enquiry of all kinds and in particular we need more research which studies both men and women together. It is a strange irony that the largest British enquiry into women's employment (Martin and Roberts 1984) studied only women yet it is becoming abundantly clear that for couples, women's work histories cannot be studied properly apart from those of the rest of their household.

# Notes

---

## INTRODUCTION

1. Indeed, this has been recognized in the support which the Social Science Research Council (SSRC)/Economic and Social Science Research Council (ESRC) has given to the Stratification Research Seminar, which organized the Symposium on Gender and Stratification at the University of East Anglia (July 1984). All the papers in this volume were first given at the Symposium, with a single exception — Michael Mann's paper was written later.
2. See Goldthorpe 'Note on concepts and derminology' in Affluence and the British Class Structure, *Sociological Review* Vol II No.2. and also Goldthorpe (1983: p. 466) 'Parsons then uses the term "social class" where European writers would be more likely to use that of "status groups".'
3. Lockwood's comments in this volume notwithstanding; Measurement is often viewed as theory-independent, but this is not so. Decisions as to *what* is to be measured, and the categories to be used, are themselves informed by theory (Hindess 1973). Indeed, it may be suggested that the 'gender question' illustrates this problem in a particularly acute form. The problems raised by 'measurement' are discussed at greater length by Ken Prandy in chapter 10 in this volume.
4. Goldthorpe (1984) in his 'reply to the replies', siezes with some alacrity on this apparent difference between his critics. However, the different solutions proposed by Stanworth on the one hand, and Britten and Heath on the other, are consistent with the underlying theoretical frameworks of the two sets of authors. I would not suggest, however, that the two solutions are equally valid, but it is important to recognize that the difference between them is theoretical as well as empirical and thus the debate should be engaged at the theoretical level — which Goldthorpe does not do.
5. A parallel although not identical problem is raised by the segregation of employment by gender (Murgatroyd 1982b).
6. We are aware that highlighting this particular difficulty might appear as a volte-face on the part of one of the editors (Crompton). However, her recent empirical work argues that the labour process (in this particular case, the

non-manual labour process) is a phenomenon worthy of investigation in its own right. Given that more proletarian places have been created by routinization and deskilling, it is perfectly legitimate to discuss the proletarianization of the non-manual labour *process*. However, the fact that these places have been filled largely by women is not without significance for the consequences of clerical 'de-skilling' (Crompton and Jones 1984).

7. She is not the first to make this distinction which is also utilized by a number of authors in this book. (See also Gamarnikow et al. 1983).

8. Unfortunately, we have not been able to include all of the papers given at the Symposium, nor the discussants' comments. However, we would stress that *all* contributions are reflected, to various degrees, in this volume and we welcome this opportunity of expressing our thanks to all who participated in its creation.

## CLASS, STATUS AND GENDER

1. In writing this essay I have benefited from discussions with Joan Busfield, Leonore Davidoff, Mary McIntosh and Alison Scott. That they would accept my conclusions is an altogether different matter. For their comments on the paper presented to the Symposium. I am grateful to John H. Goldthorpe, Gordon Marshall and David Morgan.

2. Weber (1968: p. 307) 'Depending on the prevailing mode of stratification, we shall speak of a "status society" or a "class society".'

3. A formidable task in its own right, and one which impatient theorists of stratification disregard at their peril. Since the Ruhr has been mentioned, see, for example, Geary (1981).

4. The two activities are naturally associated closely. Yet they remain distinct in that the description and explanation of class and status formation in its particularity has usually been the work of historians and anthropologists, whereas the work of generalizing from this array of evidence and explanatory detail has been taken on by sociologists, who risk seeking to order it in some more systematic fashion.

5. Although no one has spelled out the consequences for class and status relations of, for example, a change in favour of a more 'sex-neutral' allocation of persons to positions in the division of labour. Consequently the whole question of whether any such change would alter class and status relations significantly remains a matter of speculation.

6. And have usually had as much to do with status as class considerations. For example, middle-class suffragettes were very conscious of their status disqualification *vis-à-vis* working-class men, who were sometimes among their servants. (I owe this example to Leonore Davidoff). More generally, the view that class conflicts are not substantially motivated by status interests must now be quite anachronistic.

7. See Ortner and Whitehead (1981: p. 16):

   In the simplest societies, there are often only two principles of status differentiation: one that distinguishes between senior (or "elder" or

# Gender and Stratification

"initiated") men and juniors, ranking the former over the latter; and one that distinguishes between male and female, ranking men over women. In such simple systems, needless to say, gender as a prestige system has enormous social salience, and is interwoven with the political-economic fabric of the society in direct and transparent ways. In more complex societies, in which larger systems of nongender-based ranking (ranked lineages, castes, classes) attain asocial structural prominence and historical dynamism, and in which gender recedes into the background as a formal organizational principle, the genders remain nonetheless among the most psychologically salient of status groups.

8. Even in an imaginary society consisting entirely of male and female homosexuals, the a priori reasons for thinking that, in the absence of other differences, gender would be the basis of either class or status formation are not immediately evident; as opposed to an equally imaginary society in which all male homosexuals were capitalists and all female homosexuals proletarians (or vice versa).

9. So, as one authority puts it, 'there is no need for there to be "class consciousness" or autonomous political organization for the class struggle to take place, and to take place in every domain of social reality.' (Poulantzas 1978: p. 17).

10. An early proponent of this comparison was Myrdal (1944: Appendix 5). Following Weber, ethnic groups are considered here to include all those who 'entertain a subjective belief in their common descent because of similarities of physical type or customs or both, or because of memories of colonization and migration'. Weber also includes 'language' groups and stresses the 'ritual regulation of social life' (1968: pp. 389—90).

11. 'The struggle for suffrage imposed a spurious unity. Once gained, there was nothing to take the vote's place as a rallying point' (O'Neill 1969: p. 93).

12. What it sometimes does reveal, however, is the existence of residual categories. For example, a recent critic of the idea of domestic labour (Molyneux, 1979: p. 14) introduces the notion of 'social display' quite adventitiously into her argument in order to distinguish the work of the bourgeois housewife from that of the proletarian. This lapse is illuminating in two ways. First, it displays ignorance of the extent to which proletarian action is oriented to status interests (the distinction between the 'rough' and the 'respectable' working class being only the most obvious example); and secondly, and much more importantly, the whole idea of status has no place within the Marxist action schema.

The role of women in negotiating and maintaining status boundaries is a much-neglected topic; but one that in the present intellectual climate will not be a popular field of research.

13. And even when it is argued that women do not constitute a class, but that 'those engaged in unpaid domestic labour' do 'share a common class position', it is still concluded that 'housewives as a group do not see themselves as a class or have the basis for organizing collectively to defend their interests, because they are isolated and dependent on the male breadwinner' (Gardiner 1976: p. 119). Note that the same conclusion is arrived at from the rather different premises of 'patriarchy': it 'appears as if each woman is oppressed

by her own man alone' and 'it is hard to recognize relations among men and between men and women as systematically patriarchical' (Hartmann 1981: p. 19).

14. For example 'Patriarchal power can be characterized in terms of organizing and rationalizing social relations based on male superiority and female inferiority which, *at one and the same time,* take an economic and familial form, and which pervade the major institutions and belief systems of the society.' (Lown 1983: p. 33).

15. Still exemplary in this respect is Elizabeth Bott's (1957) analysis of the relations between conjugal roles and social networks. See also Whitehead (1976), for empirical typology of gender relations.

16. Weber does not dwell on the role of illegal or extra-legal violence (or the threat of it) in maintaining status boundaries, although it has always been a major means of keeping the lower orders in their place. Even today, in rural India, such sanctions against 'untouchables' are commonplace. In this respect too, the situation of women is analogous to that of a status group, although the incidence of domestic violence, rape, and sexual harrassment is difficult to determine.

17. As opposed to being unintended consequences of action, a possibility raised by (Walby (1983: p. 165) who argues that "If a structure or set of practices is patriarchical in its effects, then it is useful to describe it as a patriarchical structure or set of patriarchal practices.'

18. Schoolteaching and white-collar work are the only two major occupations whose sexual composition has undergone a substantial and fairly rapid change in recent times. Yet in neither case would it be easy to prove that fluctuations in the relative social standing of the occupation was due primarily to the extent of its 'femininization', as opposed to the effects of other factors such as the rationalization of office work, the professionalization of the teaching profession and changes in the supply and social origins of qualified labour — not to mention the status-enhancing features of the occupations with which it had traditionally been compared.

19. One rather crucial piece of evidence, much cited, but apparently not equally well scrutinized, is a paper by Haavio-Mannila (1969). The major finding of this study is that people's estimations of the status of occupations (especially 'traditional', in contrast with 'modern' occupations) is affected to a statistically significant degree by the sex of their incumbents — though not to such an extent as to affect the normal rank ordering of these occupations. Moreover, this finding could well have been an artefact of the research methods, as the author readily admits when she writes that her questions (which prevented interviewees from ranking any category the equal of any other) 'may have somewhat influenced the results. For example, male and female representatives of the same occupational group were not allowed to be given the same rank. Thus the inequality of the sexes is, perhaps, accentuated'. This careful qualification seems to have been ignored by commentators on the original, for example, by Murgatroyd (1982b: p. 578).

## GENDER, CLASS AND STRATIFICATION

1. I should like to thank the Lancaster Regionalism Group and participants in the ESRC Symposium on Gender and Stratification for helpful comments on earlier versions of this paper.
2. These are:

    1 Equal pay and job opportunties
    2 Equal educational opportunities
    3 24-hour nurseries
    4 Free contraception and abortion on demand
    5 Financial and legal independence
    6 An end to discrimination against lesbians
    7 An end to male violence

    There is also a preamble which stresses the importance of sexual self-determination.
3. This analysis can be extended to those cases where a daughter performs domestic services for her father. This is again an instance of an exchange, in which the daughter gives labour and indirectly receives her maintenance in exchange. This is a situation which was more common in earlier times in Britain than today.
4. However, the effect of being husband-free needs to be distinguished carefully from that of participation in paid work in which husband-free women of 'working age' are more likely to be engaged than married women.

## CLASS ANALYSIS, GENDER ANALYSIS AND THE FAMILY

1. We are curiously confirmed in this by the recent growth of interest in the 'informal' sphere (Pahl; 1985 Gershuny 1983) and the household economy (Burns 1975). The protagonists on the commodity and labour market have to date been predominantly male. Indeed they have been male by definition, since the quality of being full economic subjects, of having full access to the market, is what distinguishes men (as a gender-and age-group) in our definition from women, children and the old. Only with the recent profound changes in capitalism and the massive rise in male unemployment, with the associated growth in men's involvement in non-market activities, has there been concern with this sector of the economy and a recognition of the vast nature of its scale.
2. Researchers might choose, as economists concerned solely with the market have done, to ignore what goes on inside the family *for certain purposes*. From the point of view of the market for example the family can be taken as a unit of supply and demand and can be presented as a single individual bringing things to the market or removing things from it, regardless of who does the exchanging.
3. The drawing of lots is practised in various small groups established for particular purposes (for example to play games, or for commando raids);

recruitment by authoritarian decision is found in many workplaces, for example in the army or in the appointment of cabinet ministers: and co-option in recruitment to religious orders.

4. What is in question is not so much the legitimacy of hereditary transmission as a whole, as its legitimacy in particular places. This implies not a rejection of the principle of hereditary transmission, but a limiting of its action. It involves establishing the areas and processes in which it *may not* play, which in fact implicitly delimits those areas where it *may licitly* play.

5. Two major criteria are used to distinguish (and to oppose) caste and class: caste systems are supposedly 'closed' and class systems are supposedly 'open'; and individual caste membership is held to be based exclusively on birth, while class membership is held not to be. However, while castes (groups or positions which are defined as closed) *are* recognized as transmitted hereditarily, classes are not defined symmetrically: it is never stated that a class society is defined by the fact that the positions within it are *not* hereditary, or that they *should* be acquired in some other way. The distinction between caste and class is therefore not as marked as appears at first sight, and it is in fact a question of a difference of degree and not of nature.

6. The critical case of only daughters requires particular attention. Some interesting indications have been provided by Michael Fogarty and the Rapoports (1971) in their studies of women in 'top jobs' and 'dual-career families'.

### THE RELATIONS OF TECHNOLOGY

*What Implications for Theories of Sex and Class?*

1. Funded by the Equal Opportunities Commission and the Economic and Social Research Council 1983—4 and carried out at the Department of Social Science and Humanities, the City University, London EC1.

### HOUSEHOLDS, LABOUR MARKETS AND THE POSITION OF WOMEN

1. The research was funded by the Social Science Research Council whose support is hereby acknowledged gratefully. A general description is to be found in Harris, Lee and Morris (1985, forthcoming).

2. See Morris, L. D. in the bibliography. These items, though not all published yet, are available as working papers from Steel Project, Department of Sociology, University College of Swansea, Swansea, SA2 8PP.

3. It is necessary to add 'normally' since the advent of modern electronic office procedures and communications makes possible the existence of geographically dispersed work groups in some instances.

4. Ignoring the 34 per cent who had withdrawn from the market, 42 per cent had experienced this chequered type of work history compared with 27 per

cent who had been (chiefly) unemployed, and 23 per cent who had been chiefly employed (Harris *et al.* 1985).

5. General Household Survey 1980, table 5.10. Those workers continuously in employment between redundancy and the last contact with them two and a half years later were twice as likely (46 per cent) to have an employed spouse than those continuously without work (23 per cent).

6. For discussion see Morris forthcoming, b).

7. On the importance of contracting see Fevre (1985).

8. This is not to assert that women's inferior position in the public sphere is merely the result of their location in the private sphere. Rather it is to claim that women's position in the domestic sphere is an important element in their social structural location which determines their labour-market position. Labour-market position constitutes a relation between a worker and the employment structure; social structural location involves the relation between worker characteristics and employment practices.

### DOMESTIC RESPONSIBILITIES AND THE STRUCTURING OF EMPLOYMENT

1. This paper is based on research conducted for a doctoral degree at the University of Cambridge, and I would like to express sincere thanks to my supervisor, Sandy Stewart, for his guidance and support. Thanks, also, to John Holmwood for his useful comments on earlier drafts of this paper.

2. In thinking about this problem, I have found the arguments presented in Stewart, Prandy and Blackburn (1980), and in Holmwood and Stewart (1983), to be especially interesting.

3. The interview data for this research was collected during the spring and summer of 1979. Access to interview postal workers and telephonists was obtained thanks to the kind permission of the Union of Postal Workers (now the Union of Communication Workers), the Post Office and British Telecommunications. A total of 144 interviews were conducted and included the following numbers in the different subgroups in the sample:

   Day telephonists: female (24) male (14)
   Night telephonists: female (6) male (20)
   Postal workers: female (39) male (41)

   The history of employment in the two areas was constructed from primary sources supplied by the union and the management, various secondary sources and interview material. These sources are documented in the thesis manuscript.

4. In 1971, 53 per cent of employed men were in occupations with at least 90 per cent male workers, and 51 per cent of employed women were in occupations in which the labour force was at least 70 per cent female (Hakim 1979: p. 24).

5. This combination of circumstances — support for equal pay and opposition to female employment — seems not to be unique to the history of the postal job. Cockburn (1983a) found that male compositors opposed the employment of female compositors while at that same time insisting on equal pay for

them. While Cockburn interprets this as a 'contradiction' in the position of the male printers, I would argue that, as with the postmen, it is a consistent strategy on their part.

6.  None of the other groups in the sample contain such a substantial proportion of Black workers. Racial minorities comprise 10 per cent of the postmen, 5 per cent of the male night telephonists and 17 per cent of the female night telephonists. All the day telephonists are white.

7.  The fact that this latter group of telephonists are in a job which requires no educational qualifications, which offers minimal career prospects and which is poorly paid, appears out of line with the relative advantages they have in terms of social background. Of all the sample, however, it is this group which has at least commitment to its current employment. Many in this group expressed intentions to move to another employer, or to another job with their current employer, more frequently than workers in the other groups.

8.  On the night-telephonist shift, women and men were equally likely to work overtime and for similar numbers of hours. Half of the night telephonists work overtime on a regular basis, and those that do overtime average 21 hours overtime per week. The number of overtime hours is particularly high because the regular hours for night telephonists are, effectively, 32 hours per week, compared to 43 hours for postal workers. Roughly two thirds of postmen, and over half of the postwomen, work overtime on a regular basis and each group averages 14 hours of overtime per week.

9.  A further difference exists between the full-wage and component-wage jobs in terms of the extent to which incumbents are supporting unwaged household members. Among the men in the full-wage jobs, 26 per cent are providing the only wage in households which include dependents, as are 18 per cent of the women. None of the men and one of the women, in the component-wage job are the sole wage-earners in households with dependents. This difference will appear even more sharply when the social circumstances of people on recruitment to the full-wage and component-wage jobs are discussed.

10. The significance level of Chi-square (raw and corrected) is less than 0.001, Phi=0.53.

11. Percentages are derived from *General Household Survey 1979* (HMSO, London; 1981), table 5.8. Percentages do not add to 100 due to rounding error in the original table.

12. Black single women may be employed in component-wage jobs other than the one included here. The absence of single Black women in the sample, and the lower proportion of Black women in the telephonist job, are perhaps explained by the nature of this particular job. As previously stated, a relatively unaccented voice is chacteristic of telephonists, and they are assessed on their English speaking abilities. Those with a distinctive manner of speech, or with English language difficulties, may be at a disadvantage as possible applicants for the telephonist job.

13. Chi-square (raw) is significant at 0.02 and Chi-square (corrected) is significant at 0.04, Phi=0.28.

14. Chi-square (raw and corrected) is significant at 0.01, Phi=0.40.

## WOMEN AND THE 'SERVICE CLASS'

1. I would like to thank Jon Gubbay, Gareth Jones, Mick Mann, Nick Abercrombie and John Urry for their comments on earlier drafts of this chapter.
2. See Young, (1981). A recent development from the 'dual systems' model is an approach which stresses the need to examine the construction of gender and class as a single system. Although I cannot pursue this argument here, I would be in broad sympathy with this objective.
3. I have outlined recently, at some length, my theoretical and empirical doubts as to whether the 'service class' can be said to exist as such — however this 'class' is defined (Crompton and Jones 1984). Indeed, I have suggested that, on closer examination, the 'service class' as defined by Goldthorpe (1982) and Abercrombie and Urry (1983), represents a grouping of 'capitalist' and 'structurally ambiguous' class 'places', and that (in part as a consequence of this fact) there exist considerable tensions and conflict *within* the supposed 'service class'. My discussion of the gender division of labour on which the 'service class' rests however, is couched not at the level of 'place', but rather seeks to explore the impact which possible changes might have on service-class *practices*. It may be viewed, therefore, as further evidence for my more general arguments relating to the *lack* of stability and coherence within the 'service class'.
4. Unless it is (incorrectly) interpreted as a straightforwardly 'human capital' thesis (Breughel 1978, 1979). However, as I make clear in a fuller exposition (Crompton and Jones 1984), 'human capital' explanations, in the case of 'women's work', are often interpreted best as ideological *justifications* of the status quo, rather than explanations.
5. There are, in fact, a number of conceptual difficulties in applying this argument to the 'service class'. In particular, service-class males will not, characteristically, create surplus value directly, but will be employed to achieve, directly or indirectly, the appropriation of surplus value.
6. As the information we were able to collect was not complete in all cases, the numbers quoted (relating to cases) may vary slightly from those quoted in other contexts. This research is fully reported in Crompton and Jones (1984). Interviews were carried out with 165 of the women.
7. Eleven per cent of girls in 1981 left school with 5 or more O level passes, compared with 9 per cent of boys, and 28 per cent with at least one O level, compared with 25 per cent of boys (*Education Statistics for the UK*, 1983 ed., table 12).
8. The data in table 9.2 was compiled with the assistance of Ms. K. Sanderson. The data does not reveal the greatest single change which occurred during the 1970s in the pattern of women's post-school qualifications i.e. the cutbacks in teacher training. These cutbacks, however, have not been reflected in an overall decline in the rate at which women are improving their acquisition of qualifications. This topic is being explored further in current research.

### SIMILARITIES OF LIFE-STYLE AND THE OCCUPATIONS OF WOMEN

1. This chapter is based on research funded by the Economic and Social Research Council (ESRC).

### INDUSTRIALIZATION, GENDER SEGREGATION AND STRATIFICATION THEORY

1. I wish to acknowledge a major debt to Leonore Davidoff and Sonya Rose who generously shared their time and ideas with me while I was writing this chapter. I am also grateful to Hal Benenson, Ludi Jordanova, Hani Shukrallah, Richard Williams and Christel Lane for their comments.
2. See the labour-processes literature, e.g. Edwards (1979).
3. There are theories which maintain that women's abilities are natural, e.g. nimble-fingeredness (Becker 1957).
4. These include secretarial, telephonist and sales assistant jobs, nursing, teaching, hairdressing, laundry and cleaning, dressmaking, cooking. These occupations accounted for 67 per cent of total female employment in 1911 and 66 per cent in 1971 (Joseph 1983).
5. Tilly and Scott (1978) note that the law endorsed male adultery, female fidelity and the use of physical violence by men against their wives. Many have noted the use of physical coercion to achieve greater productivity within the household economy and in the factories (Pinchbeck 1981; Dodd 1967).
6. Although households did contain some non-nuclear members they usually consisted of apprentices and servants (see Davidoff, chapter 12).
7. The evidence on gender segregation and wage differentials in pre-industrial agriculture and craft production is mixed. See discussion in Middleton (1983) and Clark (1982).
8. Women were only allowed entry into the guilds by virtue of their status as wives and were only allowed full trading privileges once they were widows. Many wives did not therefore serve full apprenticeships and those that did were appreciated for less time than boys or men (Clark 1982).
9. The pressure on housewives' time in the sweated trades raised the opportunity cost of subsistence labour so that it became cheaper to buy ready-made goods. Also their removal from the land deprived them of access to raw materials.
10. Levine has shown that the age of marriage lowered and family size increased as a result (Levine 1977). See also Middleton (1979).
11. In the sixteenth and seventeenth centuries wages were set by local magistrates in line with economic needs, ability to work and the level of inflation. There were deliberate attempts to protect wages from the pressure of market forces. Thus married men earned more than single men and both earned more than women (Clark 1982: pp. 65—70). This principle was endorsed by the system of poor relief which set allowances according to the number of dependents within the family.

12. As individual piece-rates developed within the outworking system, women's wages were influenced by their concentration in subsidiary, productive roles and the supply price of their labour. These factors could only have combined because of gender segregation. Thus one of the most crucial tasks in the early industrialization of textiles, spinning, was one of the lowest-paid occupations (Berg 1984).

13. Rose (1984) shows that in the case of hosiery production the conflict led to a deliberate policy of 'gendering machines'. Where there was less segregation in the production process and no gender-based wage differentials there was less political conflict between men and women and both were active in struggles over wages (Clark 1982).

14. Lord Ashworth, a major textile entrepreneur, a Quaker and a major supporter of factory legislation restricting the hours of work of women and children, provides a good example. Ashworth considered that men should be able to earn high enough wages so that they could keep their wives at home, and saw this as a reason for increasing the size of men's looms and their workload. Ashworth showed particular concern about the moral and social life of his textile communities (Boyson 1970).

15. Schooling had been extended considerably prior to these dates but it was voluntary and fees had to be paid (Barnard 1961; Simon 1960; Thane 1982).

16. There were of course some enlightened institutions which paved the way for later reforms, but they were the exceptions (see Simon 1960).

17. Middle-class girls were educated by governesses at home (Dyhouse 1981).

18. Most of the material on gender segregation in Peru will be based on my own research in Lima (see Scott 1984).

19. The annual growth rates of GDP between 1940–72 averaged at 5.5 per cent per annum and per capita GDP doubled in spite of population growth. Urban growth rates were around 5.2 per cent per annum.

20. At the time of the Conquest (1492) Spain was still a feudal society. Many of the *conquistadores* had pretensions of joining the nobility through their exploits overseas. Cortés is said to have declared 'Had I wished to till the land I should have stayed at home.'

21. Domestic service was institutionalized rapidly in urban households and rural estates on the basis of Indian labour. Also, many urban trading and manufacturing activities were performed by Indians rather than by the Hispanic bourgeoisie (Burkett 1978).

22. Even as land became privatized, communal institutions remained important for the organization of community labour and negotiations with the regional state apparatus. Women's exclusion from office-bearing within the community, even when they held property, had important implications. It appears to have been produced partly by lack of contact with Mestizo culture, especially monolingualism and illiteracy (Bourque and Warren 1976).

23. Voluntary associations arose in urban areas, consisting of kin groups and other members of migrants' villages. Their purpose was to provide a contact network for migrants and to mobilize political and financial support for the village of origin.

24. Both countries have a similar history of foreign penetration of the economy,

punctuated by periods of nationalism. The composition of industrial output is also similar. However, since the 1970s Egypt has had a greater reliance on oil and substantial emigration to the Gulf States (see Hansen and Radwan 1982).

25.   The only occupations which are dominated by women are domestic service and nursing. Note however that in 1960, over 33 per cent of domestic servants were men (Youssef 1974).

26.   Mabro and Radwan (1976) report very low female participation in small-scale employment. According to their survey, only 7.4 per cent of small producers were women and most of these were in rural areas in domestic activities such as dressmaking, spinning and weaving.

27.   Grounds for divorce for men include disobedience, neglect of duty and nagging! (Fakhouri 1972). For women they are desertion, impotence and only recently, cruelty (El Saadawi 1980). Divorce rates have traditionally been high in Egypt and mostly initiated by men (Eccel 1984; Youssef 1974).

28.   A woman's testimony in court is worth only half that of a man's.

29.   'For most Arab men, to even think of a wife working outside the home is nothing more nor less than a direct reflection on his position and prestige as a male, and an afront to him as a man. The maleness of a man or his manliness is still considered to reside mainly in his capacity to rule over his wife, to dominate her, to cater for her needs financially, and not to allow her to mix with other men in offices, in the streets or in public transport' (El Saadawi 1980: p. 192).

30.   Women's rights to education, employment and suffrage have been extended gradually during this century. Family law has also been somewhat modified. However, large discrepancies between men's and women's rights still remain (see El Saadawi 1980).

31.   Female sexual mutilation (clitoridectomy) and family-honour crimes (killing of wives or sisters for sexual promiscuity) are still frequent in the countryside (El Saadawi 1980; Fakhouri 1972, Eccel 1984).

32.   Nationalism has surfaced at different times during the nineteenth and twentieth centuries. Its zenith was during Nasser's regime, 1952−70. Female emancipation has often been linked to nationalism.

33.   The earliest educated women were taught by private tutors, in foreign mission schools or abroad. Their occupations typically consisted of teaching in elite schools. Even today 90 per cent of professional women are in teaching or nursing (El Saadawi 1980).

34.   The educational system has been extended gradually since compulsory primary schooling was introduced in 1933. The major expansion was during the fifties and sixties. Today Egypt has one of the most extensive systems in the Middle East. Since 1960, female enrolments have been rising faster than men's and the male-female discrepancy in enrolments has been falling steadily (Sanyal *et al.* 1982).

35.   The generalizations in this section refer to the Ga and Akan ethnic units in the south of Ghana. They comprise about half the Ghanaian population and reside in the area which includes the main urban and industrial cities

including Accra, the capital. Obviously there are variations of detail in the different ethnic groups, but I have tried to rely only on features that are common to most of them.

36. Loans of money for business purposes between spouses are expected to be repaid and interest is often charged on them (Robertson 1976).

37. Not only is there help with the day to day care of children on the compound, a specific institution of fostering exists whereby children are brought up temporarily by female relatives other than the mother (Date-Bah 1984; Robertson 1976). Another frequent practice is for urban women to send their children to be brought up on the family farm by the grandmother. The facility with which children are passed around may be related to their economic value. Van Hear reports that most cocoa farms could not exist without child labour and that this had led to the practice of child pawning (Van Hear 1982).

38. The main export crop was cocoa, which was organized on the basis of petty commodity production and was relatively labour intensive (see Okali 1983). I am grateful to Anne Whitehead of Sussex University for information on some of these points.

39. 'Trading is *the* female vocation and the major means by which Ga women may accrue wealth and power and through which they are encouraged into the capitalist economy' (Westwood 1984). In one coastal town, Labadi in 1960, 74 per cent of all women were in trade and 91 per cent of all traders were female (Mullings 1976). In another town, in 1952, 70 per cent of all women were in commerce (Smock 1977; p. 183).

40. Female participation rates are not only high, (63.6 per cent) they vary little with age and marital status (Date-Bah 1984).

41. In 1970, primary-school teaching, typing and sales assistant occupations were only 30—45 per cent female. However, nursing, receptionist and punch-card operator jobs are around 70 per cent female (Greenstreet 1981).

42. The degree of Africanization of the colonial apparatus was an important factor in expanding recruitment of Ghanaians to public-sector posts and in developing the educational system. Smock suggests that this was due to the inhospitable climate which did not encourage white settlement (Smock 1977: p. 181).

43. The educational system was extremely elitist. There was a differentiation between public and private schools, along British lines, the latter being boarding schools. Smock quotes Griffiths: 'Education appears to have become the basis for a kind of social and economic sexual inequality from which Ghanaian society has previously been free' (Smock 1977: p. 182).

44. The missionaries petitioned the British government to pass a special marriage ordinance for Christians. This is still recognized in Ghanaian law (Smock 1977; p. 186).

45. The extent of this marginalization process has however been less extreme in southern Ghana than in other parts of Africa (Boserup 1970).

46. Women were apparently pressurized by their husbands not to go into trading since it had become a low-status occupation (Date-Bah 1984).

47. Education has been used to exclude women from holding their traditional offices. Mullings reports that a traditional female office of leadership was on the verge of becoming obsolete because women could not meet the requisite educational qualifications imposed by the chief (Mullings 1976; p. 254).

## THE ROLE OF GENDER IN THE 'FIRST INDUSTRIAL NATION'

### Agriculture in England 1780—1850

1. This chapter is based on a project funded by the Economic and Social Research Council. It concentrates on the counties of Essex and Suffolk and is balanced by a comparative study of Birmingham by Catherine Hall (North East London Polytechnic). The general argument is a joint effort and I am indebted to her throughout. I also thank Janet Gyford for Essex material and Sonya Rose, Alison Scott and Michael Mann for helpful comments. Would readers please note that many bibliographic references are given in the notes to this chapter and *not* in the main Bibliography.
2. Harold Perkin, *The Origins of Modern English Society*, (London: Routledge and Kegan Paul, 1969).
3. A. D. Gilbert, *Religion and Society in Industrial England: church, chapel and social change 1740—1914*, (London: Longman, 1976).
4. R. J. White, *Life in Regency England* (London: Batsford, 1963).
5. E. P. Thompson, 'Patrician society, plebian culture', *Journal of Social History*, vol. 17, no. 4 (Summer 1974), pp. 382—405.
6. D. C. Coleman, 'Gentlemen and players', *Economic History Review*, vol. xxvi (1973), pp. 92—116.
7. Mark Girouard, *The Return to Camelot: chivalry and the English gentleman*, (New Haven: Yale University Press, 1981).
8. L. S. Presnell, *Country Banking in the Industrial Revolution*, (Oxford: Clarendon Press, 1956).
9. J. Collyer, *A Practical Treatise on the Law of Partnership*, (London: Sweet and Maxwell, 1840), p. 72.
10. R. J. Morris, 'The middle class and the property cycle during the Industrial Revolution', in T. C. Smout (ed.), *The Search for Wealth and Stability*, (London: Macmillan, 1979).
11. Sample of 623 wills from Birmingham and Witham, Essex.
12. From the present research, the average age at marriage was 29 years for men and 26.5 for women. See also C. Ansell, *On the Rate of Mortality at Early Periods of Life, the Age of Marriage and other Statistics of Families in the Upper and Professional Classes*, (London, 1874).
13. L. Davidoff and C. Hall, *Family Fortunes: Men and Women of the English Middle Class, 1780—1850* (London, Hutchinson, forthcoming).
14. Ibid. Average family size couples with children was 7.4.
15. N. McKenrick, 'Commercialization and the economy', in N. McKenrick *et al.* (eds), *The Birth of a Consumer Society: Commercialization of 18th Century England*, (London: Europa Publications, 1982).
16. R. J. Morris, 'Voluntary societies and the British urban elites in the Industrial Revolution 1780—1800', Unpublished MS.

17. Although women owned property, it was usually in a passive form such as the trust or annuity. Women's position exemplifies the 'social closure' resulting from controlling property as possessions rather than as active capital. See the general discussion, although not applied to women in: F. Parkin 'Social Closure as Exclusion' in *Marxism and Class Theory: a bourgeois critique*, (Tavistock, 1979), p. 53.

18. For the distribution of arable farming see: P. J. Perry, *A Geography of Nineteenth Century Britain*, (London: Batsford, 1975, p. 165. A recent article challenges the usual divisions within agriculture in this period but the argument in relation to large farmers still stands. Mick Reed 'The peasantry of nineteenth-century England: a neglected class?' *History Workshop Journal*, issue 18 (Autumn 1984), pp. 53–76.

19. Ann Kussmaul, *Servants in Husbandry in Early Modern England*, (Cambridge: Cambridge University Press, 1982).

20. J. Obelkevich, *Religion and Rural Society: South Lindsey 1825–1875*, (Oxford: Clarendon Press, 1976), p. 46.

21. H. Benham, *Some Essex Water Mills*, (Colchester: Essex County Newspapers, 1976).

22. J. Booker, *Essex and the Industrial Revolution*, (Chelmsford: Essex County Council, 1974).

23. By 1859 a local competition in practical skills for farmers' sons attracted only three entrants. Obelkevich, *Religion and Rural Society* p. 50.

24. J. Harriott, *Struggles Through Life Exemplified*, (London: C. and W. Galabin, 1807).

25. John Hanson, Journal, (manuscript), 1829, kindness of Jean Harding, Great Bromley, Essex.

26. A. J. Brown, *Colchester in the Eighteenth Century*, (Colchester: privately printed, 1969).

27. H. Coleman, *Jeremiah James Coleman: a memoir*, (London: privately printed, 1905). L. C. Sier, *The Blomfields of Dedham and Colchester*, (Colchester: privately printed, 1924). Census sample.

28. James Oakes, Diary (manuscript), West Suffolk Record Office, HA 521/1–14.

29. A. J. Brown, *Essex People 1750–1900*, (Chelmsford: Essex County Council, 1972).

30. Witham File.

31. R. G. Wilson, *Greene King: a business and family history*, (London: Jonathan Cape, 1983).

32. G. Sturt, *William Smith, Potter and Farmer 1790–1858*, (Firle, Sussex: Caliban Books, 1978).

33. John Cullum, *The History and Antiquities of Hawkstead and Hardwick*, (London: Nicols and Son, 1813), p. 252.

34. A. Young, *General View of the Agriculture of the County of Essex*, (London: Sherwood, Neely and Jones, 1807), vol. 1, p. 45.

35. Witham File.

36. H. N. Dixon, diary (manuscript) kindness of Janet Gyford, Witham, Essex.

37. *Select Committee on Agriculture*, vol. IV, (1833), question 10624.

38. C. Shrimpton, 'The landed society and the farming community of Essex in

the late 18th and early 19th centuries', (Ph. D. diss., University of Cambridge, 1966).

39. Jane Austen, *Emma*, (London: Dent Dutton, 1976), p. 23.
40. William Cobbett quoted in Perkin, *The Origins of Modern English Society*, p. 93.
41. J. J. Hecht, *The Domestic Servant Class in England*, (London: Routledge and Kegan Paul, 1956).
42. *Obelkevich*.
43. Charles Tayler, *May You Like It, by a Country Curate*, (London: Seely, Hatch and Nesbit, 1823).
44. Sturt, *William Smith, Potter and Farmer 1790—1858*.
45. C. Binfield, *So Down to Prayers: studies in English Nonconformity 1780—1920*, (London: Dent and Co., 1977).
46. C. Marsh, *The Life of the Rev. William Marsh, D. D.*, (London: J. Nisbet and Co., 1867); and Sier, *The Blomfields of Dedham and Colchester*.
47. Young, *General View of the Agriculture of the County of Essex*, p. 66.
48. M. Karr and M. Humphries, *Out on a Limb: an outline history of a branch of the Stokes family, 1645—1976*, (Essex: privately printed, 1976).
49. W. and H. Raynbird, *On the Agriculture of Suffolk*, (London: Longman, 1849), p. 132.
50. Obelkevich, p. 53.
51. M. Reeves, *Sheep Bell and Plough Share: the story of two village families*, (London: Granada, 1980).
52. Jane Ransome Biddell, Manuscript Collection, Ipswich Record Office, HA2/D/1.
53. Seabrook and Bunting family records, kindness of M. Mallowartarchi, Colchester, Essex.
54. Biddell, Manuscript Collection.
55. M. Briggs, *The English Farmhouse*, (London: Batsford, 1953).
56. N. Harvey, *A History of Farm Building in England and Wales*, (Newton Abbott: David and Charles, 1970).
57. E. Mercer, *English Vernacular Houses: a study of the traditional farmhouses and cottages*, (London: Royal Commission on Historical Monuments, HMSO, 1975), p. 74.
58. Robert Baker, *On the Farming of Essex*, (London: Pamphlet printed from *Journal of the Royal Agricultural Society*) 1844, p. 31.
59. In a sample from the 1851 manuscript census from Essex and Suffolk, 16 per cent of farms employed four or more men. Of those who employed labour the average number was 8.2 census sample. Essex had one of the highest ratios in the country of employed men per farm — England 1: 4.7; Essex 1: 8.4. J. Saville, 'Primitive accumulation and early industrialization', *Socialist Register*, vol. VI (1969), p. 257.
60. M. Bayly, *The Life and Letters of Mrs Sewell*, (London: J. Nesbit and Co., 1889), p. 31.
61. John Glyde, 'The autobiography of a Suffolk farm labourer', in *The Suffolk Mercury*, 1894.
62. Royal Institute of British Architecture, *Rooms Concise: glimpses of the small domestic interior 1500—1850*, (London: RIBA Exhibit, 1981).

63. Anon., 'Diary of a farmer's wife on the Warwick/Leicestershire border', Heslop Collection, University of Birmingham, MS 10/iii/15, 1823.
64. E. Simcoe, *A Short History of the Parish and Ancient Borough of Thaxted,* (Saffron Walden: Hart and Son, 1934).
65. Ancient Free and Accepted Masons, *Bye-laws of the Angel Lodge, Colchester No. 59,* (Colchester: S. Hoddon, 1835). Bro. S. F. Watson, *A History of British Union Lodge No. 114, Ipswich 1762—1962,* (Ipswich: W. S. Cowell, 1962).
66. N. Goddard, 'Agricultural societies' in G. E. Mingay (ed.), *The Victorian Countryside,* (London: Routledge and Kegan Paul, 1981), vol. 1.
67. Raynbird, *On the Agriculture of Suffolk.*
68. J. Gyford, 'Men of bad character: property crime in Essex in the 1820s', (M. A. diss. University of Essex, 1982).
69. Peter King, 'Prosecution associations in Essex, 1740—1800' quoted by kind permission of the author.
70. A. J. Brown, Department of History, University of Essex, personal communication.
71. E. Vaughan, *The Essex Village in Days Gone By,* (Colchester: Benham and Co., 1930), p. 29.
72. J. E. Oxley, *Barking Vestry Minutes and Other Documents,* (Colchester: Benham and Co., 1955), p. 28.
73. J. P. Fitzgerald, *The Quiet Worker for Good: a familiar sketch of the late John Charlesworth,* (Ipswich: Darlton and Lucy., 1985), p. 15.
74. B. A. Holderness, 'The Victorian farmer' in G. E. Mingay (ed.), *The Victorian Countryside,* (London: Routledge and Kegan Paul., 1981), vol. 1.
75. Glyde, 'The Autobiography of a Suffolk Farm Labourer'.
76. J. Thirsk and J. Imray, 'An improved corn and cattle market at Saxmundham', in J. Thirsk and J. Imray (eds), *Suffolk Farming in the 19th Century,* (Ipswich: Suffolk Record Society, 1958).
77. S. Golding, 'The importance of fairs in Essex, 1750—1850', *Essex Journal,* vol. 10, no. 3 (1975) pp. 50—66, esp. p. 62.
78. R. Surtees 'Analysis of the hunting field' in E. W. Bovill, *The England of Nimrod and Surtees 1815—1845,* (London: Oxford University Press, 1959), p. 91.
79. White, *Life in Regency England.*
80. D. Wilson, *A Short History of Suffolk,* (London: Batsford, 1977), p. 126.
81. J. Oxley Parker, *The Oxley Parker Papers: from the letters and diaries of an Essex family of estate agents in the 19th century.* (Colchester: Benham and Co., 1964).
82. John Oxley Parker from Essex was one of the founder members. F. M. L. Thompson, *Chartered Surveyors: the growth of a profession,* (London: Routledge and Kegan Paul., 1968).
83. M. Roberts 'Sickles and scythes: women's work and men's work at harvest time', *History Workshop Journal,* no. 7 (Spring 1979), pp. 3—27.
84. K. D. Snell, 'Agricultural seasonal unemployment, the standard of living and women's work in the south and east, 1690—1860', *Economic History Review* no. 34 (1981), pp. 407—37.

85. John Glyde, *Suffolk in the 19th Century: physical, social, moral and industrial,* (London: Simpkin, Marshall and Co. n.d.), p. 367.
86. Obelkevich, p. 50.
87. G. E. Fussell, *The English Dairy Farmer 1500—1900,* (London: Frank Cass, 1966).
88. Ivy Pinchbeck, *Women Workers in the Industrial Revolution 1750—1850,* (London: Frank Cass, 1969).
89. J. Player, *Sketches of Saffron Walden and its Vicinity,* (Saffron Walden: G. Youngman, 1845), p. 57.
90. E. W. Martin, *The Secret People: English village life after 1750,* (London: Phoenix House, 1954). For a different outcome see: Joan Jensen 'Women and industrialisation: the case of buttermaking in 19th-century mid-Atlantic America', (Women and Industrialisation Conference, Bellagio, Italy, August 1983).
91. J. Twamley, *Dairying Exemplified on the Business of Cheese Making,* (Warwick: J. Sharp, 1784), p. 13.
92. Ibid., p. 10.
93. Mrs Lovi, 'Method of ascertaining the richness of milk', *Farmers Magazine* vol. 21, (August. 1820), p. 63.
94. William Marshall, *The Review and Abstract of the County Reports of the Board of Agriculture,* (London: Board of Agriculture), vol. III *Eastern Department 1818,* p. 463.
95. R. Bretnall, 'Manuscript diary of a Witham farmer', *Essex Record Office,* D/DBS, F.38.
96. M. Hardy, *Diary,* (Norwich: Norfolk Record Society, 1968). It is interesting to note that 'farmer' connotes a man. There is no feminine equivalent except 'lady farmer'. The women living on farms have to be called farmer's wife, daughter, sister, niece as the Registrar's Office noted when giving directions for collecting the census.
97. Mary Alice Parker, Diary (manuscript), 1867, kindness of William Lister, Leicester.
98. H. N. Dixon, 'Reminiscences of an Essex county practitioner a century ago', *Essex Review,* vol. XXV, (1916), p. 71.
99. Christy Miller, 'The history of banks and banking in Essex', *The Journal of the Institute of Bankers,* (Oct. 1906), pp. 319—30.
100. Shrimpton, *The Landed Society,* p. 221.
101. A. F. Fairhead, *The Fairhead Series,* (Essex: privately printed, n.d.), 1—10.
102. 158 wills from Witham in Essex, 1780—1855.
103. J. Thirsk and J. Imray, 'Suffolk farmers at home and abroad', in J. Thirsk and J. Imray (eds), *Suffolk Farming in the 19th Century,* (Ipswich: Suffolk Record Society, 1958), vol. 1.
104. Biddell — see also Reeves, *Sheep Bell and Plough Share.*
105. Bayly, *The Life and Letters of Mrs Sewell.* This pattern is confirmed in George Eliot's *Adam Bede* where Mrs Poyser, farmer's wife, has taken in Hetty Sorrel, her husband's niece, to train in dairying and also gave a home to her own orphaned niece, Dinah, in return for child care and general household duties.

106. Oxley Parker, *The Oxley Parker Papers*.
107. Sample of 1851 Manuscript Census for Essex and Suffolk.
108. Fairhead, *The Fairhead Series*.
109. Sample of wills and census. Mrs Clements, 'Essex farmers' accounts, 1783—1795', *Essex Review*, XLVII, (1938/39), p. 87.
110. E. L. Jones, *Agricultural and Economic Growth in England 1650—1815*, (London: Metheun, 1967).
111. 'Mr Gifil's love story', in George Eliot *Scenes from Clerical Life*, (Edinburgh: William Blackwood, 1856), vol. 1, p. 158.
112. Oxley Parker, p. 107.
113. Thomas Hardy, *Far from the Madding Crowd*, (London: Macmillan, 1969), p. 102.
114. Shrimpton, p. 170.
115. Revd. J. Fielding, *A Series of Letters Addressed to the Church and Congregation Assembling at the Great Meeting, Coggeshall*, (Coggeshall: privately printed, 1815).
116. Anonymous farmer's wife.
117. C. Phythian-Adams 'Rural culture' in G. E. Mingay (ed.), *The Victorian Countryside* (London: Routledge and Kegan Paul, 1981), vol. II.
118. Bayly.
119. Maria Charlesworth, *The Female Visitor to the Poor*, (London: Seeley, Burnside and Seeley, 1846).
120. H. Newby, *Green and Pleasant Land? Social change in rural England*, (London: Hutchinson, 1979).
121. William Green, *Plans of Economy or the Road to Ease and Independence*, (London: J. Hatchard, 1804), p. 10.
122. G. E. Mingay, *English Landed Society in the Eighteenth Century*, (London: Routledge and Kegan Paul, 1963), p. 246.
123. J. Stovin, *Journals of a Methodist Farmer*, (London: Croom Helm, 1982), p. 182.
124. Sue Ann Armitage 'Wash on monday: the housework of farm women in transation', (Unpublished paper, 1982), kindness of the author.
125. J. Thirsk and J. Imray, op. cit. (see fn. 103).
126. Which may help to explain why domestic service, a 'quasi-familial' role, became heavily feminized in the late nineteenth century. See L. Davidoff 'Mastered for life: servant and wife in late Victorian and Edwardian England' in *Journal of Social History*, vol. 17, no. 4. (Summer 1974), pp. 406—28.

# Bibliography

Abercrombie, N. and Turner, B. S. 1978, 'The dominant ideology thesis. *British Journal of Sociology* vol. 29, no. 2 reprinted in A. Giddens and D. Held (eds), *Classes, Power and Conflict*. London: Macmillan, 1982.

Abercrombie, N., Hill, S. and Turner, B. S. 1980, *The Dominant Ideology Thesis*. London: George Allen and Unwin.

Abercrombie, N. and Urry, J. 1983, *Capital, Labour and the Middle Classes*. London: George Allen and Unwin.

Acker, J. 1973, 'Women and social stratification: a case of intellectual sexism', in J. Huber (ed.), *Changing Women in a Changing Society*. Chicago University of Chicago Press.

Acker, J. 1980, 'Women and stratification: a review of recent literature'. *Contemporary Sociology*, 9 (Jan.). pp. 25−39.

Alexander, S. 1983, *Women's Work in Nineteenth Century London. A Study of the years 1820−50*. London: The Journeyman Press and the London History Workshop Centre.

Alexander, S. and Taylor, B. 1980, 'In defence of "patriarchy" '. *New Statesman*, (1 Feb.).

Allen, S. 1982, 'Gender inequality and class formation', in A. Giddens and G. Mackenzie (eds), *Social Class and the Division of Labour: essays in honour of Ilya Neustadt*. Cambridge University Press.

Allen, S., Sanders, L. and Wallis, J. (eds) Cambridge, 1974. *Conditions of Illusion*. Leeds: Feminist Books.

Althusser, L. 1971, 'Ideology and ideological state apparatuses'. *Lenin and Philosophy and Other Essays*. New York: Monthly Review Press.

Amsden, A. H. 1980, *The Economics of Women and Work*. Harmondsworth: Penguin.

Anderson, M. 1971, *Family Structure in Nineteenth Century Lancashire*. Cambridge, Cambridge University Press.

Anderson, M. 1985, 'The emergence of the modern life cycle in Britain'. *Social History*, 10, pp. 69−87.

Arber, S., Dale, A., and Gilbert, G. N. 1984, 'Evaluating alternative measures of social class: does gender make a difference?'. Paper presented to BSA Conference, Bradford, April.

Armstrong, P. 1982, 'If it's only women it doesn't matter so much', in J. West (ed.), *Work, Women and the Labour Market*. London: Routledge and Kegan Paul.

Bailyn, L. 1978, 'Accommodation of work to family', in R. Rapoport and R. N. Rapoport (eds), *Working Couples*. London: Routledge and Kegan Paul.

Bain, G. S. and Price, R. 1972, 'Who is a white-collar employee?'. *British Journal of Industrial Relations*, vol. 10, pp. 325—39.

Banks, D. 1981, *Faces of Feminism*. Oxford: Martin Robertson.

Barnard, H. C. 1961, *A History of English Education from 1760*. London: University of London Press.

Barrett, M. 1980, *Women's Oppression Today*. London: Verso.

Barrett, M. and McIntosh, M. 1980, 'The family wage: some problems for socialists and feminists'. *Capital and Class*, 11 (Summer).

Beauvoir, S. de 1949, *The Second Sex*. Harmondsworth: Penguin.

Bechhofer, F. 1981, 'Substantive dogs and methodological tails: a question of fit'. *Sociology*, 15, pp. 495—505.

Becker, G. 1957, *The Economics of Discrimination*. Chicago: University of Chicago Press.

Beechey, V. 1978, 'Women and production: a critical analysis of some sociological trends in women's work', in A. Kuhn and A. Wolpe (eds), *Feminism and Materialism*. London: Routledge and Kegan Paul.

Beechey, V. 1979, 'On patriarchy'. *Feminist Review*. no. 3.

Beechey, V. 1983a 'What's so special about women's employment? A review of some recent studies of women's paid work'. *Feminist Review*, no. 15.

Beechey, V. 1983b 'Part time work' Paper given to the BSA Sexual Divisions Group in Oxford, December.

Beechey, V. and Allen, R. 1982, *The Woman Question*, U221 Unit 1. Milton Keynes: Open University Press.

Bell, C. and Newby, H. 1976, 'Husbands and wives: the dynamics of deferential dialectic', in D. L. Barker and S. Allen, *Dependence and Exploitation in Work and Marriage*. London: Longman.

Benenson, H. 1984, 'Women's occupational and family achievement in the US class system: a critique of dual-career family analysis'. *British Journal of Sociology*, vol. XXXV, no. 1.

Berg, M. 1984, 'Domestic manufacture, women and community in the eighteenth century'. Mimeo.

Beteille, A. 1965, *Caste, Class and Power*. Berkeley: University of California Press.

Blackburn, R. M. and Mann, M. 1979, *The Working Class in the Labour Market*. London: Macmillan.

Blau, F. and Jusenius, C. 1976, 'Economists approaches to sex segregation in the labour market: an appraisal', in M. Blaxall and B. Reagan (eds), *Women and the Workplace*. Chicago: University of Chicago Press.

Bolton, R. and Mayer E. (eds) 1977, *Andean Kinship and Marriage*. Washington DC: American Anthropological Association.

Boserup, E. 1970, *Women's Role in Economic Development*. London: George Allen and Unwin.

Boserup, E. 1975, 'Employment of women in developing countries', in L. Tabah (ed.), *Population Growth and Economic Development in the Third World*, vol. I, Brussels: Ordina Editions.

Bott, E. 1957, *Family and Social Network*. London: Tavistock.

Bottomore, T. B. 1962, *Sociology, A Guide to Problems and Literature.* London: George Allen and Unwin.

Bottomore, T. and Goode, P. (eds and trans.) 1978, *Austro-Marxism.* Oxford: Clarendon Press.

Bourdieu, P. 1962, 'Célibat et condition paysanne'. *Etudes rurales,* 5—6.

Bourdieu, P. and Passeron, J.—C. 1964, *Les héritiers.* Paris: Editions de Minuit.

Bourque, S. C. and Warren, K. B. 1976, 'Campesinas and communeras: subordination in the Sierra'. *Journal of Marriage and the Family,* (Nov.).

Boyson, R. 1970, *The Ashworth Cotton Enterprise.* Oxford: Oxford University Press.

Branca, A. 1975, 'A new perspective on women's work: a comparative typology'. *Journal of Social History,* vol. 9.

Braverman, H. 1974, *Labor and Monopoly Capital: the degradation of work in the twentieth century.* New York: Monthly Review Press.

Breughel, I. 1978, 'Bourgeois economics and women's oppression'. *m/f,* 1, pp. 103—11.

Breughel, I. 1979, 'Women as a Reserve Army of Labour: a note on recent British experience', *Feminist Review,* vol. 3.

Britten, N. and Heath, A. 1983, 'Women, men and social class', in E. Gamarnikow *et al.* (eds), *Gender, Class and Work.* London: Heinemann.

Brown, R. 1982, 'Work histories, career strategies and the class structure', in A. Giddens and G. Mackenzie (eds), *Social Class and the Division of Labour: Essays in honour of Ilya Neustadt.* Cambridge: Cambridge University Press.

Broyelle, C. 1979, *La Moitie du Ciel. Le mouvement de liberation des femmes aujourd' hui en Chine.* Paris Editions Denoel/Gonthier.

Burkett, E. C. 1978, 'Indian women and white society: the case of sixteenth century Peru, in A. Lavrin (ed.), *Latin American Women, Historical Perspectives.* Westport: Greenwood Press.

Burns, S, 1975, *The Household Economy.* Boston: Beacon.

Carchedi, G. 1975, 'On the Economic Identification of the New Middle Class'. *Economy and Society,* vol. 4, no. 1.

Carchedi, G. 1977, *On the Economic Identification of Social Classes.* London: Routledge and Kegan Paul.

Casey, K. 1976, 'the Cheshire cat: reconstructing the experience of medieval women', in B. Caroll (ed.), *Liberating Women's History.* Urbana: University of Illinois Press.

Cavendish, R. 1982, *On the Line.* London: Routledge and Kegan Paul.

Chiplin, B. and Sloane P. J. 1982, *Tackling Discrimination at the Workplace.* Cambridge: Cambridge University Press.

Chisholm, L. and Woodward, D. 'The experiences of women graduates in the labour market', in R. Deem (ed.), *Schooling for Women's Work.* London: Routledge and Kegan Paul.

Chodorow, N. 1979, 'Mothering, male dominance and capitalism', in Z. Eisenstein (ed.), *Capitalist Patriarchy and the Case for Socialist Feminism.* New York: Monthly Review Press.

Chueca, M. 1982, 'Mujer, familia y trabajo en villa El Salvador'. Paper presented to the Seminar 'Analysis y Promocion de la Participacion de la Mujer an en la Actividad Economica', Lima, 2—5 March.

Clark, A. 1982, 1919, *Working Life of Women in the Seventeenth Century.* London: Routledge and Kegan Paul.

Clarke, B. *et al.* 1979, *Working Class Culture.* London: Hutchinson.

Cockburn, C. 1977, *The Local State.* London: Pluto Press.

Cockburn, C. 1981, 'The material of male power'. *Feminist Review,* no. 9.

Cockburn, C. 1983a, *Brothers — male dominance and technological change.* London: Pluto Press.

Cockburn, C. 1983b, 'Caught in the wheels'. *Marxism Today,* (Nov.).

Cohen, G. 1977, 'Absentee husbands in spiralist families'. *Journal of Marriage and the Family,* vol. 39, pp. 595—604.

Collver, A. and Langlois, E. 1962, 'The female labour force in Metropolitan areas: an international comparison'. *Economic Development and Cultural Change,* X (Jul.).

Costello, C. 1983, 'Working women's consciousness and collective action'. Paper presented at the Annual Meeting of the American Sociological Association, Detroit, Michigan, August 1983.

Coyle, A. 1982, 'Sex and skill in the organisation of the clothing industry' in J. West (ed.), *Women, Work and the Labour Market.* London: Routledge and Kegan Paul.

Crewe, I., Robertson, D. and Sarlvik, B. 1981, 'A Description of surveys conducted by the BES Research Project', Technical Paper 1981: 1. Department of Government, University of Essex.

Crompton, R. and Jones, G. 1982, 'Clerical "proletarianisation": myth or reality', in G. Day, *et al.* (eds), *Diversity and Decomposition in Labour Markets.* Aldershot: Gower.

Crompton, R. and Jones, G. 1984, *White-collar Proletariat: deskilling and gender in the clerical labour process.* London: Macmillan.

Crow, G. 1981, 'Whither the mistresses of business administration?'. *Personnel Management,* vol. 36—39 (Sept.).

Curran, M. 1984, 'Women's job changes, men's careers'. Paper given to the BSA Sociology of Work and Industrial Relations Group, London, June.

Currell, M. 1974, *Political Woman.* London: Croom Helm.

Dahrendorf, R. 1959, *Class and Class Conflict in an Industrial Society.* London: Routledge and Kegan Paul.

Dale, A., Gilbert, G. N. 1984, 'Integrating women into class theory'. Stratification and Employment Group, Department of Sociology, University of Surrey, mimeo.

Daniel, W. W. 1981, 'A clash of symbols: the case of maternity legislation'. *Policy Studies,* vol. 2, part 2 (Oct.).

Date-Bah, E. 1984, 'Sex segregation and discrimination in Accra-Tema, causes and consequences', in R. Anker and C. Hein (eds), *Sex Discrimination and Sex Segregation in Urban Labour Markets of the Third World.*

Davidoff, L. 1973, *The Best Circles.* Beckenham: Croom Helm.

Davidoff, L. 1974, 'Mastered for life: servant and wife in Victorian and Edwardian England'. *Journal of Social History,* (Summer).

Davidoff, L. 1976, 'The rationalization of housework', in D. L. Barker and S. Allen (eds), *Dependence and Explotation in Work and Marriage.* London: Longman.

Davidoff, L. Esperance, J. and Newby H. 1976, 'Landscape with figures. Home and community in English society', in J. Mitchell and A Oakley (eds), *Rights and Wrongs of Women.* Harmondsworth: Penguin.

Davies, M. 1974, 'Woman's place is at the typewriter: the feminization of the clerical labour force'. *Radical America,* vol. 8, no. 4.

Davies, K. and Moore, N. E. 1945, 'Some Principles of Stratification'. *American Sociological Review,* vol. 10, no. 2.

Deane, P. 1979, *The First Industrial Nation,* 2nd ed. Cambridge: Cambridge University Press.

Degler, C. 1980, *At Odds: the family in America from the Revolution to the present.* New York: Oxford University Press.

Delphy, C. 1977, 'The main enemy: a materialist analysis of women's oppression'. *Explorations in Feminism,* no. 3.

Delphy, C. 1981, 'Women in stratification studies', in H. Roberts (ed.), *Doing Feminist Research.* London: Routledge and Kegan Paul.

Delphy, C. 1984a, 'Women in stratification studies', in *Close to Home.* London: Hutchinson.

Delphy, C. 1984b, 'Hereditary transmission'. Mimeo.

Delphy, C and Leonard, D. 1982, 'Marxism, the division of labour and the oppression of women'. Paper presented at BSA Conference Manchester.

Dodd, W. 1967, *The Factory System Illustrated.* London: Frank Cass.

DuBois, E. C. 1978, *Feminism and Suffrage: the emergence of an independent women's movement in America 1848–1869.* Ithaca, NY: Cornell University Press.

Dworkin, A. 1983, *Right Wing Women.* London: Women's Press.

Dyhouse, C. 1981, *Girls Growing up in Late Victorian and Edwardian England.* London: Routledge and Kegan Paul.

Eccel, C. 1984, *Egypt, Islam and Social Change: Al Azhar in conflict and accommodation.* Berlin: Klaus Schwarz Verlag.

Edgell, S. 1980, *Middle Class Couples: a study of segregation, domination and inequality in marriage.* London: George Allen and Unwin.

Edwards, R. 1979, *Contested Terrain.* London: Heinemann.

Eisenstein, Z. 1979, *Capitalist Patriarchy and the Case for Socialist Feminism.* New York: Monthly Review Press.

Eisenstein, Z. 1981, *The Radical Future of Liberal Feminism.* New York: Longman.

El Saadawi, N. 1980, *The Hidden Face of Eve.* London: Zed Press.

Elias, P. and Main, B. 1982, *Women's Working Lives: evidence from the National Training Survey.* Warwick Institute of Employment Research.

Eliasberg, G. 1974, *Der Ruhrkrieg von 1920.* Bonn: Bad Godesberg.

Elshtein, J. B. 1981, *Public Man, Private Woman.* Oxford: Martin Robertson.

Engels, F. 1884, *The Origins of the Family, Private Property and the State,* 1972 ed. London: Lawrence and Wishart.

Erikson, R. 1984, 'Social class of men, women and families'. *Sociology,* vol. 18. no. 4.

Fakhouri, H. 1972, *Kafr El-Elow, an Egyptian Village in Transition.* New York: Holt, Rinehart and Winston.

Feminist Anthology Collective 1982, *No Turning Back.* London: Women's Press.

Fevre, R. 1985, 'Contract work in the recession', in S. Wood and K. Purcell (eds), *The Changing Experience of Work: Restructuring and Recession.* London: Macmillan.

Finch, J. 1983, *Married to the Job: wives' incorporation in mens' work.* London: George Allen and Unwin.

Finch, J. and Groves, D. (eds) 1983, *A Labour of Love: women, work and caring.* Henley: Routledge and Kegan Paul.

Firestone, S. 1971, *The Dialectic of Sex.* London: Jonathan Cape.

Flexner, E. 1974, *Century of Struggle.* New York: Atheneum.

Fogarty, M. and Rapoport, R. and Rapoport, R. 1971, *Sex, Career and Family.* London: George Allen and Unwin.

Friedman, S. and Sarah, E. (eds) 1982, *On the Problem of Men.* London: Women's Press.

Gamarnikow, E., *et al.* 1983, *The Public and Private.* London: Heineman.

Gardiner, J. 1976, 'Domestic labour in capitalist society', in D. Barker and S. Allen (eds), *Dependence and Exploitation in Work and Marriage.* London.

Garnsey, E. 1978, 'Women's work and theories of class and stratification'. *Sociology,* vol. 12, no. 2, Reprinted in A. Giddens and D. Held (eds), *Classes, Power and Conflict* London: Macmillan 1982.

Garnsey, E. 1981, 'The rediscovery of the division of labor'. *Theory and Society,* vol. 19, pp. 337–58.

Geary, D. 1981, 'Identifying militancy: the assessment of working-class attitudes towards state and society', in R. Evans (ed.), *The German Working Class 1888–1933:The Politics of Everyday Life.* London: Croom Helm.

Gershuny, J. K. 1983, *Social Innovation and the Division of Labour.* Oxford: Oxford University Press.

Giddens, A. 1973, *The Class Structure of the Advanced Societies.* London: Hutchinson.

Giddens, A. 1981, *The Class Structure of the Advanced Societies,* 2nd edn. London: Hutchinson.

Gilman, C. P. 1966, *Women and Economics.* New York: Harper and Row.

Ginsburg, N. 1979, *Class, Capital and Social Policy.* London: Macmillan.

Glastonbury, M. 1978, 'Holding the pens', in S. Elbert and M. Glastonbury (eds) *Inspiration and Drudgery.* London: Women's Research and Resources Centre Pamphlet.

Glucksmann, M. 1984, 'Women and the "New Industries": Changes in Class Relations in the 1930s' (mimeo). Paper presented at the ESRC Symposium on Gender and Stratification, University of East Anglia, July.

Goldthorpe, J. H. *et al.* 1969, *The Affluent Worker in the Class Structure.* Cambridge: Cambridge University Press.

Goldthorpe, J. H., (with Llewellyn, C. and Payne, C.) 1980, *Social Mobility and Class Structure in Modern Britain.* Oxford: Clarendon Press.

Goldthorpe, J. H. 1982, 'On the service class, its formation and future', in A. Giddens and G. Mackenzie (eds), *Social Class and the Division of Labour:*

*Essays in Labour of Ilya Neustadt.* Cambridge: Cambridge University Press.

Goldthorpe, J. H. 1983, 'Women and class analysis: in defence of the conventional view'. *Sociology,* vol. 17, no. 4.

Goldthorpe, J. H. 1984, 'Women and class analysis: a reply to the replies', *Sociology,* vol. 18, no. 4.

Goldthorpe, J. H. and Hope, K. 1974, *The Social Grading of Occupations.* Oxford: Clarendon Press.

Goody, J. 1983, *The Development of the Family and Marriage in Europe.* Cambridge: Cambridge University Press.

Greenstreet, M. 1981, 'When education is unequal' in K. Young and C. Moser (eds), *Women and the Informal Sector.* IDS Bulletin, vol. 12, no. 3 (Jul.).

Grimes, A. 1967, *The Puritan Ethic and Women's Suffrage.* New York: Oxford University Press.

Gross, E. 1968, 'Plus ca change? The sexual structure of occupations over time'. *Social Problems,* 16 (Fall).

Haavio-Mannila, E. 1969, 'Some consequences of women's emancipation'. *Journal of Marriage and the Family,* vol. 31.

Hacker, A. 1983, 'Where have the jobs gone?'. *New York Review of Books,* (30 Jun.).

Hakim, C. 1979, *Occupational Segregation,* research paper no. 9. London: Department of Employment.

Hamilton, R. 1978, *The Liberation of Women: a study of patriarchy and capitalism.* London: George Allen and Unwin.

Handy, C. 1978, 'Going against the grain: working couples and greedy occupations', in Rapoport, R. and Rapoport, R. N. (eds), *Working Couples.* London: Routledge and Kegan Paul.

Hansen, B. and Radwan, S. 1982, *Employment Opportunities and Equity in Egypt.* Geneva: ILO.

Harris, C. C. 1969, *The Family.* London: George Allen and Unwin.

Harris, C. C. 1983, *The Family in Industrial Society.* London: Allen & Unwin.

Harris, C. C. 1984, 'The idea of a labour market', School of Social Studies, occasional paper no. 4. University College of Swansea.

Harris, C. C., Lee, R. M. and Morris, L. D. 1985, 'Redundancy in steel', in R. Finnegan, B. Roberts and D. Gallie (eds), *New Approaches to Economic Life.* Manchester: Manchester University Press.

Harris, O. 1981, 'The power of signs: gender culture and the wild in the Bolivian Andes', C. MacCormak and M. Strathern (eds), *Nature, Culture and Gender.* Cambridge: Cambridge University Press.

Hartmann, H. 1976, 'Capitalism, patriarchy and job segregation by sex', in Blaxall, M. and Reagan, B. (eds), *Women and the Workplace.* Chicago: University of Chicago Press.

Hartmann, H. 1979, 'Capitalism, patriarchy and job segregation by sex' in Z. Eisenstein: *Capitalist Patriarchy and the case for Socialist Feminism.* New York: Monthly Review Press.

Hartmann, H. 1981, 'The unhappy marriage of Marxism and feminism: towards a more progressive union', in L. Sargent (ed.), *Women and Revolution.* London: Pluto Press.

Heath, A. and Britten, N. 1984, 'Women's jobs do make a difference' *Sociology*, vol. 18, no. 4.

Hindess, B. 1973, *The Use of Official Statistics in Sociology: a Critique of Positivism and Ethnomethodology.* London: Macmillan.

Holmwood, J. and Stewart, A. 1983, 'The role of contradictions in modern theories of social stratification'. *Sociology,* vol. 17.

Hoodfar, H. 1985, 'Patterns of household budget arrangement and management of financial affairs in a lower income neighbourhood in Cairo, Egypt'. Mimeo.

*ILO Yearbook of Statistics,* 1973; 1975; 1980. Geneva: ILO.

James, R. 1962, 'Discrimination against women in Bombay textiles'. *Industrial and Labor Relations Review,* vol. 15, no. 2.

Jenkins, R. 1983, *Lads, Citizens and Ordinary Kids.* London: Routledge and Kegan Paul.

Johnson, T. 1972, *Professions and Power.* London: Macmillan.

Joseph, G. 1983, *Women and Work.* Oxford: Philip Allan.

Kelly, J. 1979, 'The doubled vision of feminist theory'. *Feminist Studies,* 5.

Kenrick, J. 1981, 'Politics and the construction of women as second-class workers', in F. Wilkinson (ed.), *The Dynamics of Labour Market Segmentation.* London and New York: Academic Press.

Koedt, A., Levine, E. and Rapone, A. (eds), 1973, *Radical Feminism.* New York: Quadrangle.

Kohn, H. 1967, *Prelude to Nation-states: the French and German experience, 1789—1815.* Princeton: Van Nostrand Reinhold.

Kuhn, A. and Wolpe, A. 1978, *Feminism and Materialism.* London: Routledge and Kegan Paul.

Kuper, L. 1974, *Race, Class and Power.* London: Duckworth.

Kuper, L. and Smith, M. G. 1971, *Pluralism in Africa.* Berkeley: University of California Press.

Land, H. 1980, 'The family wage'. *Feminist Review,* 6.

Leete, R. and Fox, J. 1977, 'Registrar-General's social classes: origins and uses'. *Population Trends,* 8.

Lenski, G. 1966, *Power and Privilege.* New York: Harper and Row.

Levine, D. 1977, *Family Formation in an Age of Nascent Capitalism.* New York: Academic Press.

Lewenhak, S. 1977, *Women and Trade Unions.* London: Ernest Benn.

Lewis, J. 1984, *Women in England 1870—1950.* Brighton: Wheatsheaf Books.

Liddington, J. and Norris, J. 1978, *One Hand Tied Behind Us: the rise of the women's suffrage movement.* London: Virago.

Littlejohn, J. 1963, *Westrigg: the sociology of a Cheviot Parish.* London: Routledge and Kegan Paul.

Lockwood, D. 1958, *The Blackcoated Worker: a study in class consciousness.* London: George Allen and Unwin.

Lown, J. 1983, 'Not so much a factory; more a form of patriarchy: gender and class during industrialization', in E. Gamarnikow *et al.* (eds), *Gender Class and Work.* London: Heinemann.

Lown, J. 1984, *Gender and class during industrialisation: a study of the Halstead silk industry in Essex, 1825—1900.* Ph.D. thesis, University of Essex.

Mabro, R. and Radwan, S. 1976, *The Industrialisation of Egypt 1939—1973.* Oxford: Oxford University Press.

Mann, M. 1986, *The Sources of Social Power,* vol. I: *A History of Power from the Beginning to AD 1760.* New York: Cambridge University Press.

Mann, M. forthcoming, *The Sources of Social Power, vol. II: A History of Power in Industrial Societies.* New York: Cambridge University Press.

Mark-Lawson, J. 1984, 'Women and the local state, 1919—1939'. Paper presented to the Women's Research Group, Lancaster University, May.

Mark-Lawson, J., Savage, M. and Warde, A. 1984, 'Gender and local politics struggles over welfare policies, 1918—1939', in L. Murgatroyd *et al.* (eds), *Localities, Class and Gender.* London: Pion.

Marks, P. 1976, 'Femininity in the classroom: an account of changing attitudes', in J. Mitchell and A. Oakley (eds), *The Rights and Wrongs of Women.* Harmondsworth: Penguin.

Marshall, T. H. 1950, *Citizenship and Social Class.* Cambridge: Cambridge University Press.

Martin, J. and Roberts, C. 1984, *Women and Employment: a lifetime perspective. The report of the 1980 DE/OPCS Women and Employment Survey.* London: HMSO.

Masnick, G. and Bane, M. J. 1980, *The Nation's Families, 1960—1990.* Boston; Auburn House.

Mathieu, N.—C. 1977, *Ignored by Some, Denied by Others: the social sex category in sociology.* London: Womens Research and Resources Centre.

Matthaei, J. 1982, *An Economic History of Women in America.* Brighton: Harvester Press.

McGaw, J. A. 1982, 'Women and the history of American technology'. *Signs,* vol. 7, no. 4.

McIntosh, M. 1978, 'The state and the oppression of women', in A. Kuhn and A. Wolpe (eds), *Feminism and Materialism.* London: Routledge and Kegan Paul.

McNally, F. 1979, *Women for Hire: a study of the female office workers.* London: Macmillan.

Middleton, C. 1979, 'The sexual division of labour under feudalism'. *New Left Review,* nos. 113—14, Jan—April.

Middleton, C. 1983, 'Patriarchal exploitation and the rise of English capitalism', in E. Gamarnikow (eds), *Gender, Class and Work.* London: Heinemann.

Milkman, R. 1976, 'Women's work and the economic crisis'. *Review of Radical Political Economics,* vol. 8, no. 1.

Millett, K. 1977, *Sexual Politics.* London: Virago.

Mills, C. W. 1963, 'Women: the darling little slaves', in *Power, Politics and People.* New York: Oxford University Press.

Mincer, J. (1962) 'Labour force participation of married women: a study of labor supply' in National Bureau of Economic Research *Aspects of Labor Economics: A Conference of the Universities,* Princeton, US: Princeton University Press.

Molyneux, M. 1979, 'Beyond the domestic labour debate'. *New Left Review,* no. 116.

Morgan, D. 1972, *Suffragists and Democrats: the politics of woman suffrage in America.* East Lansing, Michigan: Michigan State University Press.

Morgan, D. 1975, *Suffragists and Liberals: the politics of woman suffrage in England*. Oxford: Basil Blackwell.

Morris, L. D. 1984a, 'Patterns of social activity and post-redundancy labour market experience'. *Sociology*, vol. 18, no. 3.

Morris, L. D. 1984b, 'Redundancy and the pattern of household finance'. *Sociological Review*, vol. 32, n. 3.

Morris, L. D. 1985, 'Renegotiation of the domestic division of labour in the context of male redundancy', in H. Newby (ed.), *Restructuring Capital*. London: Macmillan.

Morris, L. D. (a) forthcoming, 'Redundancy and gender roles in South Wales'. *British Journal of Sociology*.

Morris, L. D. (b) forthcoming, 'Responses to redundancy: labour market experience, domestic organisation and male social activity'. *Journal of Social and Economic Research*.

Moser, C. 1981, 'Surviving in the suburbios', in K. Young and C. Moser (eds), *Women in the Informal Sector*. Stanford: Stanford University Press.

Murgatroyd, L. 1982a, *Gender and Class Stratification*. Unpublished D.Phil. thesis, Wolfson College University of Oxford.

Murgatroyd, L. 1982b, 'Gender and occupational stratification'. *Sociological Review*, vol. 30, no. 4.

Murgatroyd, L. 1984a, 'Women, men and the social grading of occupations'. *British Journal of Sociology*, vol. 35, no. 4.

Murgatroyd, L. 1984b, 'Gender and occupational stratification', in L. Murgatroyd *et al.* (eds), *Localities, Class and Gender*. London: Pion.

Myrdal, G. 1944, *An American Dilemma*. New York: Harper and Row.

Newby, H. 1982, *The State of Research into Social Stratification*. London: Social Science Research Council.

Oakley, A. 1974, *The Sociology of Housework*. London: Martin Robertson.

Oakley, A. 1981, *Subject Women*. Oxford: Martin Robertson.

O'Brien, M. 1981, *The Politics of Reproduction*. London: Routledge and Kegan Paul.

Okali, C. 1983, *Cocoa and Kinship in Ghana*. London: Kegan Paul International.

O'Neill, W. 1969, *The Woman Movement: feminism in the United States and England*. London: George Allen and Unwin.

OPCS 1980, *General Household Survey*. London: OPCS.

Oppenheimer, V. 1970, *The Female Labour Force in the United States*. Berkeley Institute of International Studies, University of California.

Ortner, S. and Whitehead, H. 1981, *Sexual Meanings: the cultural construction of gender and sexuality*. Cambridge: Cambridge University Press.

Pagels, E. 1980, *The Gnostic Gospels*. London: Weidenfeld and Nicholson.

Pahl, R. E. 1980, 'Employment, work and the domestic division of labour'. *International Journal of Urban and Regional Research*, vol.4, no. 1, pp. 1—20.

Pahl, R. 1985, *Divisions of Labour*. Oxford: Basil Blackwell.

Pahl, R. E. and Wallace, C. 1983, 'Household work strategies in economic recession'. Mimeo.

Papenek, H. 1973, 'Men, women and work: reflections on the two-person career'. *American Journal of Sociology*, vol. 78, no. 4, pp. 852—72.

Parkin, F. 1972, *Class Inequality and Political Order*. London: Paladin.
Parkin, F. 1974, 'Strategies of social closure in class formation', in F. Parkin (ed.), *The Social Analysis of Class Structure*. London: Tavistock.
Parkin, F. 1979, *Marxism and Class Theory: a bourgeois critique*. London: Tavistock.
Parry, N. and Parry, J. 1976, *The Rise of the Medical Profession: a study of collective social mobility*. Beckenham: Croom Helm.
Phillips, A. 1983, *Hidden Hands*. London: Pluto Press.
Phillips, A. and Taylor, B. 1980, 'Sex and skill: notes towards a feminist economics'. *Feminist Review*, no. 6.
Pinchbeck, I. 1981, *Women Workers and the Industrial Revolution 1750—1850*. London: Virago.
Pollert, A. 1981, *Girls, Wives and Factory Lives*. London: Macmillan.
Pollert, A. 1983, 'Women, Gender Relations and Wage Labour', in E. Gamarnikow *et al., Gender, Class and Work*. London: Heinemann.
Poulantzas, N. 1973, *Political Power and Social Classes*. London: New Left Books.
Poulantzas, N. 1975, *Classes in Contemporary Capitalism*. London: New Left Books.
Poulantzas, N. 1978, *Classes in Contemporary Capitalism*. London: New Left Books.
Prandy, K., Stewart, A. and Blackburn, R. M. 1982, *White-collar Work*. London: Macmillan.
Rapoport, R. and Rapoport R. 1971, *Dual Career Families*. Harmondsworth: Penguin.
Rapoport, R. and Rapoport, R. N. (eds) 1975, *Working Couples*. London: Routledge and Kegan Paul.
Redstockings 1975, *Feminist Revolution*. New York: New Paltz.
Reid, I. and Wormald, E. 1982, *Sex Differences in Britain*. London: Grant McIntyre.
Rex, J. 1961, *Key Problems of Sociological Theory*. London: Routledge and Kegan Paul.
Richman, J. 1982, 'Men's experiences of pregnancy and childbirth', in L. McKee and M. O'Brien (eds), *The Father Figure*. London: Tavistock.
Riemer, E. and Fout, J. 1983, *European Women: a documentary history, 1789—1945*. Brighton: Harvester Press.
Robertson, C. 1976, 'Ga women and socio-economic change in Accra, Ghana', in Hafkin and Bay (eds), *Women in Africa*. Stanford: Stanford University Press.
Rose, S. O. 1984, 'Gender segregation in the transition to the factory: the English hosiery industry 1850—1910'. Mimeo.
Routh, G. 1980, *Occupation and Pay in Great Britain 1906—79*. London: Macmillan.
Rover, C. 1967, *Women's Suffrage and Party Politics in Britain, 1866—1914*. London: Routledge and Kegan Paul.
Rowbotham, S. 1979, 'The problem with "patriarchy" ' *New Statesman*, (21—28 Dec.). Reprinted in *Dreams and Dilemmas*. London: Virago.
Rowbotham, S. 1982, 'The trouble with "Patriarchy" ', in M. Evans (ed.), *The Woman Question*. London: Fontana.

Sachs, A. and Wilson, J. H. 1978, *Sexism and the Law*. Oxford: Martin Robertson.

Sanyal, B. C. *et al.* 1982, *University Education and the Labour Market in the Arab Republic of Egypt*. Oxford: Pergamon Press for Unesco.

Sargent, L. (ed.) 1981, *Women and Revolution*. London: Pluto Press.

Savage, M. 1984, 'Control at work', in L. Mugatroyd *et al.* (eds), *Localities, Class and Gender*. London: Pion.

Schreiner, O. 1911, *Woman and Labour*. London: Fisher Unwin.

Scott, A. MacEwen 1979, 'Aspects of job stability amongst Peruvian manual workers'. Paper given to the Development Studies Association Annual Conference, Glasgow. Mimeo.

Scott, A. MacEwen 1984, 'Economic development and urban women's work: The case of Lima, Peru', in Anker, R. amd Hein, C. (eds) *Sex Inequalities in Urban Employment in the Third World* (ILO) (to be published by Macmillan 1986).

Seccombe, W. 1974, 'The housewife and her labour under capitalism'. *New Left Review*, no. 83.

Shils, E. 1967, 'Deference' in J. Jackson (ed.), *Social Stratification*. Cambridge: Cambridge University Press.

Shils, E. 1982, *Centre and Periphery: essays in macrosociology*. Chicago: Chicago University Press.

Siltanen, J. 1981, 'A commentary on theories of female wage labour', in Cambridge Women's Studies Group (eds), *Women in Society*. London: Virago.

Siltanen, J. 1985, 'Employment and parenting: variations in experience'. Ph.D. thesis, University of Cambridge.

Siltanen, J. and Stanworth, M. (eds) 1984, *Women and the Public Sphere*. London: Hutchinson.

Simon, B. 1960, *The Two Nations and the Educational Structure 1780—1870*. London: Lawrence and Wishart.

Smith, D. E. 1974, 'Women's perspective as a radical critique of sociology'. *Sociological Inquiry*, vol. 44, no. 1, pp. 7—13.

Smith, D. E. 1983, 'Women, class and family', in R. Miliband and J. Saville (eds), *The Socialist Register*.

Smith, D. E. 1973, 'Women, the family and corporate capitalism', in M. Stephenson (ed.), *Women in Canada*. Toronto: New Press.

Smith, D. J. 1977, *Racial Disadvantages in Britain: the P.E.P. report* Harmondsworth: Penguin.

Smock, A. C. 1977, 'Ghana, from autonomy to subordination', in J. Z. Giele and A. C. Smock (eds), *Women, Roles and Status in Eight Countries*. New York: Wiley.

Smock, A. C. and Youssef, N. 1977, ''Egypt', from seclusion to limited participation', in Giele, J. Z. and Smock, A. C. (eds) *Women, Roles and Status in Eight Countries*. New York: Wiley.

Spender, D. 1980, *Man Made Language*. London: Routledge and Kegan Paul.

Spender, D. 1983a, *Women of Ideas (and what men have done to them)*. London: Ark.

Spender, D. 1983b, *There's Always Been a Women's Movement this Century* London, Boston, Melbourne and Henly: Pandora Press, Routledge and Kegan Paul.

Stacey, M. 1960, *Tradition and Change: a study of Banbury*. London: Oxford University Press.

Stacey, M. 1981, 'The division of labour revisited or overcoming the two Adams', in P. Abrams *et al.* (eds), *Practice and Progress: British sociology 1950—1980*. London: George Allen and Unwin.

Stacey, M. 1984, 'Who are the health workers? Patients and other unpaid workers in health care'. *Economic Democracy*, 5, pp. 157—84.

Stacey, M. *et al.* 1975. *Power, Persistence and Change*. London and Boston: Routledge and Kegan Paul.

Stacey, M. and Price, M. 1981, *Women, Power and Politics*. London: Tavistock.

Stanworth, M. 1984, 'Women and class analysis: a reply to John Goldthorpe'. *Sociology*, vol. 18, no. 2.

Stark, D. 1980, 'Class Struggle and the Transformation of the Labour Process: A Relational Approach'. *Theory and Society*, vol. 9.

Steel, W. F. 1981, 'Female and small-scale employment under modernisation in Ghana'. *Economic Development and Cultural Change*, vol. 30, no. 1.

Stewart, A., Blackburn, R. M. and Prandy, K. 1985, 'Gender and earnings, the failure of market explanations', in R. Finnegan *et al., New Approaches to Economic Life*. Manchester: University Press.

Stewart A., Prandy, K. and Blackburn, R. M. 1980, *Social Stratification and occupations*. London: Macmillan.

Stewart, M. and Greenhalgh, 'Work history patterns and the occupational attainment of women'. University of Warwick Economic Research Papers no. 212.

Stone, L. 1977, *The Family, Sex and Marriage in England, 1500—1800*. London: Weidenfeld and Nicholson.

Taylor, B. 1979, 'The men are as bad as their masters — socialism, feminism and sexual antagonism in the London tailoring trades, in the early 1830s'. *Feminist Studies*.

Taylor, B. 1983, *Eve and the New Jerusalem*. London: Virago.

Thane, P. 1978, 'Women and the Poor Law in Victorian and Edwardian England'. *History Workshop*, 6.

Thane P. 1982, *Foundations of the Welfare State*. London: Longman.

Thompson, P. 1983, *The Nature of Work*. London: Macmillan.

Tilly, L. and Scott, J. 1978, *Women, Work and Family*. New York: Holt, Rinehart and Winston.

Van Hear, N. 1982, 'Child labour and the development of capitalist agriculture in Ghana'. *Development and Change*, vol. 13, no. 4 (Oct.).

Vanek, J. 1980, 'Time spent in housework', in A. H. Amsden (ed.), *Women and Work*. Harmondsworth: Penguin.

Vogel, L. 1983, *Marxism and the Oppression of Women: toward a unitary theory*. London: Pluto Press.

Walby, S. 1983a, 'Patriarchal structures: the case of unemployment', in E. Gamarnikow *et al. Gender, Class and Work*. Heinemann: London.

Walby, S. 1983b, *Gender and Unemployment. Patriarchal and capitalist relations in the restructuring of gender relations in employment and unemployment.* Unpublished Ph.D. thesis, University of Essex.

Walby, S. 1984, 'Historical and spatial variations in women's employment', in L.

Murgatroyd *et al.* (eds), *Localities, Class and Gender.* London: Pion.

Walby, S. 1985, *Patriarchy at Work.* Oxford: Polity Press.

Watson, W. 1964, 'Social mobility and social class in industrial communities', in M. Gluckmann and E. Devons (eds), *Closed Systems and Open Minds.* Edinburgh: Oliver and Boyd.

Weber, M. 1968. ed. by G. Roth and C. Wittich (eds), *Economy and Society.* New York: Bedminster Press; 2 vols.

Weber, M. 1982, 'Selections from *Economy and Society,* vols. 1, 2; and *General Economic History',* in A. Giddens and D. Held (eds), *Classes, Power and Conflict,* London: Macmillan.

West, J. 1978, 'Women, sex and class', in A. Kuhn and A. M. Wolpe (eds), *Feminism and Materialism.* London: Routledge and Kegan Paul.

Westergaard, J. and Resler, H. 1975, *Class in Capitalist Society.* London: Heinemann.

Westwood, S. 1984, ' "Fear woman": property and modes of production in urban Ghana', in R. Hirschon (ed.), *Women and Property: Women as property.* Beckenham: Croom Helm.

Whitehead, A. 1976, 'Sexual antagonism in Hertfordshire', in D. L. Barker and S. Allen (eds), *Sexual Divisions and Society: Process and Change.* London: Tavistock.

Wikan, U. 1980, *Life Amongst the Poor in Cairo.* London: Tavistock.

Willis, P. 1977, *Learning to Labour.* Farnborough, Hants: Saxon House.

Wilson, F. 1983, 'The representation of gender in current indigenous thought', Centre for Development Research Project Paper A.83.6. Mimeo.

Women's Studies Group, Centre for Contemporary Cultural Studies 1978, *Women Take Issue.* London: Hutchinson.

*World Development Report, 1979.* Washington: Oxford University Press.

Wright, E. O. 1978, *Class, Crisis and the State.* London: New Left Books.

Wright, E. O. 1979, *Class Structure and Income Determination.* New York and London: Academic Press.

Wright, E. O. and Perrone, L. 1977, 'Marxist Class Categories and Income Inequality'. *American Sociological Review,* vol. 42, no. 1.

Young, I. 1980, 'Socialist feminism and the limits of dual systems theory'. *Socialist Review,* 50—1, pp. 169—88.

Young, I. 1981, 'Beyond the unhappy marriage: a critique of dual systems theory', in L. Sargent (ed.), *Women and Revolution.* London: Pluto Press.

Youssef, N. H. 1974, *Women and Work in Developing Societies.* Westport: Greenwood Press.

Zaretsky, E. 1976, *Capitalism, the Family and Personal Life.* London: Pluto Press.

# Index

Index by Meg Davies